AMERICA AND THE WORLD OF OUR TIME

America AND THE WORLD OF OUR TIME · UNITED STATES DIPLOMACY IN THE TWENTIETH CENTURY · BY JULES DAVIDS

Georgetown University

THIRD EDITION

RANDOM HOUSE, NEW YORK

To My Wife

FRANCES

and to Our Children

PAUL AND JEANIE

327.73
D251

Third Edition

First Printing

98765432

Copyright © 1960, 1962, 1970 by Jules Davids.
All rights reserved under International and Pan-American Copyright
Conventions. Published in the United States by Random House, Inc., New York,
and simultaneously in Canada by Random House of Canada Limited, Toronto.

Library of Congress Catalog Card Number: 76–97587

Manufactured in the United States of America

Printed and bound by The Haddon Craftsmen, Inc., Scranton, Pa.

PREFACE TO

THE THIRD EDITION

Almost ten years have gone by since I completed this survey of American diplomatic history in the twentieth century. Two years later, some additions were made to update the book to 1962. Since that time, we have witnessed a veritable transformation of American life and explosive developments in many parts of the world. The Cuban missile crisis; the assassinations of President John F. Kennedy, Martin Luther King, and Robert F. Kennedy; America's involvement in the Vietnam War; the intervention in the Dominican Republic; the impact of the Sino-Soviet conflict; Communist China's entry into the nuclear club; the Arab-Israeli Six-Day War; the Soviet invasion of Czechoslovakia are only a few of the events that have had far-ranging repercussions.

The changes in American society have also been vast. Tensions generated by the world upheavals have been reflected in the black power movement, in student radicalism on the college campuses throughout the country, and in demands to reduce America's commitments abroad. The technological revolution has not only computerized much of American life, exacerbated urban problems, increased air and water pollution, but has also accelerated the nuclear arms race and contributed to enlarging the role and influence of the military-industrial complex in the United States. Although we cannot ignore the deleterious effects of scientific technology, neither can we overlook its remarkable accomplishments, particularly with respect to the prolongation of life and the conquest of man's new frontier of outer space that was capped in July, 1969, by the landing of Neil Armstrong and Edwin Aldrin on the moon.

During the past eight years, many scholarly contributions have been made on almost all facets of America's diplomacy in the twentieth century. Inevitably, with the passage of time, perspectives change. This is true of my own viewpoints. Still, I find that much of the information and material of this volume remains useful. In this third edition, I have been mainly concerned with the updating of developments to the summer of 1969, and for this purpose have added three new chapters. I have also included a Bibliographical Addendum so that those readers who wish to explore various topics more fully will have a guide by which they can do so. I am most grateful to Jeannine Ciliotta of Random House for her editorial help in connection with the revisions that have been made.

JULES DAVIDS

Georgetown University
Washington, D.C.

CONTENTS

Part I · DIPLOMATIC PRELUDE:

1900-1941

1 · AMERICA ENTERS FRONT-CENTER ON THE WORLD STAGE

We stand supreme in a continent, in a hemisphere. East and West we look across two great oceans toward the larger world life in which, whether we will or not, we must take an ever-increasing share.
THEODORE ROOSEVELT, *Vice-presidential inaugural address, March, 1901*

It was bright and sunny on Friday, September 6, 1901, in Buffalo, New York. The occasion was a festive one. People turned out in large numbers to see the Pan-American Exposition in the city. President William McKinley, who had arrived the previous day, was scheduled to visit the fairgrounds. Cheerfully painted in lavish red, blue, and yellow colors, the exhibit buildings had the gay flavor of Spanish-mission architecture. Like a World's Fair on a small scale, the main attraction was a Tower of Light, four hundred and nine feet high—an impressive spectacle demonstrating the new wonder of electricity.

About four o'clock in the afternoon, McKinley decided to hold a public reception at the Temple of Music. A long line of people quickly formed outside the building. Among those who came to shake hands with the President was Leon F. Czolgosz, a twenty-eight-year-old worker of Polish descent. Mentally disturbed, young Czolgosz had for some time been obsessed with the idea of killing McKinley. However, his plan for the act had not taken concrete shape until a few days before, when he read a newspaper announcement of the President's visit to the Pan-American Exposition.

Dressed neatly, Czolgosz was an innocent-looking member of the crowd. When he entered the Temple of Music, he managed to wrap a large white handkerchief inconspicuously around his right hand to conceal the revolver he held there. The expression on his face was blank as he approached the President and extended his left hand. McKinley, smiling, was just about to grasp it with his right hand when Czolgosz pressed the "bandaged" revolver against the President's abdomen and fired two bullets. McKinley slumped down under a palm tree in the bower of the Temple of Music. With disbelief, he looked up and asked, "Am I shot?"

Czolgosz was almost lynched on the spot. The beating of the assassin stopped only when the President gasped, "Let no one hurt him." Later that evening, without remorse, Czolgosz confessed to the police that he shot McKinley "because I done my duty." He was to explain that he was an anarchist and thought it would be "a good thing for the country," because the President was "going around . . . shouting prosperity when there was no prosperity for the poor man."

Shortly after five o'clock in New York City, an excited newspaper reporter stopped J. P. Morgan as he was leaving his office building. He told the financial giant that McKinley had been shot. Incredulously, Morgan grabbed the reporter's arm and exclaimed, "What?" Without waiting for an answer, he rushed back to his office. Assistants who were still present were ordered to telephone to obtain confirmation of what had happened. But it was not necessary. A newspaper "extra" was already out, and just then a copy was brought to Morgan. He read the story slowly, and sank back in his chair muttering, "Sad . . . sad . . . sad."

Sad—sad, indeed; it marked the end of an era.

McKinley did not die immediately. For eight days his life hung in the balance. It seemed for a while he would recover. On the evening of September 6, Vice-President Theodore Roosevelt was at Isle la Motte, in Lake Champlain, where he had addressed an outing of the Vermont Fish and Game League. During the summer—the first after his inauguration—he had spent most of his time writing, traveling, and speechmaking. When he received the news that McKinley had been shot, he rushed to Buffalo. "My position was of course most delicate," Roosevelt wrote to Henry Cabot Lodge on September 9, "but I felt that the only course to follow was that which was natural, and that the natural thing was to come at once to Buffalo, where I might see how the President was getting on; and to stay here until he was on the highroad to recovery."

The doctors assured the Vice-President that they thought McKinley was out of danger. As a gesture of reassurance to the nation, on September 10 Roosevelt decided to join his family in the Adirondacks. On the night of September 12, however, McKinley suffered a relapse, and his pulse suddenly weakened. Grave anxiety arose that the President would not recover. Word was rushed to Roosevelt, but it did not arrive in the remote Adirondack area until after the Vice-President had begun to climb Mount Tahawus on the afternoon of September 13. While resting with several members of his family near the summit, Roosevelt saw a guide running and panting toward him on the trail below. He felt that something must have happened. "Sure enough," wrote Roosevelt in his *Autobiography,* "he handed me a telegram saying that the President's condition was much worse and that I must come to Buffalo immediately."

While Roosevelt arranged to hurry to Buffalo, consternation arose among the Republican party leaders and in Wall Street. A hurried conference was held in New York City on September 13 between Douglas Robinson, Roosevelt's brother-in-law, and Major George Dunn, chairman of the Republican State Committee. That evening Robinson dictated a lengthy, confidential letter to Roosevelt. It was rushed to Buffalo by special messenger. That same evening McKinley died. His last words, according to the physician who was in attendance, were: "Good-by, all. Good-by. It is God's way. His will be done."

Roosevelt had great difficulty in getting to Buffalo. He traveled some thirty-five miles by horse and wagon to the nearest railroad station. At dawn, when he reached the North Creek station platform, Roosevelt found his secretary, William Loeb, who told him that McKinley had died during the night. He arrived at Buffalo late in the afternoon. Elihu Root, the Secretary of War, advised Roosevelt to take the oath of office immediately. He did so, on September 14, in the house where McKinley lay dead. Theodore Roosevelt was now President of the United States.

Douglas Robinson's letter, which was written in the expectation that Roosevelt might become President, offered some carefully considered advice. Roosevelt was strongly cautioned to give the feeling when he took over the McKinley administration that things were not going to be changed and that he would continue the conservative tradition. "It will," said Robinson, "take a weight off the public mind." To assure the country that he intended to carry out the administration policies, Roosevelt was urged to ask McKinley's Cabinet to remain in office. "I must frankly tell you," Robinson's letter went on, "that there is a feeling in financial circles here that in case you become President you may change matters so as to upset the confidence . . . of the business world, which would be an awful blow to everybody—the West as well as the East. . . ."

The anxiety of the Republican and Big Business leaders was indeed great. Roosevelt had established a reputation for himself while governor of New York as an "untrustworthy," brash, independent-minded, "progressive" individual. Thomas C. Platt, the Republican boss of New York State, had agreed most reluctantly to Roosevelt's nomination for the governorship in 1898. But there was political magic in the name of the national hero of the Spanish-American War, and with misgivings, he gave Roosevelt his support. To be on the safe side, Platt tried to extract a promise from Roosevelt that he would not "make war on him." Roosevelt said that he had no intention of making "war on Platt or on anybody, if war could be avoided." Actually, Roosevelt was eager for the governorship and he did not wish to antagonize Platt. But he made it clear that he did not intend to let the party machine dictate to him, and that he would "administer the State Government as I thought it ought to be administered."

After he became governor, Roosevelt practically wrecked the Platt machine. As a result, Tom Platt exerted pressure on his fellow Republican bosses to get Roosevelt out of New York, "to kick him upstairs" into the Vice-Presidency where he could do the least harm. Marcus A. Hanna, a rich and successful businessman from Cleveland, Ohio, who had by 1900 become virtually the national boss of the Republican party, opposed Roosevelt's nomination. "Uncle Mark" did not want the "Rough Rider" in Washington any more than Platt desired him in New York. However, when a tremendous demonstration arose in favor of Roosevelt at the Republican National Convention in 1900, he reluctantly accepted the result and, for the sake of party solidarity, approved T.R.'s selection as McKinley's running mate. Roosevelt was far from elated at the developments. Somewhat despondent at the time, he felt that his political career had hit a dead end, and he spoke about taking up the practice of law after completing his term as Vice-President.

On the funeral train from Buffalo to Washington, little more than a year later, Hanna was especially bitter about the turn of events. He now felt he should have taken a stronger stand against Roosevelt's nomination and resisted the pressures in his behalf. "I told William McKinley it was a mistake to nominate that wild man at Philadelpha. I asked him if he realized what would happen if he should die," Hanna is reported to have complained on the train. "Now look, that damned cowboy is President of the United States."

THE "LARGE" POLICY OF THE UNITED STATES

Theodore Roosevelt's elevation to the Presidency in September, 1901, inaugurated a new era in America's political life. His youth—he was only forty-three when he took the oath of office—his dynamic personality, and his megalomania personified many of the characteristics of the United States itself at the turn of the century. A native New Yorker, born into a wealthy and distinguished family, educated at Groton and Harvard with Phi Beta Kappa honors, a seasoned traveler to Europe, a writer, a naturalist, and a politician, Roosevelt was far from the stereotyped self-educated, log-cabin-to-White-House figure that Americans for nearly a hundred years had been accustomed to electing to the highest office in the country. A colossal egoist and magnificent showman, a man whom the historian Henry Adams described as "pure act," and others as "ambitious, imperious, and arrogant," he was, above all, a human dynamo and a person who loved life and people and had at all times to be in the "swim" of things. Few will argue that Roosevelt was a vital force who reinvigorated the political process by expanding the powers of the executive, and accelerated the social and economic revolutions in the United States. "I did not usurp power," declared Roosevelt in his *Autobiography,* "but I did greatly broaden the use of executive power."

The issues which Roosevelt faced during his administrations were mainly domestic problems carried over from the turbulent decade of the 1890's: control of the trusts, regulation of the railroads, Populist demands for agrarian reform, revision of the national banking system, and the tariff. The ferment of the age was reflected in the rise of the progressive movement. Underlying the conflicts of the period was the problem of how America should properly deal with the maladjustments created by the rapid advance of industrial capitalism. Alarm was expressed that the great industrial enterprises could destroy the basis of the American democratic system. Government, the progressives said, had to adopt a more positive approach and employ experimental measures to channel economic and social progress toward sound democratic goals. They declared that political democracy was inseparable from economic democracy, and if political democracy had faltered, it was largely because economic democracy had never been tried. A two-pronged attack was directed against political corruption and the concentration of wealth and economic power. Despite his conservative and "aristocratic" background, Roosevelt drifted with the progressive tide, and became one of its most important spokesmen, supporting the aspirations of the underprivileged and those who clamored for political reform.

But the Progressive Era's mood of protest was inchoate. It lacked discipline and organized leadership, and was chiefly marked by a crusading zeal which shot off in a dozen different directions. While it included members of all classes and groups, it was essentially middle-class and urban in nature. Much more articulate and respectable at bottom than the Populist revolt, progressivism groped to awaken the Jeffersonian faith in the dignity and freedom of the individual, which the reformers felt was being crushed by the machine civilization. In one way or another, whether it was an attack against the trusts or the slums or municipal political corruption, or whether it was a fight for workmen's compensation laws or decent conditions in sweatshop factories or direct election of senators or women's suffrage, the progressives aimed at establishing a moral and ethical code which would be in accord with the principles of American democracy.

Roosevelt's moralism and abiding sense of responsibility were in tune with the spirit of his time. While he believed that combinations of both capital and labor were inevitable and frequently worked for the public good, "they must work under the law," he said, "or they will inevitably do evil." However, quite often a discrepancy existed in the practice of Roosevelt's "moral righteousness," between the word and deed, and between his conduct of domestic and foreign policy. "Justice and righteousness were determined by his own conception of justice and righteousness," states Foster Rhea Dulles. "The policy that he judged to be in the interests of the United States as a responsible member of the world community obviously conformed to moral law."[1] According to Roosevelt, it was the duty of the President to decide what was right and what was wrong. But he had only one standard of judgment—his own; and he never doubted for a moment that whatever decision he made was morally the correct one.

Straightforward and aggressive, Roosevelt, acting as his own Secretary of State, frequently ran roughshod over Congress in foreign affairs. In the conduct of diplomacy, he liked directness, and had no use for hypocrisy and artificial pretenses. But he did not tolerate undue familiarity. He insisted upon dignity and simplicity. Roosevelt changed the name of the President's home from the "Executive Mansion" to the "White House." He also frowned upon the traditional use of the title "Excellency" in referring to the President, and requested diplomats not to address him in this manner. "Let them call me 'The President,' or 'Mr. President,' or 'Sir,' " he wrote to Alvey A. Adee, the acting Secretary of State, "but not a title to which I have no right (And one, incidentally, given to every third rate German potentate or beaurocrat [sic])." While Roosevelt disliked uncalled-for familiarity, however, he did not object to a certain intimacy in his personal relations. As a matter of fact, he encouraged it, and frequently carried on important talks with ambassadors after playing a tennis match with them, or

[1] *America's Rise to World Power* (New York, 1954), p. 69.

while relaxing after a swim, or while on a long hike—sometimes through Rock Creek Park in Washington.

An important contribution of Roosevelt was in converting the United States from *a* world power to *a great* world power. In this respect, he acted as a catalyst, galvanizing America's expansionism. Until the 1890's, with the exception of the acquisition of East Florida and the purchase of Alaska, America's territorial expansion was a westward movement, taking in the vast domain from the Atlantic to the Pacific oceans. There were, to be sure, recurring suggestions about Cuba and Central America, but the growth of America's empire was essentially continental and anticolonial in nature. The Northwest Ordinance of 1787 had established a revolutionary principle for the absorption of new lands on a basis of equality with the older states, and this policy proved to be enormously successful right down to 1959 when Alaska and Hawaii were admitted as states.

After the Civil War, the development of American expansion took new twists and turns that ultimately marked a departure from the traditional concepts implicit in the Northwest Ordinance. While emphasis was placed on building up domestic markets through the settlement of western lands, the construction of railroads, and the increase of manufactures, during the 1890's agrarian and business interests were no longer confident that American markets alone could provide continued growth and prosperity. The closing of the frontier, the acute agrarian distress, and the depression of 1893 gave rise to a feeling that America's domestic problems could be solved only by making an effort to stimulate foreign trade and to further commercial expansion. With European nations embarked on imperialistic conquests, many Americans believed that the United States could not stand idly by while potential markets were being closed off.

The 1890's saw a resurgence of the idea of Manifest Destiny—the concept that it was America's mission, as Andrew Jackson had phrased it, "to extend the area of freedom." The duty of the United States was to help the weak against the powerful nations of the world and to inspire a "moral regeneration." The superiority of American democratic institutions, it was affirmed, carried with it certain responsibilities, not the least of which was to see that backward countries and peoples were protected from the clutches of power-hungry foreign nations. America's destiny had to be fulfilled. This could not be achieved, said the expansionists, if America remained insular in its outlook. Defending America's acquisition of the Philippines, Senator Albert J. Beveridge of Indiana thundered:

And of all our race, He has marked the American people as His chosen Nation to finally lead in the regeneration of the world. This is the divine mission of America, and it holds for us all the profit, all the glory, all the happiness possible to man. We are trustees of the world's progress, guardians of its righteous peace.

While the commercial impulse was primarily responsible for pointing the way to the desirability of overseas expansion, it remained for a number of leading American imperialists to give it form, substance, and direction. Outstanding among the group were people like Admiral Alfred Thayer Mahan, Senator Henry Cabot Lodge of Massachusetts, Columbia's political scientist John W. Burgess, the prominent Congregational minister Josiah Strong, the popular historian John Fiske, and Theodore Roosevelt. The individual who undoubtedly exerted the most profound expansionist influence in the 1890's was Mahan, the brilliant naval strategist. Through his books, lectures, and numerous articles, Mahan provided a synthesis which reconciled the diverse motives—economic, military, and religious—for American expansion. In substance, Mahan declared that America was at a crossroad in its history. The nation could either continue to concentrate on its continental expansion by exploiting the domestic markets to their fullest potential and nurturing its policies of isolationism, or it could expand outward, and by so doing establish itself as a great world power. There was no doubt in Mahan's mind that America's destiny required an outward expansion.

The program which the American expansionists set forth encompassed a number of specific objectives. By the 1890's, it was to be formulated into the "large policy" for the United States. Five main goals were outlined. First, a primary stress was placed on the construction of an American-controlled canal through Central America. Such a canal was held to be essential to the expansion of America's trade throughout the Far East, as well as in Latin America. However, the area that was considered potentially most lucrative for trade development was China. The second goal, establishment of American control in Cuba and elsewhere in the Caribbean region, was considered vital to the protection of the waterways leading to the isthmian canal. A third emphasis was on the acquisition of bases in the Pacific as stepping stones to the Far Eastern trade. Strategic points which were designated included Hawaii, Guam, Samoa, Wake Island, and the Philippines. As a fourth point, colonies were deemed useful, both as coaling stations and as sources of raw materials. Finally, but by no means least important, the "large policy" called for the creation of a sizable merchant marine and of a modern and powerful navy to protect America's ships and commercial interests.

Mahan propagandized strongly for the increase of America's naval power. It was in 1890 that his classic book, *The Influence of Sea Power upon History, 1660-1783,* was published. This work was based on lectures Mahan prepared for the Naval War College established in 1884 at Newport, Rhode Island. His views on sea power and its relation to national defense profoundly affected Congressional leaders, and soon stirred up a great deal of thinking on naval policy in Europe, especially in Germany, and also in Japan. In the United States, it led to a demand for larger appropriations for naval construction and for a revamping of America's strategic naval principles. Agitation to build a stronger navy was gaining momentum, and Mahan's book was timed perfectly to provide navalists with an arsenal of arguments to defend their doctrines. Emphasis was placed on the need to create a fleet of capital ships in which the United States was woefully deficient. "A fighting force," it was declared, was required not for conquest, but defense. Compared to what existed before 1890 notable progress was made in improving the "fighting" strength of the navy. But in 1897, the North Atlantic Squadron still included only three first-class battleships, two second-class battleships, and two armored cruisers.

Mahan, as well as other expansionists, recognized that the real substance of America's power lay not in naval strength per se, but rather in the foreign trade itself and in the wealth which would be acquired from that trade. An expanding foreign commerce was held to be the key to national power and prosperity. A strong merchant marine and a powerful navy to protect this merchant marine in time of war and peace were necessary to compete successfully in the world-wide struggle for markets. From Mahan's thesis flowed a number of corollaries. Among these may be noted the following: that sea power was vital to protect the neutrality of a nation; that in time of war, especially involving the United States, it was a means of ensuring neutral shipping free access to ports; that it was fundamental toward the attainment of world supremacy; and that without sea power a nation was doomed in warfare. The smashing of the Spanish fleet in Manila Bay at the outset of the Spanish-American War in May, 1898, was interpreted by many as a vindication of Mahan's theories. However, in the final analysis, what Mahan and the expansionists advocated was a policy of mercantile imperialism backed by naval power.

Roosevelt was an enthusiastic disciple of Mahan and an ardent supporter of the "large policy." He was to become an important agent in the fulfillment of the ambitious program of the expansionists. Both Roosevelt and Lodge did much to generate a spirit which contributed to the outbreak of war with Spain in 1898. This "splendid little war" placed America on the first rung of the ladder in its climb to world power. It was, of course, not wholly accidental that the fruits of the war coincided with some of the major objectives of the expansionists: control over Cuba and Puerto Rico, and the acquisition of the Philippine Islands, Guam, and the Isle of Pines (which was returned to Cuba in 1925). In 1898, the United States annexed Hawaii, and the following year occupied Wake and secured a definitive title to American Samoa as a result of an agreement with Germany and Britain.

When Roosevelt stepped in as President, the policies of American imperialism were already well established. McKinley, however, had been a reluctant exponent of this course of action. Doubts had assailed him about taking over the Philippines. In fact, it appears that at the outset of the Spanish-American War, he had little knowledge of the geographical location of the islands. He subsequently thought that the United States might require only a coaling station at Manila. The possibility that Germany or Japan might establish themselves in the Philippines— if the United States did not—did much to persuade McKinley to take all of the islands. Indeed, shortly after Germany seized Kiaochow in China in 1898, she tried to obtain America's approval for taking over the Philippine Islands, except for the area around Manila Bay. Japan likewise suggested in the summer of 1898 a possible tripartite division of the Philippines in which the United States, Germany, and Japan would each acquire a share. But these proposals were rebuffed. The German government, nevertheless, managed to extract a secret pledge from Spain during the Spanish-American War not to cede the Carolines to the United States. These islands near the Philippines, as well as the Palau Islands and the Marianas (with the exception of Guam) were sold to Germany by Spain for $4,500,000 after the treaty of peace was signed with America in December, 1898.

"The truth is I didn't want the Philippines, and when they came to us, as a gift from the gods, I did not know what to do with them," McKinley is said to have told a group of visiting clergymen at the White House in November, 1900. He explained the "tortures" of his decision; he had walked the floor of the White House night after night until midnight," and had gone "down on my knees and prayed Almighty God for light and guidance more than one night." And then it came to him one night—"I don't know how it was, but it came"—that there was no other course except to take the Philippines. That night, McKinley said, he slept soundly, and the next morning he sent for the chief engineer of the War Department (the map maker) and told him to put the Philippines on the map of the United States. "There they are," he exclaimed, "and there they will stay while I am President."

This colorful version of how America acquired the Philippines serves at least to point up McKinley's hesitation about embarking on a course of imperialism. Republican leader Mark Hanna, who strongly influenced the policies of the McKinley administration, was similarly slow to be won over to the benefits that might be derived from an imperialistic policy. What apparently convinced Hanna was the benefit that would accrue from American commerce with China. "If it is commercialism to want possession of a strategic point [the Philippines]," he said, "giving the American people an opportunity to maintain a foothold in the markets of that great Eastern country [China], for God's sake let's have commercialism."

The Democrats and their nominee for President, William Jennings Bryan, tried to make an issue of imperialism in the campaign of 1900. McKinley, however, emphasized the growing prosperity of the nation. "All we need do," declared Hanna, "is to stand pat." And, indeed, at the turn of the century the optimism and buoyant faith in America's future were great. "The year 1899 was a year of wonders, a veritable annus mirabilis, in business and production," exulted the *New York Times* in its leading editorial on January 1, 1900, and it prophesied that the next twelve months would be even better. The warm glow of prosperity helped to carry McKinley to victory and a second term.

If McKinley and Mark Hanna were less than enthusiastic about the policies of American imperialism, this was to be more than made up by the exuberance of Theodore Roosevelt. The 1890's saw only the beginning of the realization of the goals of the "large policy." Roosevelt's foreign policy was to be directed toward achieving its full aspirations. By pursuing this course, Roosevelt succeeded in greatly expanding America's interests in Latin America and the Far East, and in projecting the country forward into the center of world politics.

GETTING AN AMERICAN-CONTROLLED CANAL

The policies of American imperialism were not directly aimed at establishing a colonial empire. Colonies were only incidental to the larger goal of commercial expansion. Thus the idea of subjugation did not play a part in America's thinking. Control, it was felt, was necessary to guarantee the retention of bases, to provide an opportunity to "educate" the "backward" people in self-government, and to achieve economic stability in colonial areas. It was also deemed essential for reasons of national defense, especially in the Western Hemisphere, where it was to strengthen "hemispheric security."

Around the turn of the century, the program for America's growth of power focused on the construction of an isthmian canal. The Spanish-American War enabled the United States to turn the Caribbean into an American lake; bases were acquired in the Pacific; and with the Philippines, America was ready to expand its trade into the Far East. But the most important elements necessary to make these gains meaningful were still lacking: an American merchant marine; a strong navy; and, above all, an American-controlled canal. On December 5, 1898—five days before the treaty of peace was signed with Spain—McKinley, in his annual message to Congress, spoke about the necessity for an isthmian canal. He did not make any specific reference to location, but the Senate quickly passed a resolution requesting the President to modify the Clayton-Bulwer Treaty of 1850, in which the United States had recognized Britain's extensive interests in Central America and had agreed that any future canal be a joint Anglo-American undertaking and that it be unfortified.

Negotiations with the British began immediately and led to the signing of the first Hay-Pauncefote Treaty early in 1900. The treaty gave America the right to build a canal. But it stated that the canal, once completed, was to remain open to all nations in time of peace and war; no fortifications were to be erected near it, and a self-denial clause was inserted which pledged both countries against the exercise of political influence and territorial encroachment in Central America. Roosevelt, then governor of New York, launched a caustic attack against the treaty. "If that canal is open to the war ships of an enemy it is a menace for us in time of war; it is an added burden, an additional strategic point to be guarded by our fleet," he stated. "If fortified by us, it becomes one of the most potent sources of our possible sea strength. Unless it is fortified it strengthens against us every nation whose fleet is larger than ours. . . ." Without the right of fortification, Roosevelt argued, the canal would be a heavy liability.

The Senate agreed with Roosevelt. A move got under way to amend the first Hay-Pauncefote Treaty so that the United States could fortify the canal region, if it saw fit, in the interests of national defense. The British balked at this proposal; they felt that it would be a preliminary step which would lead to America's taking over the Central American republics. Secretary of State John Hay, deeply discouraged, disturbed by the Senate's inaction on ratification of his treaty, and hurt by the criticism of his friends and the sharp attacks of the press, submitted his resignation. He thought that by stepping out he would also avoid embarrassment to the administration in the presidential elections of November, 1900. But McKinley refused to accept the resignation, and insisted that Hay remain in the Cabinet.

Hay resumed negotiations with the British for a second treaty, and these were still in progress when McKinley was assassinated. After Roosevelt assumed the presidency, he promptly directed his attention toward obtaining a satisfactory canal treaty. Hay was urged to remain as Secretary of State and to straighten out whatever difficulties existed. The British, anxious to cultivate Roosevelt's friendship and to foster good relations with the United States, agreed to accept America's terms. In November, 1901, the second Hay-Pauncefote Treaty was signed. It declared that the Clayton-Bulwer Treaty was "superseded." Significantly, the prohibition against fortifications was omitted, although the British managed to salvage a most important point: a pledge of equal treatment for her ships.

The British privately understood that America would fortify the canal region. Two years later, the British Admiralty dismantled its naval stations in the West Indies. A vacuum was created which was promptly filled by the United States. By the second Hay-Pauncefote Treaty, America implicitly obtained hegemony over any future canal, its approaches, and the adjacent territory in Central and South America.

By 1902, the question for decision was where the canal should be constructed. For about half a century the matter of the location of the canal route had been debated and investigated. The route most favored in Washington was through Nicaragua, but no action was taken by the United States. Finally, in the 1880's, in view of the lack of American efforts, Ferdinand de Lesseps, who had earlier successfully promoted and supervised the construction of the Suez Canal, organized a private French company to build a canal across Panama. Work was begun and nearly $300 million was spent before the project failed. The savings of several hundred thousand thrifty Frenchmen disappeared in the collapse. An investigation of the affairs of the company in France disclosed a shocking degree of corruption and created a world-wide sensation in 1889. Expenses had been systematically "padded"; contractors had received millions of francs for services never rendered, and part of the French press had been subsidized. The trail of scandal led right up to the French Cabinet. The aged De Lesseps received a five-year prison sentence, but it was suspended.

The bankruptcy of the French company offered an opportunity to a private American corporation—the Maritime Canal Company of Nicaragua—to try to build a canal in Nicaragua. Ground was broken in October, 1889. For over three years work went forward on a limited scale. But because of inadequate finances—the company had a paid-in capital of only $6 million—it, too, went into bankruptcy.

Both the French and American companies were anxious to dispose of their assets in the 1890's. Only one prospective customer existed: the American government. Each tried to maneuver the United States into supporting and taking over its project. The Maritime Canal Company found an able champion of its interests in Senator John T. Morgan of Alabama. From 1894 to 1903, not a session of Congress passed without an eloquent appeal by Morgan for a Nicaraguan canal bill.

The New Panama Canal Company which took over the assets of the De Lesseps company in 1894 was fortunate in obtaining the services of two of the greatest lobbyists in American history: William Nelson Cromwell, a brilliant and tireless New York lawyer—of the famous old law firm of Sullivan and Cromwell, whose head a half-century later, John Foster Dulles, was to grace the office of Secretary of State; and the clever Frenchman, Philippe Bunau-Varilla, a former chief engineer of the defunct De Lesseps company and a stockholder in the new company. Bunau-Varilla was not employed directly by the New Panama Canal Company; he carried out his activities independently of Cromwell. Although a stockholder—and as such he stood to profit by the sale of the assets of the French company—Bunau-Varilla's interest in the construction of a Panama canal appears to have transcended personal, material gain. He was imbued with an intense and fanatical zeal for the cause of Panama; and he remained an active figure in Panama's affairs long after a financial settlement had been made with the French company.

Cromwell's greatest obstacle in building up sentiment in favor of the Panama canal was the complacency which existed over the Nicaraguan route. Ignorance with respect to Panama was very great in the United States. Comparatively few people had heard of the New Panama Canal Company. Moreover, the idea of building a Panama canal had become repugnant because of the scandal associated with the De Lesseps venture. To overcome these disabilities, Cromwell organized a press bureau in New York, and hired lecturers, magazine writers, and scientists to make the nation "Panama-conscious." Information was disseminated dealing with the work of the French company and the advantages of the Panama route. But more important than these activities were Cromwell's lobbying efforts in Congress, and the personal contacts he established with Secretary of State John Hay, Mark Hanna, and Theodore Roosevelt.

Cromwell succeeded in 1899 in inducing Congress to investigate and compare the merits of the Nicaraguan and Panama routes. After an extensive two-year investigation, the American commission endorsed Nicaragua. However, the crucial issue centered on estimated comparative costs. Originally, the French company placed the value of its assets at $109 million, which resulted in a higher estimated cost for the Panama plan. When the asking price was reduced to $40 million, which was what the American commission thought they were worth, Roosevelt prevailed upon Admiral John G. Walker, who headed the commission, to change his recommendation in favor of Panama. It is possible—but by no means proved—that Cromwell's contribution of $60,000 to the Republican campaign chest in 1900 helped considerably, not only in preventing the party from endorsing the Nicaraguan route, but in persuading Hanna, the chairman of the Republican National Committee, and Roosevelt to support a Panama canal.

In a more flamboyant fashion, Bunau-Varilla carried on a one-man campaign to dispel doubts about the Panama route. He visited the United States in January, 1901; lectured in many cities; wrote numerous propaganda articles which were published by the American press; and, like Cromwell, soon made himself known to the "right people."

Bunau-Varilla's most striking coup was accidental. Early in May, 1902, Mont Pelée on the Caribbean island of Martinique burst forth in a volcanic eruption, and destroyed the town of St. Pierre with its 25,000 people. Later that month, the press reported serious volcanic disturbances and earthquakes on the shores of Lake Managua, caused by the eruption of Momotombo, in Nicaragua. These events occurred in the midst of the Senate debate over the canal route.

Mark Hanna, who had become senator from Ohio, led the debate in support of the Panama route. On June 5, he delivered a speech—regarded as one of the most important in his political career, and based on information largely supplied to him by Bunau-Varilla and Cromwell —in which he emphasized the vulnerability of a Nicaraguan canal because of the presence of volcanoes. The next day, the Washington *Star* published a facetious cartoon showing Hanna painting volcanoes on a map of Central America.

Bunau-Varilla had a brainstorm. He hurried to a Washington stamp shop and was elated to find exactly what he had recalled: a Nicaraguan stamp, "showing," as he later wrote, "a beautiful volcano belching forth in magnificent eruption." He quickly purchased ninety of these stamps, one for every senator, and then pasted each stamp on a sheet of paper, above which he placed the words: "Postage of the Republic of Nicaragua," and below the notation, "An official witness of the volcanic activity on the Isthmus of Nicaragua." On June 16, he deposited a sheet on the desk of each senator. Bunau-Varilla wrote later that this maneuver, coming as it did at the end of the debate, was responsible for swinging the Senate vote in favor of the Panama canal route.

Three days later, the Senate passed the Spooner Amendment to the Nicaraguan bill, authorizing Roosevelt to buy the assets and concessions of the French company, and to acquire from the Republic of Colombia —in which Panama was then a province—perpetual control of a zone at least six miles wide across the Isthmus of Panama. If the New Panama Canal Company could show valid titles to the assets and concession, and if Colombia agreed to American control over the canal zone, the Spooner Amendment declared that the United States should proceed with the construction of the Panama Canal. However, if these conditions could not be met within a "reasonable time," the amendment authorized Roosevelt to build the canal across Nicaragua. Meanwhile, very quietly, a Panama Canal Company of America had been organized in New Jersey by Cromwell. With capital supplied by Wall Street bankers, purchase was made of the stock of the French company.

A major stumbling block now arose in the form of Colombia's opposition to granting the United States control over the canal zone. Actually Colombia desired the construction of the canal, but objection was voiced to the financial terms. America was willing to give Colombia $10 million and an annual indemnity of $250,000 for control of a three-mile strip of territory on either side of the canal. In addition, however, Colombia indicated that it wanted Roosevelt to use his influence in securing it another $10 million from the French company, whose concession was due to expire in October, 1904. Although President José Marroquin had extended it to 1910, this was done without the consent of the Colombian Congress. It was therefore felt that it could be rescinded. Thus, if the money was not forthcoming, some leaders in Colombia reasoned that when the concession expired they would be able to obtain all of the $40 million earmarked for the French company. In June, 1903, Cromwell told Secretary of State Hay:

The money element . . . plays a great part and the scheme of a large faction [in Colombia] is to repudiate the last Canal extension; wait until next year and forfeit the concession; then sell to the United States direct and get the whole $40,000,000 (this being boldly and frequently stated in the public prints), or else force the United States and the Canal Company to make up a purse of $20,000,000.

Roosevelt refused to be a party to this type of blackmail.

It was natural that Colombia would try to obtain as much as she could out of the deal. She could not, however, press the American government too far, since the United States might then drop the Panama project and turn to the Nicaraguan route. In January, 1903, Secretary of State Hay delivered a virtual ultimatum to Tomás Herran, the Columbian chargé in Washington. Setting forth America's terms, he stated, "I am not authorized to consider or discuss any other change whatever." Herran delayed no longer; with serious misgivings, he signed a treaty at once. The United States Senate approved the Hay-Herran Treaty, but it was rejected in August, 1903, by the Colombian Congress. Resentment at what was deemed to be America's high-handed pressures, dissatisfaction over the financial terms, and a belief that the treaty represented too great an infringement on Colombia's sovereignty were largely responsible for the action. Yet, while rejecting the treaty, the Colombian Congress urged a renewal of negotiations.

Roosevelt was furious. His letters at this time were sprinkled with references to the Colombians as "bandits," "blackmailers," and "contemptible little creatures in Bogota." In August, 1903, he told John Hay, "They are mad to get hold of the $40,000,000 of the Frenchmen." And again he wrote the Secretary of State, "I do not think that the Bogota lot of jack rabbits should be allowed permanently to bar one of the future highways of civilization."

But the question of where and how to build the canal still remained. With the rejection of the Hay-Herran Treaty, Roosevelt technically was obligated to turn to the Nicaraguan route. But his mind was made up. He was determined that the canal would go through Panama. The main problem, therefore, was *how*. John Bassett Moore, a Columbia University professor and an outstanding American authority on international law, was requested by the State Department to submit his views in writing for the President's possible use. Moore prepared an important memorandum in August, 1903, which was promptly given to Roosevelt. In it he argued that the United States already had a guarantee of "the right of way or transit across the Isthmus of Panama" on the basis of a treaty concluded with New Granada (now Colombia) in 1846. If the American government believed the Panama Canal to be the best and most practical route through Central America, he saw no reason why the problems which might be responsible for the possible rejection of the Hay-Herran Treaty could not eventually be settled by diplomatic negotiations. Moore wrote:

Some years must elapse before the canal can be completed; and it is not to be supposed that the United States would be unable meanwhile to arrange all expedient details. Once on the ground and duly installed, this Government would find no difficulty in meeting questions as they arose.

The Moore memorandum, in other words, advised the American government to insist upon its *right* to construct the Panama Canal under the treaty of 1846. It did not, however, say what the United States should do if Colombia failed to comply with the terms of the treaty. A veiled hint of a threat that some action might be required was suggested by Moore's observation that "we have usually found, when the emergency arose, that we were dependent upon our own resources for the enjoyment of the privileges which the treaty was designed to secure for us." But he made it clear that Colombia's noncompliance with the treaty of 1846 did not mean that the United States had the right to seize the canal zone. Roosevelt was deeply impressed by the memorandum, and he invited Professor Moore to dine with him at Oyster Bay early in September; but exactly what was discussed is not known.

While the United States undoubtedly had the right to construct the canal through Panama, it was reluctant to exercise this right. Before 1900, it could not do so on its own because of its commitment to Britain in the Clayton-Bulwer Treaty of 1850, which required joint construction. After this treaty was abrogated, the United States did not wish to proceed with the construction without the coöperation of Colombia. In 1902, there was reason to believe that such coöperation would be forthcoming. The obstacles which arose in 1903 were not foreseen.

Roosevelt publicly accepted Moore's solution of insisting on America's right to proceed under the treaty of 1846; but privately he favored making Panama an independent state. "For me to announce my feelings," he told President J. G. Schurman of Cornell University, "would be taken as equivalent to an effort to incite an insurrection in Panama." Nevertheless, in March, 1903, when Roosevelt expected some future trouble with Colombia, he ordered Secretary of War Elihu Root to send two or three army officers "to map out and gather information concerning the coasts of those portions of South America which would be of especial interest . . . in the event of any struggle in the Gulf of Mexico or the Caribbean Sea." It was apparent that Roosevelt contemplated sending American troops to occupy the Isthmus, and then he planned to follow the suggestion later proposed by Moore to proceed with the construction of the canal on the basis of the treaty of 1846.

Cromwell and Bunau-Varilla made Roosevelt's plan unnecessary. Bunau-Varilla managed to impress the President with the advantages of a revolution in Panama. While Roosevelt did not officially approve of such action, he intimated to Bunau-Varilla that it would receive American support. As a result, Bunau-Varilla established contact with a Panamanian revolutionary junta to set up an independent republic. In October, 1903, he worked out his plans in detail. The center of revolutionary activities became the quarters of Bunau-Varilla in Room 1162 of the old Waldorf-Astoria Hotel in New York City—in his own words, "the cradle of the Panama Republic."

On October 14, 1903, Dr. Manuel Amador Guerrero, a member of the Panama junta, came to Bunau-Varilla's room. He received full instructions with respect to the launching of the revolt, which was to begin on November 3. Bunau-Varilla gave Dr. Amador $100,000 for preliminary "bribe" expenses, a proclamation of independence, a draft of Panama's new constitution, and a code for the rebels' use in communicating with him. Finally, there was a prepared message to be sent to Bunau-Varilla from Panama, appealing to him to become the first Panamanian Minister to the United States, even though he was a French citizen. Amador said that Panama would object to the appointment of a foreigner as its Minister, but Bunau-Varilla insisted upon this condition. "Nothing remains," said Bunau-Varilla as he led Amador to the door, "but to make the model of the flag." And, in fact, that week the Frenchman's wife stitched the "flag of liberation." Modeled after the American flag, it had a yellow background instead of a white one, and two suns in place of the stars. But Panama later changed the design.

Dr. Amador returned to Panama on October 27. That night a meeting was held. The junta expressed deep disappointment that more positive assurance of American help had not been obtained. Doubt arose about going ahead with the revolt. Colombian troops, it was known, were on their way to reinforce the garrison on the isthmus. Amador, depressed, cabled Bunau-Varilla the next day and told him that Bogotan forces would arrive shortly; unless an American warship were sent to Panama to prevent the landing of the Colombian troops, he did not see how the revolution could succeed.

Bunau-Varilla immediately went to Washington. He conferred with Hay and Roosevelt and other key officials. The Secretary of State had told him a few weeks earlier that in the event of a revolt in Panama "we shall not be caught napping" and that orders had been given "to naval forces in the Pacific to sail toward the isthmus." Bunau-Varilla tried to obtain more definite information about America's plans. But he was unable to do so; while Hay and Roosevelt were sympathetic, they made no definite commitments. By some astute intelligence work, however—Bunau-Villa studied the notices of the sailings of American ships in the newspapers—he learned that three American warships were already on their way to the isthmus. He cabled Amador and told him that the U.S.S. *Nashville* would arrive at Colón on the Atlantic side within two days and, within four days, two other American vessels would drop anchor at Panama City on the Pacific side. The *Nashville,* as Bunau-Varilla predicted, reached Colón on November 2. As a result, the revolt occurred the next day as planned. It was virtually a bloodless affair and was over in a single day. The Colombian troops in Panama had been promised bribes, and American naval forces were ordered from Washington on November 2 to "prevent landing of any armed force, either government or insurgent, at any point within fifty miles of Panama." While Commander John Hubbard of the *Nashville* did not receive the orders in time to stop four hundred Colombian troops from landing at Colón, they were prevented, nevertheless, from reaching Panama because of delays in transportation purposely caused by the officials of the Panama Railroad.

On November 4, the Colombian troops that had "assisted" in the revolt were lined up, and Dr. Amador deposited in the hand of each soldier the $50 in gold that had been pledged. General Esteban Huertas, the commander of the Colombian troops at Panama City, received $30,000 in silver, and later an additional $50,000 in gold. Junior officers were given about $10,000 each. In a fiesta spirit, a gala demonstration took place, with the troops parading and snaking through the streets to the plaza of Panama City. The parade wound up at the Century Hotel. General Huertas was carried aloft in an ornate chair. When he was put down, he was practically drowned as bottle after bottle of champagne was poured over his head.

Word of the establishment of the Panama Republic came to Theodore Roosevelt on November 6. Within two hours, Secretary of State Hay instructed the American consul at Panama City to recognize the de facto government. Bunau-Varilla then persuaded Roosevelt to receive him as the Panamanian Minister. His "credentials" were accepted on November 13. Within four days, the Hay–Bunau-Varilla Treaty was negotiated. It was approved by the new Panama government on December 2, and ratified by the United States Senate on February 23, 1904. The treaty was substantially similar to the one made with Colombia, except that the canal zone was extended to a ten-mile width. America agreed to pay Panama $10 million and, beginning nine years later, an annual sum of $250,000. In return, the United States was given the right to build and fortify the canal. The $40 million for the assets of the New Panama Canal Company was not paid directly to the French company. Instead, it was turned over to the House of Morgan, which acted as the transfer agent. Who actually received the money was never made known.[2] Cromwell put in a bill for about $800,000 for his legal services; but the French Panama Canal Company's liquidators subsequently cut down his fee to about $225,000. He became sole fiscal agent of the Republic of Panama in 1905, and resigned from this position in 1937. Cromwell died in 1948 at the age of 94 and left a gross estate of almost $19 million. His later years were spent in France, where he contributed generously to the American Library in Paris.

In 1914, Secretary of State William Jennings Bryan negotiated a treaty with Colombia in which the United States expressed its regret for impairing the good relations with Colombia because of America's role in the Panama incident. It provided for a payment to Colombia of $25 million. Roosevelt opposed this treaty and declared it amounted to submission to blackmail. His friends in the Senate blocked its approval. However, in 1921, a treaty was ratified—without any expression of apology—which sanctioned the payment of the $25 million. American capitalists, it appears at this time, desired favorable oil concessions in Colombia; they were anxious to heal the old wound over Panama, and as a result, influenced the Senate to approve the treaty. In 1939, the Alfaro-Hull Treaty increased the annuity to Panama for use of the canal strip from $250,000 to $430,000, and ended America's protectorate interest in the republic. However, the treaty included a pledge of joint coöperation in the event "of any threat of aggression which would endanger the security of the Republic of Panama or the neutrality or the security of the Panama Canal." The treaty also permitted the United States to engage in expansion and to undertake new construction for the canal. During World War II, a new agreement was signed (May, 1942) which allowed America to establish military and air bases to protect canal defenses; but it stipulated that these new bases would be evacuated one year after the end of the war.

T. R. TIGHTENS AMERICA'S GRIP IN THE CARIBBEAN

Work began on building the Panama Canal in 1904. It took ten years before it was finally opened to ships, and was one of the greatest engineering feats in the twentieth century. The cost ran to $370 million, which was a great deal higher than the original estimates. No less remarkable than the technical accomplishment was the sanitary work of Colonel

[2] An attempt to ferret out "Who Really Got the American Taxpayers' $40,-000,000" may be found in Earl Harding's *The Untold Story of Panama* (New York, 1959), pp. 55-68.

W. C. Gorgas. Unsanitary conditions and disease—yellow fever and malaria—prevailed on the isthmus, and had been responsible for the death of countless Frenchmen twenty years earlier. Benefiting from Dr. Walter Reed's medical research during the Spanish-American War, which identified the mosquito as the carrier of these diseases, Gorgas managed to wipe out the deadly pestholes where the carriers bred and to make the Panama region habitable. It was one of the most impressive achievements in preventive medicine in modern history.

As the canal construction got under way, Roosevelt centered his attention on expanding America's naval power. His interest in the navy was of long standing. In his youth, Roosevelt had frequently been enthralled by the stories told to him by an uncle, James D. Bulloch, who had been involved in the *Black Warrior* incident in 1854 that almost precipitated a war with Spain. Bulloch later became a significant figure in the Confederate Navy, and had a rich store of naval adventures. Roosevelt's enthusiasm for the navy was evident when he was a student at Harvard and started to write a naval history of the War of 1812. As Assistant Secretary of the Navy during McKinley's first administration, he worked hard to make the fleet strong and efficient. In 1897, two months after he became Assistant Secretary, he told a class at the Naval War College:

Merely for the protection of our own shores, we need a great Navy, and what is more, we need it to protect our interest in the islands from which it is possible to command our shores and to protect our commerce on the high seas.

As President, Roosevelt regarded the navy as a prime essential to the growth of America's power. He was deeply disturbed that the United States ranked sixth among the world navies when he took office. In view of the country's growing world responsibilities, Roosevelt viewed this situation as intolerable. Bluntly, he warned Congress: "The American people must either build and maintain an adequate navy or else make up their minds definitely to accept a secondary position in international affairs, not merely in political, but in commercial matters." Swept along by Roosevelt, Congress by 1905 authorized the construction of ten battleships, four armored cruisers, and seventeen other vessels. Roosevelt was determined to have a navy second in size only to Great Britain's and, if possible, equal to hers. By the time he left office, this goal was almost reached. In 1909, the United States ranked second among the world naval powers, and had surpassed France, Russia, Japan, and Germany. It was rapidly closing the gap with Britain.

Naval and military power were linked by Roosevelt to foreign policy. "It is contemptible for a nation, as for an individual, to . . . proclaim its purposes," he said, "or to take positions which are ridiculous if un-supported by potential force, and then refuse to provide this force." The establishment of bases in the Caribbean and the Pacific and the building of the Panama Canal awakened new responsibilities for America. In particular, the United States had to make sure that its position would not be jeopardized by foreign powers.

Roosevelt was well aware of the nation's vulnerability, especially in Latin America and the Philippines. The chronic instability of the republics in the Caribbean and Central America was a constant source of worry. Bankruptcy and debt problems had frequently been a cause for European intervention. In the Pacific, Roosevelt was somewhat apprehensive about Japan, and the threat which her growing power might pose to the Philippines. A major concern of Roosevelt was to neutralize these dangers. Fortunately, around the turn of the century, the threat to Britain's power position by Germany in Europe and by Japan in Asia enabled Roosevelt to consolidate America's hold in the Caribbean and to further America's interests in the Far East.

During the 1890's, Britain was especially alarmed over the possible breakup of China. Her position of supremacy was being undermined by the imperialistic "scramble" of Russia, Japan, and Germany. To counter-act the encroachment, Britain looked around desperately after 1895 to find some counterweights to protect her interests. As one of the lines of her policy, she turned to America for support. Championing an "open door" in China, Britain strongly encouraged the establishment of the United States as a Far Eastern power. Britain's role was not only signifi-cant in contributing to the outbreak of the Spanish-American War—she blocked all of Spain's efforts to obtain a mediation before the onset of the war—but she was also instrumental in pressuring the United States to take over the Philippine Islands, so that they would not fall into the hands of Germany or Japan. During the Spanish-American War, Britain suggested the possibility of an Anglo-American alliance. It was turned down with reluctance by the Anglophile Secretary of State Hay because it was contrary to the traditional American policy. Nevertheless, a close unofficial entente was achieved. This was, in part, obtained as a result of Britain's willingness to accept American political hegemony in Latin America, and to withdraw from the Caribbean.

The change in Britain's attitude was reflected in the settlement of the Venezuelan and Alaskan boundary disputes, the Samoan issue, and the signing of the Hay-Pauncefote treaties. During Roosevelt's first administration, however, one point continued to rankle: the problem of European intervention in Latin America.

In 1902, Britain and Germany intervened in Venezuela to obtain payment on defaulted debts to their nationals. The two countries (later joined by Italy, Germany's nominal ally) blockaded Venezuela's ports. Two forts were bombarded; several Venezuelan gunboats captured— Germany sank two of these; and the custom houses, Venezuela's only source of revenue, were seized. Roosevelt at first maintained an aloof attitude. Privately, he characterized Cipriano Castro, Venezuela's dictator, as "an unspeakably villainous little monkey," and he had told Congress in his annual message of 1901: "We do not guarantee any state against punishment if it misconducts itself, provided that punishment does not take the form of the acquisition of territory by any non-American power."

But the Venezuelan intervention created anxiety in the United States. Fear was expressed in Washington about the possibility of occupation of the country. In October, 1902, Roosevelt directed Admiral Dewey to concentrate America's naval forces in the Caribbean. In addition, he ordered a military force—equal or superior to that of Germany— to be mustered at Puerto Rico in case of trouble. However, while military and naval preparations were made, no action was ever taken.

American public opinion seized upon the Venezuelan debt episode as a serious violation of the Monroe Doctrine. But Roosevelt rejected the implication that a European state did not have the right to intervene to enforce a debt claim, provided no acquisition of territory was involved. He was satisfied that in this case it was justified. Moreover, Roosevelt was pleased that both Britain and Germany had presented their intervention plans to Washington in advance to make sure that there would be no objections. This was the first time that such a thing had ever happened. Besides representing a tacit recognition of the Monroe Doctrine, it reflected the changed power status of America.

But popular disapproval of the intervention was very great. Nor was it quieted when the dispute was promptly referred to the Hague Court for arbitration. Britain, anxious to avoid friction, raised the question as to whether America might not assume the responsibility for the good behavior of the Latin-American republics. Germany, too, pressed the idea strongly. German banking interests were eager to set up some international administration of the Venezuelan customs. Herman Speck von Sternburg, the German ambassador in Washington and a personal friend of the President, alluded frequently to the proposal in 1903. But Roosevelt was not sure that it would work. He feared that a control of the finances of Venezuelan through American and European financial institutions would be condemned by American public opinion. He is reported to have told the German ambassador:

These wretched republics cause me a great deal of trouble. A second attempt of foreign powers to collect their debts by force would simply not be tolerated here. I often think that a sort of protectorate over South and Central America is the only way out. Personally I am absolutely against it. I would even be ready to sponsor a retrocession of New Mexico and Arizona. Foreign financial groups should make no efforts at the development of these ill-governed republics, if they lose their money, they should take the consequences.

But in 1904 Roosevelt was compelled to make a decision with respect to the extent of America's obligations under the Monroe Doctrine. Trouble this time brewed in Santo Domingo. Foreign intervention threatened as the debt-ridden country, wracked by dictatorship and revolution, was reduced to utter bankruptcy. Armed vessels of the United States and several European countries landed troops in Santo Domingo in the latter part of 1903. Yet Roosevelt hesitated about getting enmeshed in the politics of the Dominican republic. In February, 1904, he wrote:

I have been hoping and praying for three months that the Santo Domingans would behave so that I would not have to act in any way. I want to do nothing but what a policeman has to do in Santo Domingo. As for annexing the island, I have about the same desire to annex it as a gorged boa constrictor might have to swallow a porcupine wrong-end-to. . . . If I possibly can, I want to do nothing to them. If it is absolutely necessary to do something, then I want to do as little as possible.

On the same day, the Hague Court handed down its opinion in the Venezuelan debt case. In effect, the judges unanimously ruled that the powers which had used coercion to collect their debts had a preferential right in the matter of their claims. The decision thus appeared to encourage the use of force in European dealings with Latin America. The State Department quickly became alarmed at the fact that a premium had been placed on violence. During the spring of 1904, a propaganda campaign was launched to prepare the American people to accept the necessity for American intervention in Latin America to forestall future European intervention. In this way, the groundwork was laid for the "Roosevelt Corollary" to the Monroe Doctrine.

In his annual message to Congress in December, 1904, Roosevelt finally responded officially to the British and German overtures that America recognize the "obligations" of the Monroe Doctrine by protecting foreign investments in Latin America to avoid European intervention. He declared, however, that instead of any joint European and American financial supervision, the United States would alone assume the responsibility:

Chronic wrongdoing . . . may in America, as elsewhere, ultimately require intervention by some civilized nation, and in the Western Hemisphere the adherence of the United States to the Monroe Doctrine may force the United States, however reluctantly, in flagrant cases of such wrongdoing or impotence, to the exercise of an international police power.

By a clever juxtaposition of the Monroe Doctrine, the "Roosevelt Corollary" provided a justification for the right of the United States to interfere in the internal and external affairs of the Latin-American republics. The basis for this policy had already been established by Secretary of War Elihu Root, a notable jurist and soon (1905) to become Roosevelt's Secretary of State. Root was responsible for setting up the structure of government in America's overseas possessions, notably the Philippines and Puerto Rico. He is also credited with being the author of the Platt Amendment which, tacked on to an army appropriation bill in 1901, provided for the evacuation of American troops from Cuba. Unlike the situation in the Philippines and Puerto Rico, the United States was prevented from acquiring complete control over Cuba; the Teller Amendment of April, 1898—just prior to the outbreak of the Spanish-American War—had stipulated that the United States had no intention of annexing Cuba. In 1901, Washington was reluctant, because of the chronic instability of Cuban affairs, to withdraw from the island without some guarantee of the protection of America's interest. The solution which was arrived at was the Platt Amendment; under its terms, Cuba was established as a quasi-protectorate. As the price for America's military evacuation, Cuba was required to agree to the right of the United States to intervene in Cuba's domestic and foreign affairs in order to maintain Cuban independence and maintain law and order. In addition, Cuba was also required to permit the United States to purchase or lease two naval stations for its own defense as well as that of Cuba. Guantanamo Bay is still held today.

Cuba balked at this infringement of her sovereignty. But Elihu Root made it clear that unless Cuba accepted the provisions of the Platt Amendment and incorporated them in the Cuban constitution, the independence of the island could not be assured. Under the circumstances, the Cubans decided that half a loaf was better than none; the Platt Amendment was accepted. It was incorporated into the Cuban constitution of 1901, and also embodied in a separate treaty signed in May, 1903. The treaty remained in effect until 1934, when it was abrogated. During this period, the United States intervened in Cuba's affairs on a number of occasions, especially from 1906 to 1909, and again in 1911. On the whole, America tried to avoid such intervention, and it did so only when it believed it was absolutely necessary both for the protection of the interests of Cuba as well as the United States. Indeed, instances arose in which Cubans severely criticized the American government for *not* intervening. In the 1920's, especially during Hoover's administration, a relaxation of America's imperialistic policies occurred, and this was followed by a substantial alteration of United States relations with Latin America by the adoption of Franklin D. Roosevelt's "Good Neighbor Policy."

In 1904, Theodore Roosevelt, in effect, broadened the scope of the Platt Amendment and sought to apply its principles to all of Latin America. On the basis of the "Roosevelt Corollary," he intervened in Santo Domingo, and obtained an agreement with the Dominican republic to establish American financial supervision over the revenue-producing custom houses. The Senate, irritated at the high-handed manner in which Roosevelt had acted without securing their consent, refused to ratify the treaty that had been negotiated. But Roosevelt, at the height of his power and disgusted with the Senate, took matters into his own hands. In place of the treaty, he substituted a temporary executive agreement which accomplished the same purpose. Beginning in April, 1905, American custom collectors took complete charge of the Dominican revenues. Two years later, Roosevelt overcame the scruples of the anti-interventionists in the Senate and secured approval of a new treaty.

With the Platt Amendment, the signing of the Hay–Bunau-Varilla Treaty, and Roosevelt's action in Santo Domingo, a pattern was established by which America tightened its grip in the Caribbean and Central American regions.

TAFT FAVORS DOLLAR DIPLOMACY

The key to America's changed world position lay in its Panama policy. The construction of a canal through Central America symbolized not only the growth of power of the United States, but also established the direction of its foreign policy. American agriculture, industry, and finance made impressive strides during the 1890's. The nation began to experience an economic revolution of vast proportions. For the first time in its history, the United States eliminated its unfavorable trade balance, began to undersell British steel in the world markets, and exported more manufactured goods than it bought from abroad. The export of investment capital mounted. George E. Mowry records:

By 1897 American investment abroad already totaled $700 million, a figure that was increased to $2.5 billion in 1908 and to $3.5 billion by the beginning of the First World War. The United States was still a debtor nation in 1900, but the gap between international debts and credits was being closed with amazing speed. By 1914 Americans owned about as much as they owed abroad.[3]

The outpouring of capital and manufactured goods required ever-expanding markets. The Panama Canal was looked upon as a means to speed the flow of America's trade and to provide a gateway to the Far East.

With the beginning of the construction of the canal, the United States became increasingly concerned over the bankruptcy and political instability of the republics in the Caribbean area and Central America. These conditions had frequently led to European intervention in the past. After 1900, America looked for a solution to this situation. Secretary of State Philander C. Knox declared in 1912, shortly before the Panama Canal was opened:

The logic of political geography and of strategy . . . make the safety, the peace, and the prosperity of Central America and the zone of the Caribbean of paramount interest to the Government of the United States. Thus the malady of revolutions and financial collapse is most acute precisely in the region where it is most dangerous to us. It is here that we seek to apply a remedy.

Strategic considerations, financial advantage, and an attitude of benevolence toward the Latin-American•republics largely motivated America's foreign policy. The object of American diplomacy was to make the Caribbean and Central America safe—safe from European interference, safe for American capital investment, safe for the development of democratic institutions in Latin America. The methods and tactics used by the United States to buttress its policies varied and depended upon who was in the White House. They included financial control, military occupation, political interference, and the purchase of territory. But the goals remained the same.

Theodore Roosevelt set America's course, and William Howard Taft, who was inaugurated in 1909, tried to keep it on an even keel. Lacking Roosevelt's showmanship, bluster, and belligerence, Taft nevertheless appeared to inspire confidence and faith in a prosperous America. A

[3] *The Era of Theodore Roosevelt, 1900-1912* (New York, 1958), p. 4.

"big" man—described as three hundred fifty pounds of solid Republican flesh wrapped around a kindly heart—his weight was frequently the butt of many jokes. While in the Philippines as governor-general, he once wired Secretary of State Elihu Root, "Stood trip well. Rode horseback twenty-five miles to five thousand foot elevation." Root is said to have replied, "How is the horse?" Although Roosevelt bestowed upon him his mantle of progressivism, Taft was traditionally conservative in his outlook and felt uncomfortable in the role of a crusading reformer. Popular and jovial "good old Will" saw the world through Wall Street's "rosy" glasses. He graduated second in his class at Yale, and devoted much of his life to public service. A lawyer, judge, and able administrator, Taft gained a reputation for himself as one of Roosevelt's most capable "trouble shooters." In domestic affairs, unlike Roosevelt, he preferred to remain in the background. Taft respected the legislative prerogatives of Congress, and tried to maintain harmony in the Republican party. But with all of his good qualities and good intentions, Taft's timidity—his lack of decisiveness on domestic issues—and inability to grasp the implications of the political revolution of his day ultimately led to his tragic repudiation.

Although in domestic matters Taft slowed the Roosevelt revolution, this was far from the case in foreign affairs. Here his conception was clearer and more direct; he energetically encouraged Wall Street to pump capital into the countries of Latin America and the Far East, and he vigorously supported the policies of "dollar diplomacy" to establish an American financial empire in the Caribbean region. By pushing American bankers into this area, Taft hoped to supplant European interests, and further America's prosperity, while at the same time protecting the waterways to the Panama Canal and the Canal Zone. In 1909, the State Department attempted to squeeze Britain out of Honduras and Guatemala by getting Wall Street bankers to refinance the indebtedness of these countries, which were then having trouble with British bondholders. But the Senate did not approve the treaties to achieve the ends Taft and Knox had in mind. Knox was much more successful in 1910 in Haiti, where he managed to induce four American banks—among them the National City Bank of New York—to invest heavily in the Haitian National Bank.

The most serious "trouble" spot during Taft's administration was Nicaragua. This country assumed importance because of its proximity to the Panama Canal and because the United States still had hopes of building another canal through Nicaragua sometime in the future. In 1909, Nicaragua was ruled by a ruthless, ambitious dictator-president,

José Santos Zelaya, who had come to power in 1893. Zelaya, hostile to American interests, tried to extend his control throughout Central America in the early 1900's, but was foiled by the United States and Mexico. Taft and Knox were particularly disturbed when Zelaya in 1909 refinanced Nicaragua's debt through an international syndicate formed in London, which was undertaken as an obvious affront to the United States. Equally infuriating was Zelaya's threat to cancel a mining concession of some Pittsburgh capitalists for whom Secretary of State Knox had formerly been legal counsel. Knox lost little time in throwing his support behind Zelaya's political enemies and finding a pretext for intervention. An anti-Zelaya revolution, partly fomented by American firms, quickly arose. During the fighting, two American filibusters serving with the insurgents were captured while laying mines in the San Juan River. They were promptly executed. Knox broke diplomatic relations; a naval vessel was dispatched to Nicaragua; and Zelaya, realizing that he could no longer maintain his power, resigned in December, 1909, and fled the country.

A period of turmoil ensued from 1909 to 1912 which was climaxed by the dispatch of American marines to Nicaragua. Meanwhile, Knox succeeded not only in overthrowing Zelaya, but in establishing American financial control in the country. The marines soon restored order, and their forces were reduced by the end of 1912 to a legation guard of one hundred men, which remained in the capital city for about thirteen years. The action in Nicaragua bore bitter fruit. America's blatant intervention, disclosing "dollar diplomacy" in its ugliest light, created resentment and intense anti-American sentiment in Latin America. But it also showed the new force of America's power.

During the Taft period, rumblings of unrest brewed not only in Central America but, more importantly, in Mexico. For more than thirty years, the country south of the border enjoyed ostensible stability under the iron rule of Porfirio Diaz. Relations between the United States and Mexico remained, on the whole, peaceful and mutually beneficial. Diaz welcomed foreign investment, and from 1880 to 1910 encouraged an American economic invasion into the country. American interests made rapid strides in building up Mexico's railroad network. By the turn of the century, Americans controlled about 80 percent of the railroads constructed. The mining industry was also dominated almost completely by a few American firms; and because of favorable land laws, Americans acquired extensive tracts in practically every state of Mexico and used this land to establish ranches, to develop plantations, or simply to hold for speculation. Most lucrative, however, was America's domination of Mexico's oil industry. Although attempts to develop Mexico's oil deposits were begun as early as 1857, it was not until the turn of the century that success was achieved in its exploitation. Two Americans, Edward L. Doheny, who organized the Mexican Petroleum Company and subsequently became a multibillionaire, and C. A. Canfield, a prospector with Doheny, were the first individuals responsible for starting the oil boom. Within a short period of time, rival American firms (most notably the Standard Oil Company) made their appearance. To counteract exclusive American domination, Porfirio Diaz encouraged the British to enter the oil fields. Favorable oil concessions were granted, and there was organized the Mexican Eagle Company, owned by Sir Weetman Pearson (later Lord Cowdray), who was to exert a powerful influence in Mexico's affairs. By 1908, a bitter, three-cornered "oil fight" developed among Doheny, Standard Oil, and Cowdray's company.

Foreign economic penetration into Mexico produced a profound reaction, and contributed to the outbreak of the Mexican Revolution in 1910. While the causes of this revolution were deeply rooted in domestic social, economic, and political problems that went back at least a hundred years, an immediate impetus to the revolt was a nationalist upsurge directed against Diaz' policies. The Mexican dictator ruthlessly suppressed criticism and demands for reform. Idealistic and visionary Francisco I. Madero arose as a leader of the opposition groups. In 1908, he wrote an epoch-making book, *The Presidential Succession*. In this work, Madero argued that the source of Mexico's evils stemmed from Diaz' absolutism. He demanded his resignation to permit the Mexican people to be free to elect his successor.

About the time of the publication of this book, Porfirio Diaz, close to eighty and growing senile, issued a statement in which he said:

No matter what my friends and supporters say, I retire when my presidential term of office ends, and I shall not serve again. . . . I welcome an opposition party in the Mexican Republic. . . . If it can develop power, not to exploit, but to govern, I will stand by it.

Shortly after this statement was made, Madero organized a No Reëlection (or Anti-Reëlection) party. However, Madero predicted that despite Diaz' pledge, he would run for the presidency again; and he was right. The Mexican dictator announced his candidacy in 1910. Madero ran against him, and in the midst of the campaign, Diaz, alarmed at his opponent's growing popularity, arrested him. The election in June turned out to be a farce. The Mexican Bureau of Information reported that only 19,051 ballots were cast. Of these votes, Diaz received 18,829 and Madero 221.

After the election, Madero escaped from jail, crossed the Mexican border, and made plans in San Antonio, Texas, for a revolution against Diaz. Meanwhile, insurrections arose in the northern and southern parts of Mexico, led by Francisco "Pancho" Villa, a notorious bandit, and by Emiliano Zapata, one of the folk-heroes of the Mexican Revolution, who fought for agrarian and land reforms. When Madero returned to Mexico, disorder was widespread. Unable to control the situation, Diaz resigned in May, 1911, and the following month Madero made a triumphal entry into Mexico City.

Throughout the first phase of the Mexican Revolution, Taft avoided interference. Although he favored Diaz—and demonstrated America's support by an exchange of visits across the border—he was not too unhappy at first to see the "strong man" depart the Mexican scene. From 1908 to 1910, Diaz had shown a marked favoritism to British interests. As a result, American Big Business had grown openly hostile to his regime. It was hoped that Madero, who had been educated in the United States and favored American interests, might be more friendly. Unfortunately, Madero's meager efforts at political reform proved inadequate to cope with Mexico's vast economic and social problems, and America's investment became endangered. As instability increased, the attitude of the American government and American businessmen changed swiftly. Madero had great difficulty in pacifying the country, and fighting continued. In 1912, Taft mobilized twenty thousand troops on the Texas border. Warships were dispatched to take home Americans who wished to leave Mexico.

Henry Lane Wilson, the American ambassador and bitter foe of Madero, clamored for the Mexican president's resignation. Counterrevolutions flared up. Taft, irritated by the continued disorder, told Knox: "I am getting to a point where I think we ought to put a little dynamite in for the purpose of stirring up that dreamer who seems unfitted to meet the crisis in the country of which he is President."

The high point of the crisis came during Mexico's "ten tragic days" in February, 1913. A plot to overthrow Madero, in which the American ambassador was actively involved, finally succeeded. A coup d'état occurred on February 18. General Victoriano Huerta, a trusted commander in Madero's army, betrayed his chief, joining forces with Felix Diaz, nephew of the former dictator and a leader in an abortive revolt in October, 1912. Madero was arrested in the National Palace by Huerta's followers. Immediately after the arrest, Huerta and Felix Diaz went to the American Embassy. A "Pact of the Embassy" was drawn up, which outlined plans for setting up a new government. "After enormous difficulty," Wilson informed the State Department, "I managed to get them to agree to work in common on an understanding that Huerta should be the Provisional President of the Republic, and Diaz should name the Cabinet, and thereafter he should have the permanent presidency." Five days later, Huerta henchmen assassinated Madero.

Henry Lane Wilson urged immediate recognition of Huerta's government. But Taft demurred. The State Department was anxious to obtain a settlement of a number of conflicting issues with Mexico before recognition was granted. The problem of dealing with Huerta was thus left to Woodrow Wilson, who came into the White House about a week after Madero's murder.

WILSON AND MEXICO

When Woodrow Wilson assumed the presidency in March, 1913, the United States was at the high tide of the Progressive Era. His election was chiefly the result of the split in the Republican party between the Roosevelt and Taft factions. T. R., angered by Taft's "betrayal" of his progressive programs, broke with the Republican leadership, and in 1912 became an independent candidate, under the banner of the Progressive "Bull Moose" party. Taft was renominated at the Republican convention. The total popular vote of Roosevelt and Taft actually exceeded Wilson's by about a million; but because of the division of the votes, Wilson secured a decisive majority. Thus, Roosevelt's "rebellion" helped to put a Democrat in the White House after sixteen years. More significant, however, was the fact that Wilson, as President, managed to jam through Congress a Democratic legislative program which substantially modified Republican policies for the first time since the Civil War, especially on such matters as tariff, banking, and trust problems.

Wilson was a unique phenomenon in American politics. Much more so than Theodore Roosevelt, he was a study in contradictions. Born in Staunton, Virginia, Wilson spent his later life in the North; he retained the peculiar mixture of Southern gentility, conservatism, and aristocracy, combined with a Northern liberal and progressive outlook. The son of a Presbyterian pastor, Wilson was brought up in a rigid theological home environment that developed in him an acute sense of moral values. While President, he was determined to make the United States a moral world leader. Yet, ever consciously aware of moral issues in politics and diplomacy, Wilson could be cold-blooded and Machiavellian in his actions. A brilliant scholar and distinguished writer, he was far from well-rounded in his interests. He cared little for belles-lettres, art, or philosophy. Originally, Wilson had planned a career in law, but after obtaining his degree, he abandoned this plan for teaching. He received a doctorate from Johns Hopkins University, and for many years was a professor in government and history at Bryn Mawr, Wesleyan, and Princeton. In 1902, he became president of the latter institution, where he introduced the preceptorial system. He resigned in 1910 after a bitter feud with the trustees.

"Big Jim" Smith, Democratic boss of New Jersey, was anxious to find a "front man" as governor of the state to take the heat off the charges of corruption in the party. Wilson, without political experience but with a reputation for integrity and honesty, appeared an ideal choice. To Wilson, the offer of the gubernatorial nomination provided an opportunity to end his frustration at Princeton. Like Theodore Roosevelt in his relations with Tom Platt, he warned "Big Jim" that he would be strictly independent if elected; but Smith did not take him seriously. This proved to be a mistake; after becoming governor, Wilson wrecked the Smith machine and embarked on a vigorous, progressive course in his legislative policies that soon brought him the attention of national Democratic leaders and the 1912 nomination for the presidency.

Although politically unprepared for the Chief Executive's office, Wilson demonstrated a great capacity for growth. Precisely analytical and logical in his approach to problems, he brought to the White House a stubborn self-confidence and a conviction of the rightness of his course once he decided what the correct solution should be. In this respect, he had much in common with Theodore Roosevelt. Wilson had little patience with those who disagreed with him; these individuals he regarded as ill-informed, as agents of vested interests, or as simply stupid. A devoted admirer of the English parliamentary system, Wilson looked upon himself as a triumphantly elected prime minister to whom loyalty by the rank and file was something to be taken for granted. While Wilson remained President, no doubt existed about who was "boss" and leader of the country.

Nowhere was the contradiction of Wilson more sharply defined than in foreign policy. An avowed anti-imperialist, he adopted policies that in many respects were more interventionist than those of the Republican predecessors he severely criticized. He desired to help the Latin American people by giving support only to "the orderly processes of just government based upon law, [and] not upon arbitrary or irregular force [and] to cultivate the friendship . . . of our sister republics of Central and South America." Unfortunately, he deepened Latin American hostility by his "meddling" in Mexico, by his strengthening of America's protectorate control over Nicaragua, by his landing of marines in Haiti and imposing a treaty and constitution on that republic, and by his giving to the navy responsibility for governing the Dominican Republic. A further irritant was his undermining of the Central American Court of Justice when he refused to accept a judicial decision in connection with the Bryan-Chamorro Treaty of 1916 which granted the United States exclusive rights to the Nicaraguan canal route and to naval bases on both coasts.

In 1916, Wilson became alarmed that Germany might overrun Denmark and take over the Danish West Indies. He feared that these islands might be converted into a submarine base which could be used against the United States and threaten the Panama Canal. To avoid this possibility, Wilson warned Denmark that unless the islands were sold to the American government, they would be seized to prevent them from falling into Germany's hands. His pressure led to the signing of a treaty in August, 1916, by which the United States purchased the islands for $25 million; sovereignty was established in March, 1917, and the Danish West Indies became the Virgin Islands of the United States.

The most troublesome problem which Wilson faced with respect to Latin America centered on Mexico. Shocked by Madero's assassination and Huerta's despotism, he announced one week after he had assumed office that "we can have no sympathy with those who seek to seize the power of government to advance their own personal interests or ambition"; accordingly, he refused to recognize the Huerta government largely on moral grounds. By so doing, he marked a departure in the nation's traditional Jeffersonian policy, which held that recognition should be granted as soon as possible to any government that demonstrated it was in control of its territory and people. Wilson's grievance was never directed toward the Mexican people, but toward Huerta personally and his "government of butchers."

During his first administration, Wilson launched a three-pronged attack against Huerta. Diplomatically, he tried to remove Huerta by compelling him to agree to the calling of an early and free election, in which all parties could participate and any individual could run for president—except General Huerta. This advice, put forth by Wilson's confidential agent, John Lind, a former governor of Minnesota, was indignantly rejected. More damaging than the diplomatic pressures was Wilson's use of economic and financial coercion. In 1913, a financial blockade was imposed on Mexico, and American bankers were warned not to negotiate any loans to finance the Huerta government. In addition, Wilson managed to obtain Britain's coöperation in supporting the administration's economic-blockade policies when he pledged to repeal a discriminatory clause in the Panama Canal Tolls Act of 1912. This law created a strain in Anglo-American relations because of the special exemption that was granted to American coastwise shipping in the payment of tolls through the Panama Canal. Britain declared that the favoritism of the tolls act was completely contrary to the Hay-Pauncefote Treaty of 1901, which stated that "all nations" would be required to pay the same rates. To woo the British away from Huerta—Britain had granted recognition almost immediately and supported his regime to protect its vital oil interests—Wilson indicated that he would press for the repeal of the discriminatory clause. An informal understanding was worked out. Britain, more interested at the time in the long-run advantages of equal rights through the Panama Canal than in her oil interests in Mexico, went along with Wilson's policies; and Congress, on its part, repealed the discriminatory article in June, 1914.

Diplomatic pressure and economic coercion were unsuccessful in persuading Huerta to resign. As a result, Wilson, growing more stubborn and infuriated, turned increasingly to a third line of policy: the use of force. Again, he made it clear that his sole desire was to help the Mexican people. Wilson told Sir William Tyrrell, the secretary of Britain's Foreign Minister, Sir Edward Grey, "I am going to teach the South American republics to elect good men!" In February, 1914, he lifted an arms embargo to permit war materials to reach Huerta's foes—Venustiano Carranza, the leader of the Constitutionalist revolutionary movement, and Pancho Villa, both of whom had sworn to avenge Madero's murder and to carry forward his revolutionary ideals.

Tension between Wilson and Huerta reached its climax in April, 1914. On April 9, a whaleboat from the U.S.S. *Dolphin,* which had been dispatched to the Gulf of Mexico, was sent to pick up supplies at Tampico. The crew did not know it, but they landed in a no man's land—fighting was raging between Huertista and revolutionary forces around the rich oil fields in Tampico. A colonel in Huerta's army had been given orders to arrest anyone found near the warehouse dock. As the American sailors loaded the whaleboat, the colonel and a squad of Mexican soldiers approached and arrested them. They were marched a short distance through the streets of Tampico before a Mexican general stopped them. Learning what had happened, and fearing an incident with the United States, he ordered the colonel to release the Americans and told them to return to their ship.

Admiral Henry T. Mayo, the commander of the *Dolphin,* was furious when he heard what had happened. Without obtaining authorization from Secretary of the Navy Josephus Daniels, Mayo delivered an ultimatum to the Mexican general, in which he asked for a "formal disavowal of and apology for the act," and also demanded that within twenty-four hours he "publicly hoist the American flag in a prominent position on shore and salute it with twenty-one guns, which salute will be duly returned by this ship."

The incident was reported to Washington, and Wilson gave his approval to Mayo's action. However, the President extended the time period for the ultimatum to one week. Huerta, who investigated the disturbance, regarded it as a "tempest in a teapot." The colonel, acting under orders, had made a mistake; expressions of regret had been offered, and he thought the matter should be closed. However, to satisfy the United States, Huerta declared his willingness to deliver the salute, provided he had a guarantee that the salute would be returned. To prevent the possibility that this might *not* happen, he suggested that the twenty-one gun salute be fired simultaneously. Secretary of State William Jennings Bryan promptly rejected this idea: it would make the whole affair a farce. But Huerta insisted that the salute, once given, might not be returned, in which case he and his country would suffer deep humiliation. He declared that the whole matter could be quickly settled if the United States signed a written protocol guaranteeing the return salute. However, Bryan warned Nelson O'Shaughnessy, the chargé d'affaires of the American Embassy, not to sign any protocol, lest it be construed as recognition of the Huerta government. On April 19, Wilson told the Secretary of State, "Your reply to O'Shaughnessy is exactly what I would have wished it to be. In no case should any concession of any kind in detail or otherwise be made."

Meanwhile, another incident occurred in which it was reported that a mail orderly from the U.S.S. *Minnesota* was arrested and taken to jail. On April 11, while in the postoffice at Vera Cruz, the mail orderly had a heated exchange with a Mexican mail orderly. Neither could understand the other; to avoid a fight, a Mexican policeman took them both down to the station. Actually, the police judge found the Mexican at fault, and put him—rather than the American—into jail. But excitement over the Tampico incident was so great that the report to the United States was garbled.

During this hectic week, word also reached Washington that a German merchant ship, the *Ypiranga,* was due to land shortly at Vera Cruz with a cargo of arms for Huerta. Discussion arose in the administration as to whether the ship should be permitted to dock. Wilson was inclined to feel that the ship should be seized before it touched port; but he was promptly informed that this was impossible since Germany was a friendly neutral nation, and had a right to sell arms to Huerta.

On April 20, Wilson appeared before a joint session of Congress.

Solemnly, he reviewed in detail the sequence of events which led to the crisis with Mexico; he explained that America's quarrel was simply with Huerta. To make his case as strong as possible, the Tampico incident was grossly exaggerated, and Wilson erroneously reported that the mail orderly from the *Minnesota* had been arrested "and was for a time thrown into jail." Just four days earlier, Admiral Frank F. Fletcher had reported to the Secretary of the Navy that the mail orderly was not detained, that there was no cause for complaint, and that the incident was "without significance." However, Wilson was concerned not merely with the Tampico and Vera Cruz mail-orderly affairs, but more importantly, with the accumulation of grievances against Huerta. He asked Congress to give him authority to use "the armed forces of the United States in such ways and to such an extent as may be necessary to obtain from General Huerta and his adherents the fullest recognition of the rights and dignity of the United States even amidst the distressing conditions now unhappily obtaining in Mexico." After two days of debate, Congress passed a resolution and gave its approval.

Late in the afternoon of the same day that Wilson delivered his address to Congress, Bryan received a dispatch from the American consul at Vera Cruz, notifying him that the *Ypiranga* was going to dock the next morning. The Secretary of State felt that some action was imperative. After several hours of deliberation, Bryan decided to call the communication to Wilson's attention. About 2:30 A.M., Joseph P. Tumulty, Wilson's private secretary, awakened the President from a deep sleep. He also called Secretary of the Navy Daniels on the White House telephone.

In the dead of night, Wilson talked over the Vera Cruz "crisis" with Bryan and Daniels. "What do you think should be done, Daniels?" the President, half asleep but deadly serious, asked over the phone. "I do not think that the munitions should be allowed to fall into Huerta's hands," the Secretary of the Navy replied without hesitation. "I can wire Admiral Fletcher to take the customs house and prevent the shipment being landed. I think that is the proper course to pursue." Wilson paused, and then said: "Daniels, send this message to Admiral Mayo: 'Take Vera Cruz at once.'" Later, Josephus Daniels said: "The thing that determined the action . . . was the feeling that if the ammunition was landed it would strengthen the usurping president and increase the loss of life in Mexico, and the guns might later be turned upon American youths."

Early in the morning of April 21, American forces landed in Vera Cruz. The navy moved swiftly. Within a few hours, the city was occupied; but the arms cargo of the German merchant ship was not captured. Indeed, the ship was released, and it later landed at another Mexican port, where it unloaded its munitions.

While initial opposition was not great, the Mexicans, aroused by the American invasion, soon retaliated. During the next three days, disorder and casualties mounted. Martial law was proclaimed in Vera Cruz, and war appeared imminent. Most ironically, the invasion did not lead to the seizure of the *Ypiranga*'s arms; nor did it topple Huerta. He doggedly held his ground. But Wilson, fortunately, managed to extricate himself from the terrible dilemma of becoming involved in a war with the Mexican people whom he desired, above all, to help in their struggle for "liberty." On April 25, representatives of Argentina, Brazil, and Chile —the "ABC" powers—offered to mediate the dispute between the United States and Mexico. Wilson gratefully accepted.

The Mediation Commission met late in May, 1914 at Niagara Falls, Canada. Wilson continued to insist that the solution to Mexico's difficulties lay in Huerta's resignation. The prolonged discussions of the Mediation Commission enabled Wilson to withdraw American forces from Vera Cruz and to throw his support to Carranza. By July, 1914, with the counterrevolutionary forces growing in strength, Huerta finally realized that he could not maintain his power. He resigned and fled to Spain. Carranza occupied Mexico City in August. But the Mexican Revolution's blood bath continued during the next year as Carranza, Villa, and Zapata contested for control of the country. Robert Lansing, who succeeded Bryan as Secretary of State, called the representatives of the ABC powers into conference once again, and a recommendation was made to recognize Carranza as the head of the Mexican government. This proposal was acted upon in October, 1915.

Wilson's troubles were still not over. Pancho Villa, bitterly resentful over America's support of Carranza, declared a one-man war against the United States, and tried to embroil Carranza in a conflict with America. In January, 1916, he held up a train at Santa Ysabel, which carried seventeen young American mining engineers who had just crossed into Mexico from California, having received a safe-conduct from Carranza to open a mine. Sixteen were massacred in cold blood on the spot. When this attack did not bring the desired results, Villa crossed the border with a band of about four hundred followers; he raided Columbus, New Mexico, burning the town and killing seventeen Americans, among them several soldiers.

Cries arose in the United States to avenge these outrages and to capture Villa, dead or alive. Wilson ordered an expedition, headed by

General John J. Pershing, to track down the Mexican bandit leader. Carranza gave his reluctant consent to this military invasion; but he did not like it. By June, 1916, Pershing commanded a force of 12,000 men. On June 21, a skirmish with Mexican troops occurred at Carrizal, in which twelve American soldiers were killed and twenty-three captured. Angered, Wilson mobilized about 150,000 state militiamen and massed them along the border; but no other clash took place.

The Pershing expedition turned out to be a fruitless military goose-chase. Villa was never captured. As American troops penetrated deeply into Mexican territory, resentment and hostility toward the invasion increased. Carranza more persistently demanded the withdrawal of Pershing's troops, but Wilson refused. The two countries found themselves close to war. After many frustrating months, Wilson finally recalled the Pershing expedition in February, 1917. The crisis of approaching war with Germany was chiefly responsible for his action. The following month, the Mexican Congress officially installed Carranza as president and promulgated a new constitution, which embodied the agrarian, land, church, and oil reforms of the Mexican Revolution. Wilson extended *de jure* recognition and sent Ambassador Henry P. Fletcher to Mexico City; he then turned his attention to the larger crisis in Europe.

THE UNITED STATES BROADENS ITS HORIZON

From 1900 to 1917, many of the goals of America's leading expansionists were fulfilled. Primary attention focused on Latin America, particularly the Caribbean and Central American regions; but the United States also looked to the extension of its interests in the Far East. By the end of this era, America succeeded in obtaining and building an American controlled canal through Panama; quasi-protectorates were established in Panama, Cuba, Nicaragua, Haiti, and the Dominican Republic; coaling stations and naval bases were obtained in strategic locations; the Danish West Indies (the Virgin Islands) were purchased; and the Carribbean Sea was converted into an American lake.

The motives which underlay America's policies during this period were many. Commercial considerations—the enlargement of markets and areas for investment—undoubtedly remained strong. But economic factors were not solely responsible for America's new role in world affairs. Equally important was the desire of the United States to strengthen its security and the security of the Western Hemisphere. The Panama policy, in part, created new conditions, which required a closer attention to the economic and political stability of the countries close to the Canal Zone. Commensurate with its economic growth, the United States also looked toward the increase of its naval and military power.

But while America tried to advance its own interests, it was not oblivious to the need of helping and cultivating the good will of Latin America. Roosevelt, Taft, and Wilson viewed American intervention as a necessary policy, but one to be used with restraint—as much for Latin America's good as that of the United States. It was never considered as a weapon for subjugation, but rather as a means of maintaining and preserving the independence of the Latin-American republics on a more secure basis. That these republics frequently did not want America's benevolence, that they constantly suspected ulterior designs, is clear. To the extent that this was true, the interventionist policies often did irreparable damage. But in the long run, the undercurrent of America's idealism softened the hostility. Thus, in an important address at Mobile, Alabama, in October, 1913, Wilson, seeking to clarify his Latin-American policy, declared: "I want to take this occasion to say that the United States will never again seek one additional foot of territory by conquest. She will devote herself to showing that she knows how to make honorable and fruitful use of the territory she has. . . ." In 1914, he drafted a general Pan-American treaty that was intended to guarantee mutually the territorial integrity and political independence of all the Latin-American republics. But this proposal—which contained the kernel of the later Good Neighbor Policy—did not advance very far. After the outbreak of World War I, Wilson began to shift his gaze to the larger world arena and became more interested in a League of Nations to guarantee peace and the independence of nations.

During the 1920's, the United States gradually abandoned its policies of interventionism. The "Roosevelt Corollary" was repudiated. In its place, America oriented its Latin-American policy toward establishing closer coöperation on the basis of joint partnership, nonintervention, and the acceptance of the juridical equality of all nations. This change marked a revolution in the relations of the United States with Latin America, and it went far in revitalizing the Pan-American movement during the administrations of Franklin D. Roosevelt.

2 · THE FAR EAST BECKONS

I utterly disbelieve in the policy of bluff. . . . "Never draw unless you mean to shoot."
THEODORE ROOSEVELT TO PRESIDENT WILLIAM HOWARD TAFT,
Letter, December 22, 1910

The United States enjoyed a relatively free hand in the Western Hemisphere early in the twentieth century partly because of Britain's political retreat in the Caribbean and Latin America. Germany's growing threat in Europe and the encroachments of Russia, Japan, Germany, and France in China had led Britain to a shift of emphasis in her foreign policy. The possibility, however, that the great powers might carve up China created anxiety not only in Britain, but also in America. The lure of trade with the Far East had been a compelling factor in the expansionists' "large policy." While the United States concentrated primarily on enlarging its interests in Latin America, it did not want to be squeezed out of China. In 1896-97, the State Department's Bureau of Foreign Commerce had spoken hopefully of "an American invasion of the markets of the world," and it considered China to be the "most promising" area. Its annual report stated that equality of opportunity in that vast empire "would doubtless result in immense gains to our manufacturers in the demand, sure to follow, for lines of supplies and goods of various descriptions that we are preeminently fitted to provide."

Since 1784, when the *Empress of China* sailed to Canton, the attraction of the China trade had been great. Profits in the traffic of furs, seal and otter skins, raw cotton, and many other items were enormous. During the nineteenth century, this trade was supplemented by American missionary activities which exerted a profound influence upon the life of the Chinese people. During the 1850's, as trade with China increased, and steam navigation made headway, the United States began to eye

Japan and the islands in the Pacific as possible coaling stations. Interest in the Pacific region, moreover, grew greater after America's acquisition of California in 1848 and after the rise of New England's whale-fisheries industry. A consequence of these developments was the opening up of Japan by Commodore Matthew C. Perry—younger brother of Oliver Hazard Perry, famed hero of the War of 1812. An outstanding naval officer in his own right, Matthew Perry warmly espoused the expansionist doctrines of his times. He was one of the staunchest supporters of steam-propelled frigates, and had commanded the *Fulton,* the first naval steam vessel. With four men-of-war steamers, he led the famous expedition to Japan in 1853. Perry returned the following year and concluded the first American treaty with the Japanese. The long period of Japan's isolation came to an end; for the first time, foreign contacts were permitted, and two ports were opened to American trade. In 1858, however, Townsend Harris, a New York merchant with extensive interests in the Far East, managed to obtain a commercial treaty which was more favorable than Perry's. Japan opened up additional ports and agreed to a schedule of tariff duties and to a mutual exchange of diplomatic representation. This treaty became a model for other treaties negotiated by Japan in the nineteenth century.

After the Civil War, American trade with China declined. At the end of the 1890's, it was no more than 2 percent of America's world trade. Nevertheless, the pull of missionary influence which looked toward the spread of Christianity to "civilize" the Chinese, the forecasts of future commercial prospects, and expansionist propaganda exerted a powerful force on American foreign policy.

OPEN DOOR IN CHINA

During the winter of 1899, missionary and business groups in the United States clamored for a more spirited Far Eastern policy. American industries (especially textiles) developed a lively interest in the markets of northern China and Manchuria. These were the regions where German, Russian, and Japanese imperialism was most pronounced.

In 1898, Germany sent a formidable naval squadron to China after two German priests were murdered in Shantung province. She seized Kiaochow, and compelled China to recognize a German sphere of influence in Shantung. The bay of Kiaochow contained the best harbor in North China. By obtaining railroad concessions in Shantung, Germany was able to tap the North China trade and threaten Tientsin—the only treaty port in North China open to free competition which provided access to the capital at Peking.

Meanwhile, from 1895 to 1902, Russia pressed in upon China from the west and down from the north. The Russians secured a lease in Talien Bay, and took over the port of Dalny—later called Dairen. They also established a naval base at Port Arthur and planned to connect Dairen and Port Arthur by a railway. The object of Russia's moves was to link Dairen and Port Arthur to the new Trans-Siberian Railroad. She sought to unify her territories in Asia more effectively, and at the same time, to monopolize the Manchurian region.

Japan, too, edged herself onto the Asiatic mainland. After Perry's expedition and the development of foreign-trade contacts, Japan underwent a phenomenal transformation. She embarked on a rapid industrialization which exerted a profound impact on her society and economy in the latter part of the nineteenth century. However, limited in territory, with a large population and meager resources, Japan found herself dependent on the importation of raw materials. Their conversion into manufactured products became the principal means by which Japan tried to further her economic progress and build up her political power.

To obtain what she wanted, Japan looked to China. Here were the sources of many of the materials she lacked. Moreover, China was the most accessible market for the goods she wished to export. Observing the course of Western imperialism, Japan concluded that control of markets and the sources of raw materials were essential to her existence and expansion. She therefore persistently drove hard to obtain a foothold on the Asiatic mainland—peacefully, if economic penetration could be successful; forcibly, if it could not. Korea and Manchuria were her immediate goals: Korea, because it pointed a potential pistol at the heart of Japan; Manchuria, because of its soybeans, wheat, iron, and coal.

During the 1890's, Japan feared Russian and Chinese intrusion in Korea. She was apprehensive that her own plans to establish herself in this country might be frustrated. As a result, Japan, in a counterthrust, precipitated the Sino-Japanese War of 1894-95. Her swift victory led to Russia's withdrawal from Korea—made formal in 1898 in the Rosen-Nissi Agreement recognizing Japan's domination. Russia decided to concentrate instead on Manchuria. Japan, however, was not content to take over only Korea; she, too, desired control in Manchuria—a much more important objective than Korea. Signs of a rift with Russia became evident.

The maneuvers of Germany, Russia, and Japan threatened Britain's position of economic supremacy in China as well as America's hopes of commercial expansion there. In contrast to the negligible trade and direct investments of the United States, China, in the 1890's, accounted for 65 percent of Britain's total trade. Moreover, the bulk of China's trade with the rest of the world was carried in British vessels. She therefore was most concerned about the possible breakup of China into monopolistic spheres.

From 1895 to 1902, Britain developed three lines of policies with respect to the Far East: she tried to conclude bilateral treaties of alliances with her principal rivals—Germany, Russia, and Japan; at the same time, she carved out her own sphere of influence in the Yangtze Valley, the most important part of China, where her trade was greatest, and where she could exert a direct influence on the Peking government; and she sponsored an "Open Door" policy, attempting to persuade her competitors to open their spheres and leaseholds to British commerce. Down to 1902, Britain's efforts to create a balance of power by means of alliances were unsuccessful. During this period, she largely centered her attention on creating her own sphere of influence, since the principle of the Open Door, which was exclusively concerned with commercial equality, was not applicable in counteracting railroad and mining concessions. Nevertheless, to the extent that the Open Door was helpful, Britain supported this old doctrine that had guided her past policies in China.

The Spanish-American War removed the United States from the great "battle of concessions." About a month before the outbreak of the war, Britain proposed in a secret communication to President McKinley the possibility of Anglo-American coöperation in opposing the annexations or leases of territory in China by other powers. This suggestion was made again in 1899; but on both occasions the proposals were turned down, since they conflicted with America's traditional policy of nonentanglement. Britain, it should be noted, was not so much interested in an Open Door policy as such, but in checking territorial control and economic monopolization that would exclude the trade of other nations in spheres of influence.

John Hay, America's ambassador to London, was appointed Secretary of State by McKinley in the summer of 1898. Although he knew little about the situation in China, he was most anxious to help the British and foster closer coöperation. He turned to William W. Rockhill to assist him, since he had no adviser on Far Eastern affairs—a Far Eastern Division did not exist in the State Department at that time. Rockhill's role in shaping America's Far Eastern policy was to be most important at this critical juncture. A friend of the Secretary of State, he was regarded as the country's leading Sinologist and an expert on Tibet. Rockhill's earlier career had been most colorful. Most of his life had been spent abroad. He was brought up in France, and served as an officer in the French Foreign Legion. But Rockhill's passion was the study of oriental languages and religion. He made several expeditions to Mongolia and Tibet, lectured and wrote books on the Far East, and gained a certain popularity. Washington society was especially attracted to him. "It is not always that one can produce in one's own drawing room an explorer of Tibet," explained Louis J. Halle, "a man, moreover, with a mandarin moustache, a foreign accent, and an air of eccentricity."[1]

Hay had Rockhill recalled to Washington from his post as America's minister to Greece. The Secretary of State sought to have him appointed Librarian of Congress; when this failed, he secured for him the post of director general of the Bureau of American Republics (later the Pan American Union). Actually, Rockhill became Hay's private consultant on Far Eastern affairs. He had not been in China, however, for at least seven years and knew almost as little about the domestic economic and political conditions of the country as the Secretary of State. But Rockhill, with his scholar's interest in China and desire to help the Chinese people, wanted to do something to save the Manchu Empire from partition.

Two Englishmen, acting in unofficial capacities, exerted the strongest influence on Rockhill and Hay. The first was Lord Charles Beresford, who toured the Far East in 1898, and became a foremost propagandist for an Anglo-American Open Door policy in Asia. He championed the idea of a commercial alliance between the United States and Britain, "based," as he said, "on the integrity of China and the open door for all nations' trade." The following year, Beresford wrote a popular book, *The Breakup of China,* in which he set forth his arguments for an Open Door policy. The book, together with Beresford's speeches in the United States, created quite a stir.

The second Englishman, Alfred E. Hippisley, was much more closely associated with Rockhill. He was long a resident of China and had known Rockhill for many years. Hippisley was second in charge of the Imperial Chinese Maritime Customs Service, an organization established in the 1850's to regulate China's trade. An agency of the Chinese government, it was British-administered and contained representatives of other countries on its board, developing its policies independently of the British Foreign Office. In 1899, Hippisley came to the United States on leave to visit his wife's family in Baltimore. He decided to take advantage of the opportunity to see his old friend Rockhill in Washington. An authority on Chinese ceramics, Hippisley shared with Rockhill a scholar's interest

[1] *Dream and Reality: Aspects of American Foreign Policy* (New York, 1959), p. 221.

in China. But he was equally concerned about the fate of the Maritime Customs Service, whose authority was being threatened by the spheres of influence which Britain and the other great powers were setting up. Like Beresford, Hippisley wanted an Open Door policy to check the growing monopolization in China. He also desired to save the Customs Service—and, incidentally, his job. Hippisley urged Rockhill to get the United States to assume the initiative and to approach the great powers to obtain a pledge that they would not interfere with the treaty ports in their spheres of influence and would also permit commercial equality.

Rockhill, who was assigned to write a memorandum for Secretary of State Hay setting forth his recommendations for a Far East policy, was very much impressed with Hippisley's views. He asked him to prepare a paper and to help him in the formulation of his own memorandum; Hippisley was pleased to do so. Using most of Hippisley's suggestions, Rockhill drafted a report for Hay and President McKinley. On the basis of the Hippisley-Rockhill memorandum, Open Door notes were drafted to the various powers and sent by Hay in September, 1899.

The first Open Door note did not represent any striking departure in America's Far Eastern policy. It merely affirmed the principle of commercial equality and asked for a pledge on the part of the great powers to respect this principle in their spheres of interest in China. These spheres were recognized as a historical fact. The response of the powers was lukewarm. Even the British Foreign Office—which had now lost its confidence in an Open Door policy and wanted to tighten up Britain's sphere in China—was evasive in approving Hay's note. It replied that Britain would subscribe to the principles of the Open Door if the other powers did likewise. The replies of all the powers—with the exception of Italy, which did not have a sphere of influence in China—contained some qualifications. Russia's answer was most equivocal, and amounted to a virtual refusal. Despite the apparent rebuff, Hay announced that all the countries had agreed to recognize the principles affirmed by the United States. Their assent, he said, was "final and definitive." Since none of the powers had given an outright refusal, and since each reply was made contingent on agreement by the other powers, Hay's action amounted to little more than a diplomatic bluff. The Secretary of State, however, in no way intended to challenge the vested interests of the great powers in China. He was mainly concerned with putting the United States in a most favorable light as an unselfish world power whose sole desire was to uphold equal commercial opportunity in Asia.

But it was Hay's bluff that provided the basis for America's Far East policy. The principles of the Open Door were soon extended. In June of

1900, three months after Hay had expressed his satisfaction with the replies he had received to his first Open Door note, a fanatical Chinese patriotic society—the "Boxers"—incited a rebellion against foreign missionaries and concession-hunters. Encouraged by the Peking dynasty, the Boxers in a blind surge of nationalistic hatred, isolated all foreigners in North China and forced them to take refuge in the foreign legations in Peking. Widespread murder, pillage, and terrorism took place. For several weeks the foreign legations were besieged, until a military relief expedition, organized by the great powers, finally broke through and rescued the Westerners. After much bloodshed, the Boxers were dispersed. The Chinese government was held responsible, and an indemnity of $300 million was imposed by the vindictive victorious powers. It would have been much larger and would have included territorial cessions if Hay had not used his influence to modify the demands. However, each of the powers—including the United States—extracted the right to station troops at Peking and Tientsin to protect their nationals and guard the route between the two cities.

The disorders in China gave the great powers a pretext for enlarging their spheres of influence. Russia, Germany, and Japan especially tightened their holds. Fearful that partition might occur which would exclude the United States from China, Hay issued another circular note in July, 1900. Without requesting a reply, the Secretary of State declared that the "policy of the Government of the United States is to seek a solution [to] preserve Chinese territorial and administrative entity [and] safeguard for the world the principle of equal and impartial trade with all parts of the Chinese Empire." Hay's statement was indeed a far-reaching one. Intended to deal with the situation in 1900, the declaration of policy, loosely interpreted, became a guide to future administrations in their relations with the Far East. Hay himself did not envisage the implications which flowed from his second Open Door note; nor did he regard his statement as a fixed policy. In November, 1900, the Secretary of State, concerned that America might lose out in securing for itself an economic foothold in Asia, directed the American minister in China to obtain a naval coaling station and territorial concessions at Samsah Bay in Fukien province. The Japanese, however, who had prior claims in this region and feared that America's presence in Fukien, opposite Formosa—now controlled by the Japanese—might threaten the island's security and Japan's homeland, reminded the Secretary about his admonitions against territorial aggrandizement. Hay, somewhat embarrassed, quickly dropped his plans.

The larger significance of the Open Door was that it was in line with America's efforts to achieve commercial supremacy. While Hay may not have been consciously aware of this connection, it soon became clear that it helped, as William A. Williams notes, "to establish the conditions under which America's preponderant economic power would extend the American system throughout the world without the embarrassment and inefficiency of traditional colonialism."[2]

The basic problem for the United States after 1900 was how—in the face of European and Japanese monopolistic encroachments in China—the door *could* be kept open. Lacking military power to enforce its commitments to China, America was obligated either to compromise on principle or to take a stand and risk the outbreak of war. Both of these courses were distasteful, and before World War I, the United States was unwilling to accept either alternative. Instead, it tried to hold its ground by issuing moral pronouncements. At the same time, however, America sought to create those conditions that would permit economic penetration without becoming directly involved in the power conflicts in Asia To a great extent, the United States succeeded in its objectives. It managed to look after its interests, keep on the sidelines, and move cautiously into the Far East only when necessary.

THE RUSSO-JAPANESE WAR CREATES COMPLICATIONS

When Theodore Roosevelt came into office, he expressed greatest alarm over Russia's expansion in Asia. He did not see the same threat in Japan's actions, but on the contrary, welcomed Japan as a potential ally against Russia. Roosevelt did not object to Japanese control in Korea, which he frankly preferred to Korean misgovernment, Chinese interference, and Russian bureaucracy.

The Russians had pushed ahead briskly in Manchuria after 1895. They were the first to pierce the region with a railway system—the Chinese Eastern Railroad. With the railway concession had come exclusive mining privileges and the rights of administration; by 1900, Manchuria was virtually Russian territory. At the turn of the century, signs pointed to a possible further Russian sweep down into North China as far as the Yangtze—the English sphere.

The expansion of Russia in Asia precipitated a threefold reaction: Britain became fearful that Russia's encroachment would endanger the security of her Empire in the Far East and pose a threat to India; Japan, whose position in Korea was shaky, and who still looked to the Manchurian region as an area vital to her interests, eyed Russia warily; and Roosevelt became convinced that Russia represented the greatest threat to America's Open Door policy, and had to be blocked.

The pivotal country turned out to be Japan. Between 1900 and 1902,

[2] *The Tragedy of American Diplomacy* (Cleveland, 1959), p. 37.

Japan considered two possibilities to strengthen her position: an alliance with Russia, with a clear-cut division of spheres of influence, or one with Britain, aimed at driving the Russians out of Manchuria. Britain viewed the prospects of a Russo-Japanese alliance as a nightmare; it was felt that it would threaten British interests in China and the Pacific and would permit Russia to advance into Afghanistan, Persia, and the Near East. The likelihood also existed that the Russo-Japanese alliance could be expanded into a Franco-Russian-Japanese entente, with Germany acting as a silent partner. Thus, out of fear that she might be isolated both in Asia and Europe, Britain dropped whatever reservations she had toward an agreement with Japan. In 1902, she agreed to an Anglo-Japanese alliance on Japan's terms. Japan's control in Korea was recognized, and Britain agreed to support Japan in her march into Manchuria.

The conclusion of the Anglo-Japanese alliance was the prelude to the outbreak of the Russo-Japanese War in 1904-05. The accord signed, Japan demanded Russia's evacuation from Manchuria. Rather surprisingly, Russia did not oppose the Japanese pressures, and a withdrawal began. But it was suddenly halted, and Russia gave one excuse after another for delays. "No human beings, black, yellow or white," said Roosevelt, "could be quite as untruthful, as insincere, as arrogant—in short, as untrustworthy in every way—as the Russians under the present system." Japan's patience became exhausted. On February 8, 1904, without warning, Japanese torpedo boats attacked the Russian fleet at Port Arthur.

Roosevelt's attitude in connection with the Manchurian situation from first to last was sympathetic to Japan. Two days after the Port Arthur attack, Roosevelt wrote his son, Theodore Roosevelt, Jr., that it was fortunate that the Russo-Japanese War had opened most disastrously for the Russians:

For several years Russia has behaved very badly in the Far East, her attitude toward all nations, including us, but especially toward Japan, being grossly overbearing. We had no sufficient cause for war with her. Yet I was apprehensive lest if she at the very outset whipped Japan on the sea she might assume a position well-nigh intolerable toward us. I thought Japan would probably whip her on the sea, but I could not be certain, and between ourselves—for you must not breathe it to anybody—I was thoroughly pleased with the Japanese victory, for Japan is playing our game.

In a confidential note to Secretary of State Hay at this time, Roosevelt wrote that if Russia seized an American vessel, it would be his inclination "to move our Asiatic Squadron northward . . . with the intention of having our squadron bottle up the Vladivostok fleet." He ordered the navy to make plans for such an emergency.

The attack on Port Arthur was followed by a land invasion. Japan's advances were swift, and by early 1905, the Russians were in retreat. A battle at Mukden led to a complete rout of the Russian forces, and in May a great naval battle in the Sea of Japan, the major action of the war, ended in a Japanese victory. In June, both Japan and Russia accepted Roosevelt's publicly announced offer to act as a mediator in the conflict.

The rapidity of Japan's defeat of Russia astonished Roosevelt. He had expected both parties to exhaust themselves in the conflict. A powerful Japan worried him, but he was confident that the Japanese leaders would pursue a cautious policy:

If Japan is careful and is guided by the best minds in her empire, she can become one of the leaders of the family of great nations. But if she is narrow and insular, if she tries to gain from her victory more than she ought to have, she will array against her all of the great Powers, and you know very well that however determined she may be, she cannot successfully face an allied world. Now I don't believe that Japan is going to make any mistakes.

Despite his confidence in Japan, Roosevelt did not favor the complete elimination of Russia from Asia. He wanted Russia weak, but not so weak that she·would be incapable of checking Japanese designs. He wanted Japan strong, but not so strong that she would threaten the Open Door policy and America's position in the Philippines and Hawaii.

To make sure that Japan would not step out of line as far as America's interests were concerned, Secretary of War Taft, while on a mission to the Philippines, stopped off in Tokyo and negotiated an agreement with Prime Minister Taro Katsura. The Taft-Katsura secret memorandum confirmed Japan's pledge that she would not attack the Philippines; in return, the United States recognized Japan's "suzerainty" over Korea. Roosevelt was highly pleased by this clear-cut written statement. He endorsed it, and the memorandum became an informal executive agreement. "Your conversation with Count Katsura absolutely correct in every respect," Roosevelt cabled Taft in July, 1905.

The peace conference which ended the Russo-Japanese War was held at Portsmouth, New Hampshire, in the summer of 1905. The Treaty of Portsmouth, signed in September, was a striking triumph for Japan. It established her as a great world power. It also increased America's prestige, and tremendously enhanced Roosevelt's reputation as a world leader. For his work in the peace negotiations, he was awarded the Nobel Peace Prize in 1906. Yet the treaty was a patchwork affair which embittered the Russians, aroused Japan's hostility toward America, and did little to advance America's interests in Asia. Under its terms, Japan's "predominant" position in Korea was recognized by Russia, China's sovereignty in Manchuria was restored, and both Japan and Russia implicitly accepted the principle of the Open Door. Russia transferred to Japan her mining and railroad concessions in southern Manchuria, and ceded the southern half of Sakhalin Island. However, Japan had counted heavily on obtaining an indemnity, and when this was not forthcoming it created deep resentment. Riots broke out in Japan, and Roosevelt and the signers of the ignominious Portsmouth Treaty were castigated. Roosevelt wrote:

It does not seem to me that the Japanese are wise in letting everybody talk as if they had got the worst of it. They have won an astonishing triumph and have received a remarkable reward. They have secured control of Manchuria and Korea. They have Port Arthur and Dalny, and the south half of Sakhalin. In destroying the Russian Navy they have made themselves a formidable sea power—one which, in the Pacific, is doubtless a match for any nation save England. Under such circumstances, it seems to me that they are unwise, because they could not get an indemnity to which they had no real title whatever, to make it appear as if the terms of peace were utterly unsatisfactory.

Roosevelt's expectation that a "balance of power" would best advance the Open Door was rudely shaken after 1905. America's policy increasingly blocked Japan's ambitions in China. While Britain adjusted her policies toward a recognition of Japan's power position, America clung steadfastly to the support of China, and looked to China as a major stabilizing force in Asia.

TROUBLE BREWS IN CALIFORNIA

Differences between the United States and Japan were heightened in 1906-07. Japan's grudge against America for Roosevelt's part in the Portsmouth Treaty and its hostility toward immigration policies were met in the United States by an equally belligerent attitude and a determination to cut the Japanese down to "size." Feeling was particularly strong on the West Coast, especially in California, where the Japanese, as well as other Orientals, were looked upon as a threat to the economic standards of American laborers. Social prejudice was also acute. Fed by the Hearst press, jingoes, and irresponsible West Coast newspapers, propaganda whipped across the country about the "yellow peril." Tensions inevitably increased. Fighting actually broke out in the summer of 1906 between the crews of some Japanese sealing vessels and American patrols on Alaska's Pribilof Islands.

A crisis was quickly touched off in the fall of 1906 when the Board of Education of San Francisco issued an order segregating Japanese children into a separate school. The charge was made that the Japanese were crowding out Americans; but this argument was obviously ridiculous since there were only ninety-three Japanese school children in the whole city. The order was clearly inspired by ugly racial prejudice, the pressures of organized labor, and a jingo hostility toward Japan.

The segregation order's implication of racial inferiority infuriated the Japanese at home, especially after they had demonstrated their military superiority over Russia. Japan regarded the action as a deliberate insult and demanded that the situation be remedied. Roosevelt acted promptly. He sent the Secretary of Commerce and Labor to California to make a thorough investigation. Japan was quieted. The report Roosevelt received convinced him that San Francisco's Board of Education had made a seriously unwise decision. But he was powerless to rescind the order since Washington had no jurisdiction over the public schools in California. He could merely exhort San Francisco's authorities to correct their "mistake."

In his annual message to Congress in December, 1906, Roosevelt emphasized the need for fair play toward strangers within the gates. He warned that hostility toward Japan "may be fraught with the gravest consequences to the nation." Paying a ringing tribute to Japan for her remarkable progress in peace and war, Roosevelt declared that the shutting out of the Japanese from San Francisco's schools was a "wicked absurdity," since Americans had "as much to learn from Japan as Japan has to learn from us; and no nation is fit to teach unless it is also willing to learn." Americans, he said, were treated well in Japan, and not to reciprocate was "by just so much a confession of inferiority in our civilization." Roosevelt hinted that if California did not mend her ways, strong measures would be adopted. He promised to use all the forces at his command to protect the Japanese.

Roosevelt's message was a two-edged sword. While it mollified public opinion in Japan, it angered the people of San Francisco. Formerly apathetic to the segregation order, California turned its wrath on the President. "Our feeling is not against Japan," declared the San Francisco *Chronicle*, "but against an unpatriotic President who unites with aliens to break down the civilization of his own countrymen."

The President's bombshell created an uproar throughout the country.

Many, fearing that the crisis might lead to war, supported Roosevelt's stand. But the furor was not quieted until Roosevelt brought the entire San Francisco school board—paying all expenses—as well as the mayor and some local politicos to Washington. After a frank conference, the President realized that the root of the trouble was not a school issue, but the desire of the Californians to exclude Japanese from the United States. A compromise was finally arrived at in which Roosevelt promised to obtain more careful screening of Japanese immigration and the school board agreed to reinstate the children. Roosevelt fulfilled his pledge by working out a Gentlemen's Agreement with Japan in 1907-08. Tokyo agreed that it would not issue passports to Japanese workers who wished to come to the United States; Washington promised not to bar Japanese immigration completely. Japan thus controlled the emigration at its source, and in this way saved face. After 1908, Japanese immigration declined drastically, and as a rule, only professional men, students, tourists, and persons of the business class came to the United States.

ROOSEVELT SENDS THE NAVY ON A WORLD CRUISE

The trouble in California was settled by the Gentlemen's Agreement; but Roosevelt remained seriously disturbed at Japan's bellicosity. He became convinced that it might be a good idea to give Japan a demonstration of American naval power, and he decided that this purpose would be served by staging a world naval cruise. The voyage, he felt, would provide "an answer to the very ugly war talk that had begun to spring up in Japan," and also be the best example possible of "speaking softly and carrying a big stick."

During the spring and summer of 1907, Roosevelt was somewhat despondent and disheartened over the situation in the Far East. He was most disturbed about the fate of the Philippines, if a war did break out. Roosevelt had been partly responsible for the acquisition of these islands. As Assistant Secretary of the Navy, it was he who had used his influence to place George Dewey in command of the American Asiatic squadron at Hong Kong; and in February, 1898, when the Secretary of the Navy was away, sent a famous cable to Dewey instructing him to hold the American fleet in readiness to attack the Spaniards in the Philippines. When doubts arose about taking over all of the islands, it was he, too, who had urged retention under American rule.

But Roosevelt quickly became uncertain that the Philippine acquisition was a wise move. From 1899 to 1902, a Filipino insurrection, aimed at achieving independence, occurred. American forces suppressed this rebellion; but it did so at the cost of a fearful slaughter, with thousands of casualties on both sides. Sporadic resistance continued for many years. As Vice-President, Roosevelt expressed the hope that "events will speedily justify leaving them." However, when he became President, he did not take any steps in this direction. Peace was restored; Roosevelt abolished the office of military governor, and appointed William Howard Taft as civil governor—later governor general—in the Philippines. Under Taft's benevolent guidance, improvements were made in health, education, and transportation; but the islands continued to be an economic and military liability. Late in August, 1907, Roosevelt told Taft, who had succeeded Elihu Root as Secretary of War, "The Philippines form our heel of Achilles. They are all that makes the present situation with Japan dangerous. . . . I think that to have some pretty clear avowal of our intention not to permanently keep them and to give them independence would remove a temptation from Japan's way and would render our task at home easier." He thought that independence might be worked out under some kind of "an international guarantee." "I would rather see this nation fight all her life," he said, "than to see her give them up to Japan or any other nation under duress."

Taft was much less pessimistic than the President; he did not believe that war would occur with Japan. This conviction was confirmed when he visited Japan in October, 1907. It is probable, too, that Roosevelt did not expect war, that he was more disheartened by the Congressional opposition to his naval-building program and emphasized the difficulties with Japan to overcome any roadblocks. Mowry has noted:

If he did believe that war was likely, then his own secret plans, made in the summer of 1907, to sail the American battle fleet around the world are almost incomprehensible. Had Japan attacked the fleet in Tokyo Bay without warning as it had the Russian fleet, or had it attacked the Philippines and Hawaii while the fleet was in the Mediterranean, the advantage would have been all Japan's. Roosevelt's naval *beau geste* might then have proved to be one of the more disastrous moves in the history of naval warfare.[3]

The world cruise of the Great White Fleet started in December, 1907, when sixteen battleships departed from Hampton Roads, Virginia, as the bands played "The Girl I Left Behind Me." The first announcement in July had said only that the fleet was going on a "practice cruise" to San Francisco—around South America, of course, since the Panama Canal was still under construction. Congress quickly voiced its objection to this "wasteful" voyage and declared that it would strip the Atlantic seaboard of its naval defenses. The Hearst press, on its part, linked the cruise

[3] George E. Mowry, *The Era of Theodore Roosevelt* (New York, 1958), p. 189.

to the tensions with Japan, and whipped up a war scare in the country. "I do not believe we shall have war; but it is no fault of the yellow press if we do not have it," Roosevelt wrote to Senator Lodge on July 10. "The Japanese seem to have about the same proportion of prize jingo fools that we have." One can imagine the excitement which would have arisen had it been known that Roosevelt intended to extend the cruise around the world, and that before its voyage would be ended, it would cover some 45,000 miles and last for fourteen months. As it was, the departure of the battleships in December led the press to renew its opposition to the cruise, and predictions of war with Japan were made once again.

The voyage around South America was a great success. Although at first indifferent to the naval armada, the Latin-American republics became more cordial as the fleet moved southward. The first hearty welcome came at Rio de Janeiro, Brazil. The crews were entertained lavishly and taken on sightseeing tours, special editions of the newspapers were printed in English, and messages of congratulation were sent to Roosevelt. When the fleet was unable to stop at Buenos Aires, the Argentine government sent a squadron out to sea to salute it. The cruise continued without a mishap through the Straits of Magellan to Valparaiso, Chile, on to Callao, Peru, and then to Magdalena Bay, Lower California. The effect of the fleet's visit was a tremendous one on South America: for the first time in its history, the United States was providing a vivid demonstration of its ability to guarantee the security of the Western Hemisphere.

It was while the fleet was at Magdalena, in March, 1908, that Victor Metcalf, the Secretary of the Navy, announced that the cruise would continue around the world. Within a few days, Kogoro Takahira, the Japanese ambassador in Washington, delivered an invitation to the State Department for the fleet to visit Japan. It was a master stroke of Japanese diplomacy. The move undercut the rumors of war, and the world cruise was now hailed as a guarantor of peace. The reception at Yokohama was one of the most enthusiastic of the entire voyage. Thousands of Japanese lined the streets to watch the parade of the American sailors; children waved little American flags and loudly sang "The Star-Spangled Banner" in English. Posters were seen everywhere of the "dove of peace"; but in place of the face of the dove, there was a picture of Theodore Roosevelt.

While the attention of the world was fixed on the world cruise and its cordial reception in Japan, negotiations very quietly took place in Washington to remove the sources of friction in the Far East between

the United States and Japan. These discussions led to the signing of the
Root-Takahira Agreement on November 30, 1908. The executive agreement, although innocuously worded, was an important diplomatic victory
for Japan. It provided for the maintenance of the status quo in the
"region of the Pacific Ocean," respect for the territorial possessions of
America and Japan in this area, a pledge to uphold the Open Door in
China, and support "by all pacific means at their disposal the independence and integrity of China." In effect, it went one step beyond the
secret Taft-Katsura Agreement of 1905, which had given Japan a free
hand in Korea. Now, in 1908, Roosevelt indirectly indicated that he
was prepared to acknowledge a Japanese sphere in Manchuria in return
for a pledge that Japan would not undertake any aggressive action in the
Pacific region and would abide by the Open Door policy in China. By
delimiting America's 1900 commitment to the "integrity of China,"
without Hay's qualifying word "territorial," Roosevelt, indeed, left a
great deal of leeway on the matter of Japan's "rights" in Manchuria. In
his anxiety to ease the tensions with Japan and establish more cordial
relations between Washington and Tokyo, he abandoned America's
policy of maintaining the status quo in China. By so doing, in the long
run, Roosevelt inevitably weakened, rather than strengthened, the principle of the Open Door.

"DOLLAR DIPLOMACY" SEEKS TO BLOCK JAPAN

By the end of Roosevelt's second administration, America faced the
choice of acquiescing in Japan's penetration of Manchuria or resisting it.
Roosevelt had sought an accomodation as the best means to preserve a
balance of power. When Taft came into the White House in 1909, a shift
of tactics occurred. Convinced that Roosevelt's "appeasement" of Japan
was undermining America's position in Asia, Taft and Secretary of State
Philander C. Knox decided to oppose Japan's expansion with "dollar
diplomacy." This policy, it was felt, would also go far toward increasing
the stability of China and maintaining the Open Door.

During the Taft administration, the pivot of Roosevelt's balance-of-
power strategem no longer was based on the rivalry between Japan and
Russia, but rather on the encouragement of American capital investment,
especially in the railways of China. American financial penetration, it
was believed, could provide a check on Japan's encroachment and also
act as a restraining influence on the European powers. "The nations that
finance the great Chinese railways and other enterprises will be foremost
in the affairs of China," declared the State Department in 1909, "and
the participation of American capital in these investments will give the

voice of the United States more authority in political controversies in that country which will go far toward guaranteeing the preservation of the administrative entity of China."

The Taft-Knox policies were strongly influenced by E. H. Harriman and Willard Straight. During the Roosevelt period, Harriman, the great American railroad-builder, nurtured an ambitious and fantastic scheme to create a Harriman railway-steamship line that would circle the world. In 1905, he managed to obtain an agreement with Japan for joint American-Japanese control of the South Manchurian Railway, a vital link in his scheme. When the agreement was made, the railroad was still Russian property, but it was scheduled to be transferred to Japan as a result of the Portsmouth Treaty. After the treaty was ratified, Japan changed her mind about the deal with Harriman, and signed an agreement with China which excluded an American interest in the railroad. Harriman was not easily rebuffed; the rejection of his proposal increased his determination to see American economic control established in Manchuria.

Willard Straight became indirectly linked to Harriman's dream of a world railroad empire. After graduating as an architect from Cornell in 1901, Straight decided to see a bit of the world before he settled down. He went to China. He intended to remain for just a short while, but the longer he stayed, the more he liked the country and the people. He became a newspaper correspondent during the Russo-Japanese War, and in 1906, joined the State Department consular service. In a short time, he was appointed Consul General at Mukden, Manchuria. From 1906 to 1908, Straight turned the Mukden consulate into a high-pressure sales agency to encourage American capital investment in Manchuria. Motivated by a strong desire to help China, he became convinced that the territorial integrity of China could be preserved only by the increase of American trade and the investment of American capital in the internal improvements of the country. Japanese Ambassador Takahira in Washington vigorously protested Straight's propaganda activities, and demanded that his Chinese-American publicity bureau be liquidated. In 1908, primarily because of Wall Street interest rather than Japanese pressures, Straight was recalled by the State Department and made acting chief of the Far Eastern Division in Washington.

Harriman's scheme and Straight's enthusiastic support of "dollar diplomacy" dovetailed. After 1906, Harriman began a series of negotiations with the Russian government for the purchase of the Chinese Eastern Railway, which Russia was willing to sell, provided Japan also agreed to sell the South Manchurian Railway. But Japan refused. An-

gered, Harriman seriously began to contemplate using the same tactics
he employed against his competitors in America: building a parallel line
and forcing the older road to sell. However, it was one thing to compete
with an American company and quite another to deal with Japan.
Harriman recognized that it was of utmost importance to obtain the full
support of the State Department; the new Taft administration promised
to give him help.

Although Harriman died in September, 1909, the new policy of "dollar
diplomacy" was to be firmly laid down by Taft and his Secretary of State.
In May, 1909, China prepared to float a loan through an international
consortium of German, British, and French bankers to construct the
so-called Hukuang Railways to link coastal Hankow and Canton with the
interior province of Szechwan. The State Department promptly organized a powerful American banking group, which included J. P. Morgan
and Company and Harriman's firm, Kuhn, Loeb & Company. An effort
was then made to obtain American participation in the international
consortium. Willard Straight resigned from the State Department and
became the Peking representative of the American financial group. The
European bankers refused American participation, but Taft made an
unprecedented personal appeal for Chinese coöperation to Prince Ch'un,
regent for the last Manchu emperor. After a long period of negotiations
by Straight in China, a four-power consortium agreement was eventually
signed in 1911.

In addition to the Hukuang Railways, Straight arranged for the
American bankers and a British firm to build a 750-mile line between
Chinchow and Aigun in northern Manchuria. But after Harriman's
death, the American bankers lost interest in pushing into Manchuria
and withdrew. However, Secretary of State Knox, seeking to check
Japan's penetration, suggested the "neutralization" of all Manchurian
lines through joint Anglo-American action in setting up an international board. He also proposed going ahead with the Chinchow-Aigun
project on the basis of a joint participation of all "interested parties," but
without Japan. America's diplomatic moves alarmed both Japan and
Russia; in 1910, the two countries signed a treaty which defined more
closely their Manchurian spheres of influence. The Russian and Japanese
opposition effectively undermined Knox's policies and contributed to a
setback of America's prestige and of the Open Door in China. Nor were
Knox's efforts to support a plan for currency reform and industrial development in China in 1910 any more successful than his "neutralization"
scheme and Chinchow-Aigun project.

With the outbreak of Sun Yat-sen's Chinese Revolution in 1911, the policy of "dollar diplomacy" collapsed. The great powers consolidated their positions: Japan in Manchuria, Russia in Mongolia, and Britain in Tibet. In 1912, Japan and Russia signed another secret treaty, further defining their respective spheres in Manchuria and Mongolia. A new alignment of the power positions of the European countries and Japan took shape. "To my mind," cabled American Minister Calhoun from Peking, "it is no longer a question of friendly international cooperation to help China but a combination of big powers with common interests to accomplish their own selfish political aims."

WILSON TACKLES PROBLEMS WITH CHINA AND JAPAN

When Woodrow Wilson entered the White House in 1913, America had become somewhat isolated in China. The Bankers Consortium had been a singularly ineffective instrument in curbing the encroachments of the Great Powers, and Wilson promptly expressed his disdain for "dollar diplomacy." He was not, he made clear, interested in supporting any "special group or interests." Where Taft had sought to promote America's interest by encouraging financial penetration abroad, Wilson looked to a broader trade expansion. Recognizing the interdependence of nations, he felt that it was America's duty—its historic mission—not only to advance its own interests but to help other countries as well. In this respect, Wilson's policies were far more idealistic than those of his predecessors. "The idea of America," he said, "is to serve humanity."

In the Far East, Wilson viewed the Chinese Revolution with sympathy. He staunchly supported the Open Door policy, and was repelled by the imperialism of the great powers, including the United States, which undermined China's independence. When Wilson assumed office, the country was in the midst of a depression. He was convinced that this depression could be eased, the Open Door strengthened, and China's stability increased if America's overseas trade expansion could be stimulated. This could not be done, he felt, by narrowly supporting Wall Street bankers.

Two weeks after he became President, Wilson found an opportunity to define his attitude with respect to China. The American financial group was anxious to withdraw from the Bankers Consortium. In view of the chaotic conditions, they were reluctant to grant a $125 million loan to the tottering Chinese government. Unless the State Department backed up this loan, the American financiers indicated that they would withdraw from the Consortium. Wilson refused to approve their request for support. The conditions for the loan were such, he said, as to threaten "very nearly the administrative independence of China itself."

The administration could not be a party to those conditions which might invite foreign intervention. Such intervention, Wilson declared, would be most unfortunate when China was "just now awakening to a consciousness of its power and of its obligations to its people." Without Washington's support, Wall Street withdrew from the Bankers Consortium. Wilson's sympathy for the Chinese Revolution was further reflected in his recognition—the first among the great powers—of the Chinese Republic in May, 1913.

Another troublesome problem which Wilson inherited from the Roosevelt and Taft period related to the Japanese in California. The California legislature seriously considered taking steps to make it impossible for Japanese to own or lease land for agricultural purposes. Wilson, like Theodore Roosevelt, exhorted the legislators not to pass such a bill; but he found himself embarrassed not only because federal intervention was impossible in a situation of this kind, but also because the California legislature was Republican-controlled. He sent Secretary of State William Jennings Bryan to California in April, 1913, to use his powers of persuasion. This mission placated Japan, but Bryan was not completely successful. An alien land law was passed, forbidding ownership of agricultural land by persons ineligible for citizenship. No mention, however, was made of the Japanese. While less offensive than the original bill, Japan still felt affronted. Strong protests were lodged in Washington; and war talk arose again, as it had in 1907. Fortunately, Wilson's conciliatory attitude helped to subdue the crisis. But more serious tensions quickly arose in Asia.

JAPAN AND THE IMPACT OF WORLD WAR I

The outbreak of World War I brought a change in the direction of Wilson's foreign policies. He became more and more concerned with the conflict in Europe. While the Open Door continued to dominate Wilson's thinking with respect to Asia, his interest shifted away from China and toward the idea of restoring America's foreign trade by tying it to the Allied war program. The build-up of this program, indeed, led to a growth in America's prosperity—a prosperity based to a great extent on the arms trade and on loans to the belligerent powers. While economic motives were not the prime factors that influenced Wilson's hostility toward Germany, their effect cannot be discounted.

In Asia, Wilson fought a rear guard diplomatic battle against Japan. With the European powers distracted by the war, Japan found an opportunity to advance her interest in China. The only country to which China could turn to for help was the United States. Immediately after the outbreak of the war in Europe, China appealed to America to "endeavor to obtain the consent of the belligerent European nations to an undertaking not to engage in hostilities either in Chinese territory and marginal waters or in adjacent leased territories." Within four days, Secretary Bryan sounded out the powers with interests in China, including Germany, on their willingness to observe the neutrality of the Pacific Ocean and maintain the status quo in the Far East. But nothing came of this proposal. Then, in August, 1914, Japan, invoking the Anglo-Japanese Treaty of 1902 (which had been renewed in 1905 and again in 1911), declared war on Germany.

Japan's entrance into the war completely changed the status of affairs in the Far East. Moving swiftly into the German sphere around Kiaochow in East China, Japan acquired control in the Shantung peninsula. In 1914, also, she entered into a mutual understanding with Britain to divide the German islands in the Pacific that had been acquired after the Spanish-American War. It was agreed that Japan would occupy the German Pacific islands north of the equator, while British forces took over those in the south. To make sure that her claims to Shantung and the German islands would not be jeopardized, Japan later concluded a series of secret treaties with the European powers.

Using Shantung as a springboard, Japan proceeded to try to reduce China to a vassal state. In January, 1915, the Japanese presented a secret ultimatum to the Chinese government—the Twenty-One Demands, aimed at establishing Japanese economic and political supremacy in China. They called on China to give her full consent to whatever disposition was made at the end of the war to the German holdings in Shantung, to recognize Japan's special position in Manchuria and eastern Inner Mongolia, to cede or lease none of her coast to any power other than Japan, to grant Japan exclusive mining and industrial privileges in the Yangtze Valley; and to permit Japanese supervisory control over the social and political institutions of China.

Powerless to resist Japan, China made the Twenty-One Demands public. The United States was the only country capable of offering help to China, but it was not in a position to block Japan by force. Nevertheless, Bryan issued a prompt note of warning. Under no circumstances, he said, would the United States "recognize any agreement or undertaking which has been entered into or which may be entered into between the Governments of Japan and China, impairing the treaty rights of the United States and its citizens in China, the political or territorial integrity of the Republic of China, or the international policy relative to China commonly known as the Open Door Policy." Nor, Bryan declared, could America "regard with indifference the assumption of political, military, or economic domination over China by a foreign power." With respect to Manchuria, however, the Secretary of State acknowledged that "territorial contiguity creates special relations between Japan and these districts." While America's diplomatic intervention succeeded in modifying some of Japan's claims, especially those which called for Japanese supervision over the Chinese government, China was forced to accept the other demands.

During World War I, Japan concentrated her attention on obtaining Allied support for her postwar claims and America's tacit recognition to her position in Asia. By astute diplomacy, Japan went far in achieving her objectives; she signed a series of secret treaties with the European powers, and negotiated the Lansing-Ishii Agreement with the United States in November, 1917. However, the latter agreement was very ambiguously worded, and each country interpreted it to suit its own purposes. "Territorial propinquity creates special relations between countries," it stated, "and consequently, the Government of the United States recognizes that Japan has special interests in China, particularly in the part to which her possessions are contiguous." But at the same time the agreement contained an explicit pledge of respect for the Open Door and for the independence and territorial integrity of China.

Japan held that the Lansing-Ishii Agreement was an American recognition of her paramount political and economic interests in Manchuria, Shantung, and eastern Inner Mongolia, and a tacit acknowledgment that Japan could proceed with her exploitation of China, provided she did not actually annex any territory. The American government emphatically denied this interpretation, and emphasized Japan's pledge to abide by the Open Door Policy. The differences in interpretation disclosed the fundamental conflicts of national policy in the Far East which existed between the two countries. These conflicts deepened in the period after World War I.

POINT OF NO RETURN

The "large policy" of the 1890's had provided an impetus to America's expansion; but its momentum sprang from other sources, most notably from the growth of population, from the steady and tremendous increase in industrial productivity, and from the pressures which arose to enlarge domestic and foreign markets. With the rise of national wealth came increased power and a desire to assert this power to further the self-interest of the nation. As President, Roosevelt saw clearly that increased wealth, together with improvement in transportation, communication, and production, were altering life in America and its relations with other nations. "Internationally as domestically, these changes, he believed," writes John Morton Blum, "created a situation of potential chaos in which only the availability of power and, when necessary, the application of force could provide the indispensable instruments for a tolerable equilibrium."[4]

America's problem before World War I was, as it is today, how to deal with a world in "potential chaos." Roosevelt's answer was that the chaos could not be removed; it could only be brought under control. "More and more, the increasing interdependence and complexity of international political and economic relations," he told Congress in 1902, "render it incumbent on all civilized and orderly powers to insist on the proper policing of the world." Thus, while Roosevelt parted company with isolationism, he did not feel that a "concert" of the great powers was necessary to maintain world order. If each of the great powers assumed the responsibility of policing its own sphere, this end, he thought, could be achieved. In those areas where the great powers were in conflict with one another, Roosevelt believed that the best solution was to try to stabilize the situation by a "balance of power." Thus, he declared in connection with the Russo-Japanese War that Russia's elimination from Asia would be most unfortunate. "It is best," he said, "that she should be left face to face with Japan so that each may have a moderative action on the other." The Portsmouth Treaty was in his view a perfect example of the preservation of balance, since each power was made "the guarantor of the other's good conduct." And to counterbalance Japan in the Pacific he favored the increase of American naval power.

While Roosevelt was acutely conscious of the use of power to serve the self-interest of America, his successor, William Howard Taft, believed that this interest could be advanced, not by dabbling in power politics, but by promoting America's trade and overseas investments. By substituting dollars for bullets and by encouraging the extension of American financial and commercial interests, a salutary influence would be built up, he was convinced, that would go far toward preserving world peace. Taft was well aware that trade and investments required international stability. And to this end, he championed a wider application of the principle of arbitration, even to the point of restricting America's freedom of action in her foreign relations. Viewing power conflicts in somewhat narrow and legalistic terms, Taft hoped to make America a leader in a movement for world peace. By settling all inter-

[4] *The Republican Roosevelt* (Cambridge, 1954), p. 125.

national disputes on the basis of arbitration, he believed that war could finally be wiped out. But Taft won little support for his arbitration treaties, either in the United States or abroad.

Where Roosevelt looked to the control of the "potential chaos" through the "proper policing of the world," and Taft saw solutions in the promotion of economic progress and in an idealistic faith in arbitration, Woodrow Wilson was convinced that America's responsibility lay in its assertion of moral leadership. Such leadership, he felt, had to be founded on coöperation and on an acceptance of the principle that no nation had the right to interfere in the internal and external affairs of another nation. It was this principle which had to be expanded "as the doctrine of the world." For, as Wilson said, "Every people should be left free to determine its own polity, its own way of development, unhindered, unthreatened, unafraid, the little along with the great and the powerful." To Wilson, the essence of America's responsibility was to see to it that all nations were permitted to work out their way of life free from any outside coercion. When such coercion occurred, then he believed it was the duty of the United States, preferably acting jointly with other nations, to intervene to remedy the situation. Above all, he maintained that the juridical equality and moral integrity of states had to be upheld. Respect for the rights of the little nation was just as important as for those of the big powers. In some measure, America's participation in World War I, and later in World War II, was grounded on this belief. That it still exerts a powerful force is evident in the Cold War today. As Frank Tannenbaum points out:

Our quarrel with Russia is upon this ground. Our defense of Korea is explainable only on the grounds that the only kind of a world the American people can comfortably live in is one in which Korea has no more right to attack and dismember Russia than Russia has to attack and dismember Korea. . . .[5]

With America's entry into World War I, the point of no return was reached. Roosevelt, Taft, and Wilson made the United States truly a great world power; but after the war it became the greatest power in the world. The change of America's status increased its responsibilities in world leadership.

The dilemma which confronted the United States in the years before World War II lay in the fact that the American people were unwilling to accept fully the implications of these responsibilities.

[5] "The American Tradition in Foreign Relations," *Foreign Affairs,* Vol. 30 (1951), p. 34.

3 · WORLD WAR I: PROBLEMS
OF WAR AND PEACE

The isolation of the United States is at an end not because we chose to go into the politics of the world, but because by the sheer genius of this people and the growth of our power we have become a determining factor in the history of mankind. . . .
WOODROW WILSON, *Speech, September 6, 1919*

The conflict of the great powers in the Far East formed a backdrop to the great struggle in Europe. Three new world powers had arisen at the end of the nineteenth century—Germany, the United States, and Japan. The combined impact of their rise portended a shake-up of the existing world order, challenging as it did the supremacy of Great Britain in Europe and Asia. The test of Britain's ability to maintain her position came with the outbreak of World War I. Her failure to do so signified the beginning of a new era.

America was oblivious in 1914 to the new role which would be thrust upon her by the events in Europe. Only the vaguest awareness existed that the old balance of power was being shattered. However, Theodore Roosevelt sensed it in 1906 when he intruded in the Moroccan crisis. Imperialist France had been preparing to take over the weakly independent country of Morocco. Germany, traditionally hostile to France, resisted this move. Kaiser Wilhelm II, who desired to keep an Open Door in Morocco for German merchants, assured the Sultan of help against French aggression. Since Britain had signed an important accord with France in 1904 and supported French claims, the crisis pointed to a possible war. Tensions seemed to reach a breaking point. The Kaiser appealed to Roosevelt to suggest that the powers meet to discuss the matter.

Roosevelt hesitated about getting involved in the dispute; the United States did not have any direct interest in Morocco. But the situation worried him, and he therefore arranged a conference at Algeciras, Spain, in January, 1906. Roosevelt felt that it was important to try "to keep matters on an even keel in Europe." But he appeared to be more concerned about Germany's ambitions than those of France. In his instructions to the American delegation, he urged them to support discreetly the Atlantic powers.

The Act of Algeciras, signed in April, 1906, represented a compromise; but one more favorable to France than to Germany. Morocco's independence was upheld, and Germany and the other powers were guaranteed an Open Door. France, however, was given control over the Moroccan police. This control enabled her in 1911 to defy Germany once again and finally to take over Morocco.

Roosevelt was bitterly criticized for meddling in the affairs of Europe and Africa. He replied that he would intervene anywhere if it meant preserving world peace. The United States, T. R. believed, could not remain aloof from the conflicts in Europe that might lead to war and dangerously threaten America's interests in other parts of the world. He was convinced that European equilibrium depended on America's support of Britain and France in curbing an insurgent Germany. If Britain could not maintain the balance of power, then, he thought, America would have to do so. "In fact," Roosevelt stated in 1911, "we ourselves are becoming owing to our strength and geographic situation, more and more the balance of power of the whole globe."

If Roosevelt thought in these terms, few Americans agreed with him. The United States had done well for itself by keeping clear of Europe's quarrels; only danger could result from getting mixed up in European politics. In 1914, most Americans were not interested in what was happening in Europe. When the Archduke Franz Ferdinand, heir to the Austro-Hungarian throne, was assassinated in June at Sarajevo, it hardly caused a ripple in the American newspapers. Even when war erupted in Europe, most Americans were only remotely concerned with the world-shattering crisis.

President Woodrow Wilson reflected the existing sentiment in the country when, on August 4, he issued a proclamation of neutrality. "The United States," he declared, "must be neutral in fact as well as in name. . . . We must be impartial in thought as well as in action." The war, he later said, was one "with which we have nothing to do, whose causes cannot touch us." While the sympathy of many Americans was clearly with the Allies, and Wilson's injunction to be "impartial in thought" was impossible to fulfill, most people agreed with the policy of neutrality.

Between 1914 and 1917, the United States became more and more drawn into the conflict in Europe. Despite the desire to keep out of the war, circumstances arose that ultimately led to America's intervention. These circumstances resulted from many things—anti-German hostility had built up progressively since the 1880's, while a pro-British entente had grown very strong—but three factors may be singled out for special attention: the violations of America's neutrality; the effect of the build-up of economic ties with the Allies; and the failure of Wilson's peace efforts.

THE NEUTRALITY MIRAGE

Nothing frustrated Wilson more than the violations of American neutrality by Britain and Germany. Although Britain never officially proclaimed a blockade against Germany, she took steps early in the war to control effectively neutral commerce that might aid the enemy. She alleged that Germany was illegally placing mines in open waters. This action, she declared in November, 1914, compelled her to consider the "whole North Sea . . . a military area." Britain then proceeded to mine that sea thoroughly. She warned all neutral ships to enter the North Sea by way of the Straits of Dover, and to stop at a British port for directions through the mine fields. The detention at the British port was irksome. Frequently, sailing directions were withheld from American vessels that were suspected of carrying "contraband." The British widened the definition of contraband so that foodstuffs, cotton, tobacco, and countless other items which Germany normally imported and which America shipped to the European continent were included on its lists.

The United States protested sharply against Britain's control of neutral commerce. Cotton and tobacco farmers in the South and agrarians in the Middle-West and West were especially angered. The extension of the blockade, visit-and-search procedures, the British blacklist, and censorship of neutral mail aroused widespread indignation throughout the country before 1917. While these measures led to a great loss of property and vigorous complaints, the British did not take America's protests seriously. From Britain's point of view, the control of neutral trade was absolutely essential in the life-and-death struggle with Germany.

Protests were brushed aside in part because of the strong, pro-British attitude of Walter Hines Page, the author-editor who was American ambassador in London. Convinced that the Allies were fighting America's battle for democracy and greatly charmed by Britain's Foreign Minister, Sir Edward Grey, Page had little use for those who would weaken Britain's war effort. He was especially contemptuous of State Department protests in connection with violations of American neutrality rights. Recalling an incident that occurred, Grey later wrote that on one occasion Page came to him with a State Department dispatch in which Washington asked what the British were going to do about putting an end to their "blockade" practices. Page said he was "instructed" to read the message to the British Foreign Minister. "He read, and I listened," Grey stated. "He then said: 'I have now read the despatch, but I do not agree with it; let us consider how it should be answered.' "

While Britain's control of neutral commerce was frustrating, Germany's use of submarine warfare proved to be more alarming. Germany declared that this new weapon was justified because of Britain's illegal blockade and because it was necessary to retaliate against Britain's policy of starving Germany's civilian population. Evidence indicates that Germany would have embarked on submarine warfare with or without the blockade. Plans to do so in the event of a conflict had been made before the outbreak of World War I. In the United States, the submarine —coming out of the sea from nowhere, and suddenly sinking an unarmed ship at sight without warning—was viewed as totally immoral, illegal, and dastardly. In view of Britain's blockade, the legality and morality of the submarine as a tactical weapon in warfare was a moot point, and one which could not be settled easily. Nevertheless, when Germany announced in February, 1915, that it would establish a war zone around the British Isles and destroy all enemy merchant ships encountered within that area, the State Department promptly warned that if American lives or ships were lost, Germany would be held to "strict accountability."

Secretary of State Bryan, who was the most genuinely pro-neutral individual in Wilson's Cabinet, realized that British infractions and Germany's unrestricted submarine warfare would place the United States in an impossible position. He suggested in February, 1915, that a way out might be found if Britain permitted the distribution of American foodstuffs to Germany, in return for which Germany would lift her submarine campaign. The German government agreed to Bryan's plan. However, it insisted on its right not only to import foodstuffs (which would be distributed to the civilian population through American agencies), but also on its right to import certain raw materials. Britain, fearful that

Bryan's plan would prolong the war, was unwilling to make any concessions. She refused to raise the "hunger blockade."

Under the circumstances, Bryan came to the conclusion that Americans voyaging on the seas in time of war should do so at their own risk:

We can hardly insist that the presence of an American on a British ship shall operate to prevent attack unless we are prepared to condemn the methods employed as improper in warfare. . . . Can an American by embarking upon a ship of the Allies at such a time and under such conditions impose upon his government an obligation to secure indemnity in case he suffers with others on the ship?

It was this question which was most crucial. Much of America's cargo was being transported on British vessels; Americans were traveling on belligerent passenger ships. Could Germany be held to "strict accountability" if her submarines torpedoed and sank such vessels? Bryan said that once Americans had been warned not to travel on belligerent ships, she could not; Wilson wavered, and then concluded that she must. The traditional right of freedom of the seas, he felt, had to be upheld. "Once accept a single abatement of right," Wilson declared, "and many other humiliations would certainly follow, and the whole fine fabric of international law might crumble under our hands piece by piece."

Wilson's determination to maintain America's national honor was fateful. A turning point came with the sinking of the British passenger liner *Lusitania*. On May 1, 1915, the German Embassy advertised in New York newspapers warning Americans not to travel on British passenger vessels which ventured into the waters around the British Isles. Telegrams were sent to several passengers preparing to sail on the *Lusitania* urging them to cancel their trip. On May 7, off the Irish Coast, the *Lusitania* was hit by a torpedo fired without warning from a German submarine. Lieutenant-Commander Schwieger later stated that the sighting of the *Lusitania* was the result of pure chance. He was about to turn back when, according to his log, "four funnels and two masts of a steamer" came into the periscope's view. Had the *Lusitania* steered a "zigzag" instead of a straight course—which she was supposed to do to make it difficult for a submarine to take careful aim—it is probable that she would not have been hit. Schwieger, in an excellent position, fired his last torpedo. When the ship keeled over, "the name *Lusitania* . . . visible in golden letters" was seen. The liner sank with unusual rapidity—about eighteen minutes—carrying down with her 1,198 men, women, and children, among them 128 Americans. The speed with which the *Lusitania* went under led to the suspicion that the ship, one of the largest passenger vessels afloat, carried munitions.

The tragedy created a wave of indignation throughout the United States. Emotional hysteria and anti-German feeling reached a high pitch. Because Germany had tried to warn Americans not to sail on the *Lusitania,* many persons believed the sinking was a calculated plot. While sympathy was deep and heartfelt, however, few newspapers clamored for America's entrance into the war. Profoundly shocked, Wilson affirmed the "indisputable" right of American citizens to sail the high seas.

Wilson's strong notes of protest disturbed Secretary Bryan. By stubbornly clinging to the doctrine of "strict accountability," he saw the President taking the United States down the road to war. Bryan decided to resign. Wilson tried to dissuade him, but he realized that the Secretary of State had grown, as he said, "more and more out of sympathy with the administration in its controversies with Germany." William G. McAdoo, the Secretary of the Treasury, warned Bryan that his resignation would ruin him. After reflecting for a moment, Bryan said: "I believe you are right. I think this will destroy me; but whether it does or not, I must do my duty according to my conscience, and if I am destroyed, it is, after all, merely the sacrifice that one must not hesitate to make to serve his God and his country."

Wilson accepted the Secretary of State's resignation with a "feeling of personal sorrow," but the country regarded it with indifference. The President's course was widely supported, and Bryan, who desired peace at all cost, was suspected of being pro-German.

Germany did not abandon her campaign of unrestricted submarine warfare against unarmed ships. She refused to pay indemnities for the sinking of the *Lusitania,* claiming that the British vessel was an armed merchantman. Secret orders, nonetheless, were issued to submarine commanders not to attack passenger liners. But in August, 1915, another British passenger ship, the *Arabic,* was torpedoed. Two Americans were killed. This time, Count Johann von Bernstorff, Germany's ambassador to the United States was so alarmed at the public's reaction that he feared the submarine campaign would bring America into the war. On his own initiative, he issued a public statement declaring that no more passenger ships would be sunk by U-boats without warning, provided the liners did "not try to escape or offer resistance." Bernstorff was reprimanded by the German government for his unauthorized statement; but his advice was heeded. Germany apologized for the attack on the *Arabic,* agreed to pay an indemnity, and after months of negotiation also conceded its "liability"—without an apology —for sinking the *Lusitania*. The matter, however, was still not settled when the United States went to war.

For the next seven months, no other incident occurred. The war, meanwhile, had ground to a bloody halt as the German armies after invading Belgium had been stopped in their offensive drive toward Paris. The military stalemate turned into a nightmare of trench warfare, and continued without letup until the armistice was signed in November, 1918.

After the attack on the *Arabic,* relations between the United States and Germany improved. They were rudely shattered in March, 1916, however, when an unarmed French passenger liner, the *Sussex,* was torpedoed and badly damaged. It managed to reach port, but the explosion caused some eighty casualties, including injury to several Americans. Wilson, incensed at the violation of Germany's pledge, sent an ultimatum to Berlin. Germany, he said, must keep her promise not to sink unresisting passenger ships without warning, or the United States would sever diplomatic relations. Germany yielded; but with a proviso: in the so-called *"Sussex* pledge," she declared that her campaign of unrestricted submarine warfare would be abandoned, but this would be done only if Britain abided by "the laws of humanity" and relaxed, in effect, her "hunger blockade."

Wilson accepted the *Sussex* pledge as a binding commitment, ignoring the proviso attached to it. In so doing, the impression arose that the President had won a complete diplomatic victory and had put an end to unrestricted submarine warfare. Wilson's prestige increased enormously. By throttling Germany and averting hostilities, he had shown that America's rights of neutrality could be upheld without resorting to the use of force. Actually, however, Wilson had boxed himself into a trap; for once committed, he had no choice—should Germany resume her submarine attacks—except to carry through his ultimatum threat, break diplomatic relations, and declare war. Such proved to be the case after the German announcement was made in January, 1917, that an all-out, unrestricted submarine campaign would be launched against the Allies.

THE ECONOMIC STAKE

While submarine warfare was the catalyst which was responsible for plunging America into the war in Europe, the agents of the catalyst were the strong ties that bound the United States to an Allied victory. Common linguistic, cultural, and intellectual bonds had created a sympathy for Britain's cause which was heightened by an astute propaganda campaign. By censoring all cablegrams to the United States and understanding better than Germany how to influence the American mind, Britain succeeded in convincing many Americans that the Allies were fighting their fight and defending the ideals of Western civilization, which German militarism was threatening to destroy. But more powerful than British propaganda—American opinion was already clearly anti-German—were the economic ties. At the outset of the war, the American economy was in a depressed condition. It had not been able to shake off the economic setback of 1907. The war in Europe in 1914 made things worse. The British blockade cut off German markets, and the diversion of American shipping created hardships. Unemployment was great. Relief came in 1915 when Allied war orders began to pour in, and the demand for agricultural foodstuffs mounted. Slowly the depression lifted, and an unprecedented war-born prosperity took its place.

While the Allies at first paid for their supplies and munitions out of their own funds and the cancellation of the huge debits of the United States in Europe, these sources quickly became exhausted. Unless America provided credits or loans, it was apparent that the Allies would not be able to sustain themselves in a long war and that the wartime boom in the United States would collapse.

Early in the war, the United States made it clear that American citizens had a legal right to sell munitions to all belligerent powers. However, because of the British blockade, it was impossible to send munitions to Germany. Since America would become an "arsenal" only for the Allies, Secretary of State Bryan argued that a correct policy of neutrality required an embargo on the arms trade. Congress, in fact, contemplated such a step; but it met with vigorous opposition, and no law was ever passed. The legal sanction of the munitions trade was vital to the industrial boom.

Wilson and Bryan recognized the legality of the munitions trade, but in 1914 they refused to sanction loans to belligerent powers. In August, the House of Morgan was called upon to float a French loan of $100 million to help pay for the purchase of American goods. When J. P. Morgan requested State Department approval for this loan, Bryan emphatically refused it. Loans to the Allies, he said, would make America a party to the conflict. Wilson agreed with Bryan, and Morgan cabled France that the loan could not be arranged. In October, however, under strong pressure from the banking interests, Wilson reversed the State Department's ruling. He privately informed certain bankers that it was permissible to advance credits—but not loans. The distinction, indeed, was a fine one. Later, after Bryan's resignation, Wilson, without making a point of the issue, told the bankers informally that they could lend money outright. A $500-million Anglo-French issue was floated by popular subscription in 1915. A total of about $2.3 billion was advanced to the Allies in cash and credit by the time America finally entered the war. Germany, on the other hand, obtained only $27 million. In the words of Charles C. Tansill,

The successful flotation of the Franco-British loan in October, 1915, made it possible for the Allied Governments to pay for the purchase of munitions that were indispensably necessary for the projected offensive of 1916. It also bound the business interests in the United States to the cause of the Allies, for it served as the foundation of a financial structure that was evoked Aladdin-like from the lamp of fabulous war profits.[1]

By 1917, it became clear that America's economic structure and prosperity had been linked to an Allied victory. When Germany decided upon an all-out attack in a do-or-die stand in January, it imperiled not only the Allies, but the United States.

WILSON'S PEACE EFFORTS

The great passion of Woodrow Wilson was to exert America's moral leadership in world affairs. Such leadership, he thought, could best be demonstrated by removing force as an instrument in national policy and substituting a world parliament to preserve peace. Antimilitaristic in his outlook, Wilson liked neither large standing armies nor military training. Only slowly and with misgivings was he won over to the need for supporting a preparedness program.

Although devoted to British traditions and in sympathy with the Allies, Wilson felt that it was America's duty to serve humanity by acting as a mediator to end the war by a negotiated peace. In January, 1915, he sent his intimate personal adviser, Colonel Edward M. House—a Kentucky rather than a military "colonel" and a foxy, Texas politician—on a mission to Europe. House had promoted Wilson's presidential aspirations before 1912 and had been chiefly responsible for his nomination. When Wilson entered the White House, he virtually became a member of the family. Acting as an Assistant President without portfolio, he enjoyed Wilson's implicit confidence. "Mr. House is my second personality," Wilson once stated. "He is my independent self. His thought and mine are one."

Serving as the President's eyes and ears, Colonel House—who was

---

[1] *America Goes to War* (Boston, 1938), p. 114.

even more strongly pro-Allied than Wilson—sounded out the British, French, and Germans on ending the war. Germany appeared to be anxious to discuss Allied peace terms "verbally and secretly" in January, 1915, and House was urged to come to Berlin. However, he first went to England. It was apparent that the British were not ready; they managed to delay House's trip to Germany to such an extent that whatever hope existed for a negotiated peace died.

Wilson was quite upset by House's procrastination; he cautioned him not to allow the British government to determine when it was best for him to go to Germany, since they were probably waiting for events in the field to obtain an advantage. "If the impression were to be created in Berlin that you were to come only when the British government thought it the opportune time for you to come," Wilson said, "you might be regarded when you reached there as their spokesman rather than mine." But this advice was not heeded. House did not arrive in Berlin until March; by that time, the opportune moment in which Germany might have accepted a "reasonable" Allied proposal had passed.

Early in 1916, Colonel House again went to Europe on a peace mission. Sir Edward Grey had become intensely interested in establishing a parliament of world powers—a league of nations—and he dropped the hint as to whether the United States would not abandon her isolation to assume a position of leadership in such an organization. The idea immediately appealed to Wilson and Colonel House. Deeply interested in the possibility of outlawing future wars, House suggested including the "elimination of militarism and navalism" in any proposed peace terms. During House's second visit to England, much discussion centered on lofty, idealistic goals on which there was mutual agreement; some differences arose, however, on the matter of specific peace terms. After again sounding out the French and Germans, Colonel House returned to Britain, and a plan was worked out for American mediation. This was contained in the House-Grey secret agreement of February, 1916. When the moment was opportune, Grey stated in the memorandum that was drawn up, France and England would propose to Wilson "that a Conference should be summoned to put an end to the war." If the Allies accepted, and Germany refused, it was understood that the United States then "would *probably* enter the war against Germany." Should the conference fail to secure a peace, the memorandum indicated, "the United States would [probably] leave the Conference as a belligerent on the side of the Allies." Wilson included the bracketed "probably" before he approved the agreement.

With so many *probably*s, the House-Grey memorandum could not represent a binding pledge. It nevertheless virtually committed the United States to the Allied coalition. But the machinery for mediation was never put into effect. Throughout 1916, neither Britain nor France thought that the moment was "opportune." Both countries were confident that they could deliver a knockout blow to Germany and impose their own peace terms without American interference.

Wilson decided at the end of 1916 not to wait for British and French overtures. He planned to take the initiative and appeal to the belligerent powers to agree to a negotiated peace. However, just as he was ready to send out his notes, Germany, in a surprise move on December 12, issued a statement in which they declared their willingness to talk terms. The offer by the Germans was not made out of weakness. They were confident of an impending victory and expected the Allies to reject their terms; in that case, they planned to renew their offensive to smash France and Britain in the West. The decision was also reached—in the event negotiations failed—to risk America's entrance into the war in order to harass the British supply lines. "The conditions they had secretly in mind," states John Morton Blum, "asked the Allies in effect to surrender, to cede territory along the Baltic, in the Congo, in Belgium, France and Luxembourg."[2]

Despite Germany's announcement of her willingness to negotiate with her enemies, Wilson sent his own message to the belligerent powers on December 18. It was in a more modified form than the note he had originally prepared. Germany responded to the President's appeal, she called for a conference, but said she did not want neutrals involved in determining peace terms. Germany indicated, however, that after the conference she would be willing to join with the United States in the creation of an international organization. Since Wilson's message was timed so closely with Germany's offer to negotiate, Britain and France suspected German-American collusion. They rebuffed the President's appeal, and demanded instead indemnities and the destruction of Germany.

In a last, desperate effort to bring the belligerents to their senses, Wilson decided to speak to the world. Addressing the Senate on January 22, 1917, he delivered a poignant and memorable address. Representing as he felt, "the silent mass of mankind everywhere," Wilson called for a peace everlasting. He bluntly warned that only a "peace among equals," a "peace without victory," could bring a permanent settlement and an end to all wars. Permanent peace, he said, had to be based among other things on the equality of rights of all nations, on

[2] *Woodrow Wilson and the Politics of Morality* (Boston, 1956), p. 126.

the freedom of the seas, and on world disarmament. It could only be possible if a league of nations were established.

Whatever hope existed that the belligerent powers would listen to Wilson's voice—and it was a very faint hope—was smashed one week later, on January 31, when Germany proclaimed the resumption of her campaign of unrestricted submarine warfare.

ROAD TO WAR

Four days after the announcement, Wilson appeared before Congress and dramatically declared that steps had been taken to end diplomatic relations with Germany. During the next three weeks, American ships refused to sail the Atlantic. Jittery ship captains insisted on arming their merchant vessels before going to Europe. A virtual economic paralysis gripped the country. To break the bottleneck, Wilson came before Congress again and asked the legislators to enact without delay an Armed Ship Bill to give the President authority to arm American merchant vessels.

Congressional sentiment overwhelmingly supported Wilson's request. But eleven anti-interventionist Senators, led by insurgent Republicans George W. Norris and Robert M. La Follette, filibustered the bill to death. "A little group of wilful men," charged Wilson publicly, "had rendered the great government of the United States helpless and contemptible." The President failed to get Congressional authorization. Nevertheless, Wilson, by executive order, sanctioned the arming of American ships, and in March instructed the merchantmen that they could shoot submarines at sight in the war zone.

A war fever soon took hold of the country. On March 1, the American press headlined the notorious Zimmermann note that had been intercepted by British intelligence and turned over to Wilson the previous week. The President, deeply shocked, made the note public. From this message, the American people learned that Arthur Zimmermann, Germany's Foreign Minister, had instructed the German minister in Mexico to propose an alliance with Mexico in case the United States entered the war. In return for Mexico's coöperation, Zimmermann promised that Germany would seek to restore the "lost provinces" of Texas, New Mexico, and Arizona. He also urged Mexico to persuade Japan to join in the scheme. The disclosures of the Zimmermann note stirred up a wave of bitter anti-German feeling, especially in the Southwest and along the Pacific Coast, where such sentiment had previously been very mild.

Japan's role was hard to explain, but no doubt it contributed to the hostility against Germany in the West. She was an ally of Great Britain, and her apparent complicity seemed to point to a double cross. Japan quickly denied this charge, and she excused her participation in the scheme by stating that her only purpose was to obtain information about the plot. She repudiated any connection with Germany. However, it is probable that Japan was not averse to coöperating with Germany against the United States—not the Allied European powers—whose policies conflicted with her own expansionist ambitions.

The German announcement of unrestricted submarine warfare created a critical turn in the war in Europe; but far more ominous—especially to Britain and France—was the unexpected outbreak of the March Revolution in Russia, which threatened the collapse of the whole Eastern Front. From 1914 to 1917, Germany had been compelled to fight the war on two fronts. Although the Eastern Front remained subsidiary to that in the west, she was constantly faced with the problem of having to shift troops and supplies from the east to the west, and vice versa, depending on the tide of the war. The inefficiency of her ally, Austria-Hungary, and the lack of dependability of Slavic troops in that empire's army increased Germany's responsibility and led to a constant deployment of her troops. The Eastern Front for the most part remained fluid, with constant movement and utterly confused strategy. Battles generally seesawed, with the Russians defeating the Hapsburg forces, and the Germans retrieving the loss by defeating the Russians. To the Western Allies, however, the Eastern Front was of inestimable importance since it prevented the Germans from inflicting a knockout blow in France.

Fear arose in March, 1917 that the new Russian regime might negotiate a separate peace with Germany, and withdraw from the war. In this event, hundreds of thousands of veteran German troops could be shifted to the West in time for the spring and summer offensives. The military balance thus might be tipped decisively in favor of Germany. British and French strategy dictated keeping Russia in the war at all cost, and encouraging prompt American intervention. To keep Russia in the war, Britain, France, and the United States immediately recognized the new Provisional Government that replaced czarist authority.

News of the overthrow of the Czar was warmly welcomed in America. Russia, it was believed, like all the Allies would now be fighting for the cause of democracy.

The March Revolution (February in Russian terminology, since our Gregorian calendar was not adopted in that country until 1918) was the first of two distinct overturns to occur in Russia in 1917. It was a spontaneous insurrection which aimed chiefly at replacing the Czar's incom-

petent government with more moderate, progressive leaders. It was over
very quickly, with relatively little bloodshed. Its program was directed
toward the adoption of mild reforms espoused by the middle class.

Dissatisfaction was especially great in Russia early in 1917. The
exhausting war left its inevitable toll. Inflation, strikes, and food short-
ages created a rising popular fury. Talk of signing a separate peace with
Germany mounted. On March 10, a movement against the regime grew
in intensity, spurred on by a strike of thousands of workers at Petrograd's great Putilov Works. The cry arose, "Down with Autocracy!"
M. V. Rodzianko, the president of the Duma, Russia's limited parliamentary body, warned Czar Nicholas II of the seriousness of the situation. But the autocrat did not listen. "That fat Rodzianko has written me
some nonsense," Nicholas said, "to which I shall not even reply." The
movement soon turned into an insurrection, and the insurrection into
a widespread revolution. The Duma leaders demanded Nicholas' abdica-
tion and hoped to name his brother, the Grand Duke Michael, regent.
Nicholas, surprisingly, agreed. However, opposition to monarchism was
so great that Michael refused to take the crown except from a Constitu-
ent Assembly. As a result, Russia became a de facto republic, with its
new Provisional Government headed first by Prince G. E. Lvov, a noted
liberal.

The new regime put into effect a number of political reforms; but no
change was made in Russia's foreign policy. The Provisional Government
assured the Allies that Russia stood by her treaty obligations. The war,
it declared, would be continued much more energetically than had been
the case under the leadership of the Czar.

Nikolai Lenin, the future Communist leader, was in Switzerland with
several associates when news came of the fall of the monarchy and the
formation of the Provisional Government. He had spent much of the
war years in this country, developing his ideas on capitalism and imperialism. He came to the conclusion that a true Marxist party must
come to power in Russia to end the war in the interest of the working
class. Eager to return to Russia, he found that no Allied country would
permit him to cross its territory. Germany, eager to overlook no opportunity to disrupt the Russian war effort, obliged by putting the Lenin
party in a sealed railroad car which crossed into Denmark. Lenin made
his way through Sweden and Finland, and reached Russia in April.
Lenin's revolutionary program was at first regarded as visionary, im-
practical, and ludicrous by the majority socialist factions. In the chaos
of the time, Lenin's fiery oratory, his incessant plea to "End the War"
and to give "All land to the Peasants" won increasing support. The

breach between the revolutionary groups widened, and by May Lenin's demands were approved by the Bolsheviks; the attack against the wavering Provisional Government grew stronger.

In July, Lvov resigned as Premier, and was succeeded by Alexander Kerensky, a conservative, right-wing socialist, who had been Minister of Justice in the Provisional Government. Kerensky followed an even more moderate course than his predecessor. He was completely opposed to any radical change in the social order. Faced by dissension within his cabinet, growing disorder in the country, and the rising power of the Bolsheviks, Kerensky was easily overthrown in the November (Bolshevik) Revolution. On November 8, 1917, Lenin came to power and set up the Soviet government. The new Soviet regime destroyed the Provisional Government, introduced sweeping measures, and set about avowedly creating a "dictatorship of the proletariat."

The first phase of the Russian Revolution in March, 1917, coincided with the crisis in American-German relations. After adopting the policy of "armed neutrality," the American people waited for an "overt act." It came quickly. On March 12, the American steamer *Algonquin* was torpedoed. Within a week, three other American ships homeward bound from Europe were sunk. The drive for war with Germany gathered momentum. Plagued by doubt, Wilson finally made up his mind. He issued a call to Congress to convene on April 2—two weeks earlier than scheduled—to receive a communication from the Chief Executive on matters of "national policy which should be taken immediately under consideration." In his war message, Wilson reviewed the steps that led to the grave crisis with Germany. His speech, a model of splendid prose, reasserted his moral convictions. He did not blame the German people, but its rulers.

It is a fearful thing to lead this great peaceful people into war . . . But the right is more precious than peace, and we shall fight for the things which we have always carried nearest our hearts—for democracy . . . for the rights and liberties of small nations, for a universal dominion of right by such a concert of free peoples as shall bring peace and safety to all nations and make the world itself at last free.

On April 6, 1917, Congress declared war against Germany.

America's intervention and Russia's continuance in the war turned the military tide. With Russia still fighting, Germany was unable to use her full military force on the Western Front in the summer of 1917. After the German offensive was checked, American military support became decisive. For the Allies could then rely on America's growing power to assure the final defeat of Germany. By the time the Bolsheviks seized control of Russia and promptly agreed to an armistice with Germany, the immediate danger had passed. "If the Allies had been left to face the collapse of Russia without being sustained by the intervention of the United States," wrote Winston Churchill later, "it seems certain that France could not have survived the year, and the war would have ended in a Peace by negotiation or, in other words, a German victory."

A PEACE PROGRAM

As soon as the United States entered the war in Europe—as an "Associate," and not as an "Allied" power—preparations began to work out the details of a peace program. Wilson created a small group of private citizens (chiefly in the academic fields) under the direction of Colonel House, known as the "Inquiry" committee. Throughout 1917 and 1918, this group accumulated information on territorial and other questions which it believed would be most important when the final peace treaty would be drawn up. Many members of the "Inquiry" went along with Wilson to Paris after the armistice was signed and acted as an advisory board. They continued to remain in Europe until the treaties with the enemy powers—Germany, Austria, Hungary, and Bulgaria—were completed.

America's peace program centered largely on two points: the creation of a League of Nations, and Wilson's Fourteen Points, which the President enunciated in January, 1918. In many respects, the idea of the League of Nations and a number of Wilson's Fourteen Points were revolutionary in scope. They aimed, in effect, at breaking down the whole fabric of the European balance-of-power system. It soon became apparent that the concept of a League which Wilson had in mind differed greatly from that of Britain and France. These victorious Allies conceived of the League mainly as an organization to maintain the status quo and to keep Germany and the other defeated nations from renewing aggression. A wide gap existed between Wilson and the European powers, especially France, on the matter of the problems of security. This was partly due to the relatively small material losses suffered by the United States during the war compared to those of Europe. Despite the great number of casualties, America had prospered during the war years; Britain and France, on the other hand, had not only suffered more serious losses, but were in economic distress. It was difficult, moreover, for France to think of Germany as a thoroughly defeated nation when the latter had experienced no territorial devastation and had ended the war by an armistice. Germany still remained a threat that was feared. Wilson knew that it would be difficult for him to persuade the Allies to forget their purely national grievances, but he hoped that they would do so in supporting a League of Nations which would truly become a world parliament. The Covenant of the League of Nations that was finally drafted contained only the form, but not the substance, of what Wilson had in mind.

The great disparity between Wilson's views and those of the Allies was also evident in the emasculation of the Fourteen Points. Wilson demanded certain long-range reforms in international affairs: the abandonment of the European practice of entering into secret treaties; the establishment of freedom of the seas, except insofar as the seas should be closed to an aggressor nation by collective action; the lowering of tariff barriers to promote equality of trade conditions among nations; a general reduction of armament; and an impartial adjustment of colonial claims without reference to imperialist annexation ambitions. He championed the right of the self-determination of nations, with such conditions and guaranties to make independence possible.

The great end of Wilson's program was the reform of international society. But he was quite vague on *how* this reform could be brought about. He placed his faith in the League of Nations; once it became a functioning organization, he believed, it would be capable of channeling the necessary readjustments and would chart the way to future reforms.

Considerable opposition developed in the United States toward Wilson's peace program. It was principally dominated by Massachusetts' Republican Senator Henry Cabot Lodge, who had become a bitter political foe of Wilson, and for a brief period, until his death in 1919, by Theodore Roosevelt. Both Lodge and T. R. did not object to American participation in European affairs; they were not isolationists in the popular meaning of this term. Neither felt that the United States should withdraw from Europe, but they did believe that Wilson's peace program was naïve, too idealistic, and not in accord with the power realities of the world order. They thought that the United States should guarantee the peace; that it should endorse an alliance with France against Germany; and that it should support Belgium with armed force if necessary. They wanted the United States to stand committed to the independence of Poland and the Baltic states. In other words, they wanted America frankly to recognize its ties with the security problems of Europe and act accordingly. On the important matter of the structure of the peace, therefore, a major difference between Wilson and leaders of the Republican opposition was that the President wanted to promote good feeling in Europe and a fundamental reform in international society to the end that the Germans would not wish to attack other nations again; the

Lodge-Roosevelt plan put little faith in reform and relied principally on armed might as the bulwark of security.

Wilson's fatal error lay not so much in his peace program—for there was much in it on which both political parties could agree—but in his resolve to go in person to Paris to negotiate the treaty. In taking on the burden, Wilson overlooked the necessity of getting a representative delegation of Democrats and Republicans. Even if this had been done, it is doubtful whether the results would have been any different at Paris, but the fact that it turned out to be Wilson's show sharpened the opposition's attack against the President.

THE CURTAIN IS RAISED ON THE PARIS CONFERENCE

World War I brought Britain, France, the United States, Japan, and Italy together in the defeat of the common enemy. Victory soon disclosed the great differences in their national policies. When the great powers—and the lesser ones—gathered together at Paris in 1919 in one of the largest peace conferences in world history, these conflicts soon came to the forefront. Quite suddenly, the military battlefield was transformed into a diplomatic battlefield. In this new arena, each power maneuvered to obtain maximum concessions for itself. Except for a few topics suggested by Wilson, no agenda or over-all plan existed for the Paris Peace Conference.

In his *Autobiography,* Lincoln Steffens, the outstanding journalist of the muckraking era, described a conversation, held on the third day of the meetings, between Georges Clemenceau, the "Old Tiger" of France, British Prime Minister David Lloyd George, and Woodrow Wilson. It is doubtful that the conversation actually occurred in the manner set down so vividly by Steffens; nevertheless, it conveys some idea of the difficulties which arose at Paris.

One can picture Premier Clemenceau at the time. Blunt and acid in his expression, the proud patriot of France was squat and stooped with the weight of his seventy-seven years. He wore a gray walrus mustache, and a fringe of white hair encircled a bald spot protected by a black skull-cap; gray gloves covered his eczema-ravaged hands. Clemenceau's eyes were tired but alert, and his powerful, jutting jaw intruded quickly whenever a defense of France was called for. A cynic, he looked upon the idealistic Wilson with amused contempt. "I can get on with you," he once told Colonel House. "I can understand you. But talking to Wilson is something like talking to Jesus Christ." And again, "God gave us His Ten Commandments and we broke them. Wilson gives us his Fourteen Points—we shall see."

At the meeting with President Wilson and Prime Minister Lloyd

George in Paris, as Steffens tells the story, the Old Tiger declaimed: "There has been a great deal of talk about a peace to end wars forever, and I am interested in that. But I would like to know whether you gentlemen meant it, the permanent peace?"

Wilson and the suave Lloyd George assured him that they did.

"So," said Clemenceau, "you really mean it! Well, it is possible we can do it; we can make permanent peace—but we French cannot believe you mean what you say."

Patiently, Wilson and Lloyd George repeated their assurances.

"All right," muttered Clemenceau. "We can make this permanent peace. We can remove all the causes of war. Have you counted the cost of such a peace?"

"What cost?" Wilson and Lloyd George wanted to know.

"Well," Clemenceau allegedly replied, "if we give up all future wars, if we are to prevent war, we must first give up our empire and all hope of empire. You, Mr. Lloyd George, you English will have to come out of India, for example. We French will have to come out of North Africa. You Americans, Mr. President, will have to come out of the Philippines and Puerto Rico, and leave Cuba alone. We can go to these and other countries as tourists, traders, travelers. We cannot any more govern them and exploit them, or have the inside track in them. We cannot longer possess the keys to trade routes and the sphere of influence."

Clemenceau asked if the British Prime Minister and the American President were willing to pay these prices. No, they protested; no, no, they did not mean *exactly* that.

"Then," the Old Tiger declared, banging his fist sharply on the table, "then you don't mean permanent peace. You mean war!"

And, in a sense, Clemenceau was to be right. For out of the Paris Peace Conference there was to emerge a pattern of disunity among the major victorious powers—a pattern which soon wrecked all hope for a "permanent peace."

The Conference dealt mainly with five big problems: the question of French security against another German attack; the problem of reparations; the Shantung issue and Japan's claim to the German Pacific islands north of the equator; the disposition of Germany's colonies; and the annexationist claims of Italy. All of these problems were intimately tied to the most fundamental issue raised at Paris: the creation of the League of Nations.

Woodrow Wilson wanted to draft the Covenant of the League before the great powers discussed specific questions. It had to be the foundation for a just and durable peace. But Clemenceau insisted on talking

about the League later. He felt that France had to be sure that her
security would be guaranteed. Wilson would not hear of this. The League,
he said, had to come first and be made an integral part of each peace
treaty. He would not budge. Wilson was afraid that if the drafting of the
Covenant was put off, it might be shelved. He did not wish to take any
chances; the creation of the League of Nations was bound up with all
of the basic principles he had set forth as necessary for an enduring
peace. Its establishment became his overriding concern at the Paris
meetings. By his prestige, diplomatic skill, and sheer force of will, Wilson
won his point.

One of the first things the Peace Conference did was to establish a
special committee to draft the Covenant of the League of Nations. Wilson
served as chairman, and Colonel House was a member of the commission. Although representatives of the great powers and smaller states
were on the committee, the drafting of the Covenant became a pre-
dominantly Anglo-American enterprise, with Wilson dominating the
proceedings. The President succeeded in embodying many—but not all
—of the idealistic principles he had set forth in his Fourteen Points.
The heart of the League Covenant was Article 10, in which the signatory
members pledged themselves "to respect and preserve as against external
aggression the territorial integrity and existing political independence
of all members of the League." The principle of arbitration was firmly
laid down in Article 13. Member nations agreed "to carry out faithfully
awards or decisions made, and to refrain from waging war on a nation
complying with such awards or decisions." Economic penalties were to
be imposed "upon those nations which waged war in disregard of their
promises to submit their disputes for arbitration or judicial settlement."
The Covenant also specified that the Council might recommend to League
members the adoption of certain military measures against the aggressor
nations.

The principles that international engagements must be "open
covenants," and that there must be a reduction of armaments in the
interest of preserving world peace were contained in the League
Covenant. Wilson had called in his Fourteen Points for "a free, open-
minded, and absolutely impartial adjustment of all colonial claims."
While this was impossible at the Paris Conference, Article 22 set up a
mandate system which at least contemplated that colonial powers would
exercise a tutelage pointing to the eventual granting of independence
under the supervision of the League of Nations. Three classes of mandated areas were defined—later designated as "A," "B," "C"—depending upon their stage of development and the extent to which the colonial

peoples could manage their own affairs. Wilson was less successful in obtaining endorsement for the principles of the "freedom of the seas" and the reduction of tariff barriers. Article 23, however, stated that "equitable treatment" would be maintained "for the commerce of all Members of the League." The League Covenant also provided for the general supervision over slavery and forced labor, and over the traffic in drugs, arms, and munitions.

Wilson labored long and hard on the drafting of the Covenant of the League of Nations. Proudly, he presented it to the entire Conference in February, 1919. A noble machinery, he firmly believed, had been created to adjust international disputes without recourse to war. Wilson was convinced that it would be his—and America's—supreme achievement. But the great fight for his ideals—in Paris and in the United States— still lay ahead: to obtain the full support of the great powers at Paris, and to win the confidence of the American people to endorse commitments in Europe and elsewhere to maintain world peace.

The Allied leaders, less idealistic than Wilson, and more concerned with the spoils of war and *their own*—rather than the world's—security, were frankly skeptical about the League's guarantees. This was especially true with respect to France. For Clemenceau did not believe that the League of Nations could provide an answer to France's problems. Security for France meant one thing: a weakened, crippled Germany. The Franco-Prussian War of 1870-71, and the terrible destruction of World War I on French soil lived in her memory. Germany's defeat in 1918, Clemenceau felt, was not enough. The armistice, indeed, had come at a time when most Germans were by no means certain that Germany was badly beaten. She still occupied large conquered areas and had not suffered home-front devastation. France was painfully familiar with Germany's recuperative capacity. She knew, too, the deep-seated desire that would remain for a future war of revenge. Germany, and Germany alone, Clemenceau believed, was the great threat to the peace of the postwar world. The French premier would not be sidetracked by Wilson's League of Nations. He clearly and forcefully set forth France's demands. The French program called for the political and territorial dismemberment of Germany by establishing an independent Rhineland Republic; it demanded the annexation to France of Alsace-Lorraine and the Saar; and it provided for permanent disarmament and heavy German reparations.

Wilson was convinced that Clemenceau's extreme demands would sow the seeds for a future war. However, he recognized that to obtain France's support for the League, compromises and concessions would be necessary. Subsequently, Wilson faced the same problem in connection with the demands of the other powers at Paris. In each case, he was compelled to give ground; but he never surrendered completely. What is remarkable is that he managed to salvage as much of his program as he did. Britain, likewise, opposed the French program. While Britain, at first, favored crippling indemnities, she did not want Germany to be completely crushed. She counted on a sizable reparation to help make up her wartime losses, but she also felt that her recovery depended on restoring her European markets. In this respect, Germany was still needed to stabilize the European economy. Japan and Italy did not participate actively on the question of French security or the German problem, but the opposition of Wilson and Lloyd George succeeded in whittling down the French proposals.

Clemenceau did not obtain all that he wanted. He secured a permanent demilitarization of the left bank of the Rhine. But he did not obtain a Rhineland Republic, nor did he achieve the extreme indemnities he sought—far more crippling than those Britain suggested. In fact, because of Wilson's insistence, the problem was referred to a Reparations Commission for more intensive study, and the amount of Germany's indemnity was not determined at Paris. Alsace-Lorraine was restored to France, and French control was established over the Saar coal mines; but the Saar region itself was placed under the jurisdiction of the League of Nations for fifteen years.

Lloyd George tried to allay France's fears. He talked to Colonel House and later to Woodrow Wilson. Britain, he said, would be willing to support France if Germany launched another invasion. Would America join Britain in offering France such a guarantee? Without such a commitment, he was certain that Clemenceau would not endorse the League Covenant. After much reflection, Wilson agreed to sign a special Treaty of Guarantee. Britain and America, it was decided, would each negotiate a separate treaty with France. Each would pledge that it would come to the aid of its ally if an "unprovoked movement of aggression" by Germany occurred. However, Lloyd George insisted upon an "escape clause"—if America failed to ratify the alliance, he said, Britain would not be obligated to help France.

The maneuver worked. With a guarantee of a tripartite treaty, Clemenceau became more pliable and supported the League Covenant, although he continued to remain rather cynical about the new machinery for peace. Clemenceau had no objection to a League of Nations, or a League of Allies, or a league of whatever one wanted to call it, provided it exercised effective power. Wilson's milk-and-water scheme he was sure could not. What he wanted was a league in which a French general would be in command of an international army and take vigorous action at the slightest sign of German aggression. In his view, an effective league was one which would be a military alliance of the big powers, and not a sop to placate world opinion.

Clemenceau was later severely criticized for anchoring French policy to the Treaty of Guarantee. A certain doubt existed that Wilson could obtain Senate approval of the treaty since it represented a striking departure from America's "no entangling alliances" tradition. The prevailing mood in the United States was such as to give little confidence that a change would take place. Clemenceau took the gamble, and lost: the treaty later died ignominiously in the Senate Committee on Foreign Relations, which did not even refer it to the Senate floor for debate. The rejection of the security treaty led France to search for other means to strengthen her security. She decided to develop a bilateral system of alliances with the countries surrounding Germany. This course was difficult to reconcile with the Wilsonian principles of the League of Nations, to which Clemenceau had outwardly committed France. Later, she was to be accused of hypocrisy and inconsistency. But, at the time, France was convinced that Britain and America did not really understand her problems on the continent.

Wilson's greatest battle lay not so much in Paris but in the United States, where he had to rally the American people to his cause. Here he did not fare too well. His position had already been seriously compromised even before he sailed to France in December, 1918. A month earlier, Wilson had suffered a humiliating personal political defeat in the Congressional elections; the Republican party triumphantly took over control of both Houses. The defeat was made more bitter by the fact that, in October, Wilson had addressed an appeal to the country calling for a Democratic majority. He stressed the point that if the Republicans won, it would be interpreted abroad "as a repudiation of my leadership."

After presenting the draft of the Covenant of the League of Nations to the Peace Conference in February, 1919, Wilson decided to return to the United States. He felt that his great work was over; he could sign a few bills in Washington before resuming with the Conference negotiations and, most important, "educate" the American people by explaining what had been accomplished. The attack against Wilson's program began before the President stepped foot on America's shores once again. The Republican opposition was especially biting in their criticism. "The greatest triumph for English diplomacy in three centuries of English diplomatic life," declared Senator William E. Borah with reference to the League Covenant. Wilson was soon subjected to a rigorous cross-examination on the League of Nations before a gathering of the Senate and House committees concerned with foreign affairs. Republican leaders sensed a vulnerable target to discredit the administration, and they opened fire. The strength of the opposition was revealed on March 4, when Lodge read on the Senate floor a signed statement by thirty-nine Senators or Senators-elect—this was six votes more than was necessary to defeat a League treaty—which declared that "the constitution of the league of nations *in the form now proposed* to the peace conference should not be accepted by the United States." The proposal for a League of Nations, these Republicans stated, should not be considered until a peace treaty had been made; and, under no circumstances, should the League Covenant be embodied in the treaty. In effect, this statement killed America's participation in the League.

In 1919, there were a number of things which tragically worked against Wilson. The war was over, and the country was in the throes of postwar economic adjustment. The harsh experiences of battle had been a sobering experience, and most Americans were anxious to forget the past. Wilson would not let them; to him, the war could not be over until a sound foundation for peace was erected. "This nation went into this war to see it through to the end, and the end has not come yet," he said. "This is the beginning, not of the war but of the processes which are going to render a war like this impossible." However, with all of his splendid oratory, Wilson could not dispel the disillusion. The attitude slowly crystallized and then hardened into the belief that the best way to avoid involvement in a future war was to have as little to do with the rivalries of the European powers as was possible. Here were contained the seeds for the later isolationist reaction. "If I have had a conviction throughout my life with which it has been possible for me to be consistent at all times," said Senator Borah, one of the leaders of the so-called "irreconcilables," "it has been the conviction that we should stay out of European and Asiatic affairs. I do not think we can have here a great powerful, independent, self-governing Republic and do anything else. . . ."

The lines quickly became drawn. Wilson was warned that before the League Covenant would ever be considered certain changes would have to be made. These included: the right of the members to withdraw from the League; a specific article declaring that the League could not have jurisdiction in domestic matters, especially on such questions as the tariff and immigration; and a declaration safeguarding the Monroe Doctrine. Wilson took this warning to heart. When he returned to Paris in April, he secured the adoption of these amendments. He succeeded without making any of the drastic changes in the League Covenant which other nations proposed, but he paid a heavy price by having to make concessions in other matters.

Wilson obtained what he wanted: the League Covenant was made an integral part of the Versailles Treaty. He would not, under any circumstances, bend to the Republican criticism that the League be separated from the treaty of peace. "You cannot dissect the covenant from the treaty," Wilson defiantly declared, "without destroying the whole vital structure." In the end, however, he obtained neither America's participation in the League of Nations nor approval of the treaty.

Senator Henry Cabot Lodge's implacable personal hatred for Wilson and his desire to further his own political advantage set the stage for the final showdown. Lodge did not directly attack the Versailles Treaty or the League Covenant. Instead, he said, he wanted to "Americanize" them by including fourteen amendments and reservations. His principal target was Article 10—the Article Wilson considered fundamental to the League Covenant—which stated that League members would take collective action to put down future aggressors. Lodge insisted that a clause be inserted reserving to Congress the authority to approve the use of American military forces for any such purpose. He wanted to be sure that the Article would not supersede the Constitution. But Wilson did not feel that it was necessary. Stubborn, and hating Lodge as much as the senator detested him, the President refused to compromise.

In a desperate effort to beat down Republican opposition, Wilson decided to tour the country to build up popular support in his favor. He hoped, in this way, to shift a number of senatorial votes to his side. On a barnstorming trip, without pulling his "punches," the President warned that failure to make the League work would lead to another war. Popular enthusiasm was very great. But Wilson's outbursts, frequently tactless and offensive, against the "irreconcilable" Republicans solidified the determination of many senators to vote against the treaty.

After touring through the Old Northwest, the Upper Mississippi Valley, and the Far West, Wilson, physically and emotionally exhausted from the strain, summoned up his strength and spoke to a crowd at Pueblo, Colorado, in September, 1919. He pleaded, with tears in his eyes—amidst the deafening cheers of his audience—for a League of Nations to end war, and then his health suddenly gave way. He collapsed on the train that night and was rushed back to Washington. A few days later a stroke paralyzed one side of his body and made him a pitiful invalid. Rumors spread that the President was dying or had become insane. But from his sickroom, Wilson's voice was still heard. He called on loyal Democrats to defeat the Lodge reservations. He was willing to accept "mild" Democratic reservations; but not the "strong" Lodge reservations which he felt did not "provide for ratification but, rather, for the nullification of the treaty." But broken physically, Wilson could not press the fight. The end had come. In November, 1919, the Versailles Treaty with the League of Nations embodied in it was voted down by the Senate. "The United States had renounced the great effort, for which it had itself provided the leadership in the person of Woodrow Wilson," as Foster Rhea Dulles expressed it, "to substitute for the rivalries and military alliances of the past a new system of collective security. In spite of its world war experience, it was prepared to fall back upon isolationism."[3]

Whether America's participation in the League of Nations would have changed the subsequent course of events is purely conjectural; the chances are that it might have. But certainly something more was needed than participation—a desire to exert world leadership and to take on the burdens which such leadership required. Such a desire was clearly lacking. It was only when further bitter experience took place as a result of America's involvement in World War II that the American people fully realized that they could not stand alone—that no country could be an "island unto itself"—and that its fate was inextricably bound up with the fate of other nations. Wilson's grievous error was that he was too far ahead of the spirit of his time. His tragedy in the end—when he stood physically broken, lonely, deserted, a dying voice —was America's tragedy.

"LET THE BOCHE PAY FOR THE WAR"

Many of the issues at the Paris Peace Conference transcended the questions as to whether or not a League of Nations would be established or whether America would join the international organization on its own terms. The manner in which these problems (largely affecting Europe) were resolved created repercussions which echoed through the corridors of the years that led to World War II. Among the most serious of these problems was the issue of reparations; and tied up with reparations was the "war guilt" of Germany. Her war guilt—that she and she alone was responsible for the outbreak of World War I—was the keystone on which the Versailles Treaty was erected.

While the Great War progressed and built up in fury during four

[3] *America's Rise to World Power* (New York, 1954), p. 124.

bitter years, one thought dug deeply into the consciousness of Western Europe: if the Allies succeeded in the final defeat of Germany, she was going to pay, and pay heavily, for the damages that had been inflicted. It was Prime Minister Lloyd George, in his reëlection campaign of 1918, who set the tone on reparations. "We have an absolute right to demand the whole cost of the war from Germany," he said. "We propose to demand the whole cost of the war. . . ." This line was picked up enthusiastically by France. The newspaper *Dépêche,* of Toulouse, declared that "without indemnities . . . France would be ruined for centuries." The cry arose that Germany must pay "to the limit of its capacity," or else "Germany wins the war in losing it, and the word 'justice' has no meaning."

Removed to some degree from the heated emotionalism generated by the war, Woodrow Wilson viewed the question of reparations more dispassionately than the Europeans. On board the *George Washington* in December, 1918, three days before it reached France, he was to tell the members of the "Inquiry" committee that the Americans would be the "only distinterested people at the Peace Conference." What Wilson had in mind was that the United States did not covet any of the spoils of the war. However, it was misleading to say that the Americans were "disinterested," which was far from the case. Nevertheless, the word disclosed an attitude of mind on the part of the President that was most important. It was his intention to weigh all the facts on problems and without prejudice coldly determine what was right. At Paris, there is no doubt that he labored harder and more diligently than any other leader. Often he worked late into the night without regard for his failing health. Contrary to popular impression, he listened to his advisers and to those whom he respected. He sought earnestly to make up his own mind independently, and very often he disagreed with his advisers; but he did not ignore them.

Wilson's greatest difficulty was in reconciling principle with expediency. Because the Peace Conference was usually concerned with matters of expediency rather than those of principle, and because the pressures to reach expedient solution were often intolerably great, he frequently found himself at a loss to know what to do. The unwieldy size of the conference meetings and the need for speed in reaching decisions—the President could not be absent for an indefinite period from Washington—compelled him to resort to the secret diplomacy which he had condemned in his Fourteen Points. At times Wilson wanted to throw up his hands and simply go home where he could get away from the fetid air of Paris. At one point when the conference was deadlocked, he threatened to do just that. The liner *George Washington* was held in readiness. The Americans "were going home to mother," a French spokesman snickered; but the deadlock was broken. Although Wilson threatened to go home, actually he knew he could not. And it was a good thing that he remained. Who can say what the results might have been had his moderating influence not been present at Paris? Nevertheless, on a number of crucial points Wilson succumbed to the pressures of expediency. One of these was the question of reparations.

Estimating the amount of claims against Germany for damages in the war occupied a good deal of the attention of the wartime leaders at the Peace Conference. Clemenceau suggested the utterly fantastic sum of $200 billion. The British were a little bit more moderate in their proposal: two British experts, called the "heavenly twins," proposed the merely astronomical figure of $120 billion. (At the time the entire public debt of the United States, even after financing the war, was only about $24 billion.) American advisers were convinced that Germany could not manage to pay more than $30 billion at the outside. While there was a great deal of talk about Germany's reasonable capacity to pay, it was apparent that neither Britain nor France was especially interested in being reasonable. What they wanted to know was how much they could squeeze out of Germany.

"The wrongs, the very deep wrongs, committed in this war will have to be righted," Wilson had told Congress in December, 1917. "That, of course. But they cannot and must not be righted by the commission of similar wrongs against Germany and her allies." Wilson now agreed that the Allies should receive a reparation for the material damages caused by the war, but not an indemnity for its entire cost. Such a reparation, he felt, should be a fixed sum, within Germany's capacity to pay, and definitely not to exceed $30 billion. Clemenceau strenuously objected to a fixed sum; any stated amount, he thought, would be considered too low by Frenchmen, in which case he might be committing political suicide, or too high, in which case Germany might balk at signing the treaty of peace. He preferred a little mystery to keep the Germans dangling on the hook. All of Wilson's persuasive powers proved useless.

The impasse was finally broken when it was decided to turn the whole matter over to a Reparations Commission, which was authorized to determine by 1921 what the amount should be. But the problem was still not completely resolved. How would the Commission determine the amount? Would she do so on the basis of Germany's capacity to pay, or on the basis of extracting as much as the Allies believed Germany owed them? France demanded the latter alternative, and insisted that pensions to dependents of Allied soldiers killed and the cost of the lives lost be included in the category of material damages; Britain straddled the fence; and Wilson argued that the reparations be limited to the cost of the actual physical damage. The Reparations Commission finally determined the amount of reparations without regard to Germany's capacity to pay; damages included pensions, but not the cost of lives lost. In May, 1921, the Reparations Commission handed Germany a bill for about $33 billion. Of this amount, about two-thirds—$20 to $23 billion—was for pensions and allowances.

While a fixed sum was in the end worked out, the question still remained as to *how* Germany was to pay it. As it turned out in the twenties, this problem became America's headache.

JAPAN PRESSES HER CLAIMS

The Japanese delegates remained very quiet throughout the proceedings at Paris until the issue of the disposition of Germany's possessions in the Far East came up. Then Japan made its presence heard—and felt— especially when Wilson vehemently objected to her claims. Japan's strategy was directed toward embarrassing the President by insisting that an article on racial equality be included in the League Covenant. This controversial question became a "hot potato" at the conference. While Wilson was sympathetic to the idea of abolishing racial discrimination, he no doubt recalled the racial issue in California in 1913 and did not want the matter injected into American domestic politics where the criticism might be voiced that the League of Nations would interfere with United States immigration policies. Japan dropped her insistence on the racial-equality article, but she did so only when she was assured of a favorable Shantung settlement. Her rights were confirmed; however, she had to agree explicitly that the territory was under China's sovereignty. On this matter, Wilson, who had tried to uphold the principle of the integrity of China, suffered a serious personal defeat.

More alarming from the President's point of view than the problem of racial equality and the Shantung issue was the matter of the disposition of the German Pacific islands. Japan had "insured" that there would be no contest on her 1914 understanding with Britain (under which Japan was to occupy the islands north of the equator, while Britain took over those in the south) by concluding a series of secret bilateral treaties in February-March, 1917, with Britain, France, Russia, and Italy. These secret treaties almost wrecked the Paris Peace Conference.

The fact that the treaties were secret was not, in itself, disturbing—

although Wilson clearly did not like it, for it was precisely this type of secret diplomacy that he fulminated against in his Fourteen Points, insisting that covenants should be openly arrived at. What was upsetting was that Wilson sought to deny Japan's claims based on the secret treaties. The existence of the treaties was well known in Washington. As a matter of fact, British Foreign Minister Arthur Balfour had shown a map to Colonel House in April, 1917, with the territorial lines of the secret treaties clearly marked out. Moreover, they were published by the Soviet government in full before the war ended.

The United States was well aware that a "deal" had been made between Japan and Britain, and that at Paris both countries would assert their claims to the division of the Pacific German islands. An American naval-planning committee, in fact, submitted a memorandum to the Chief of Naval Operations in December, 1918, and suggested that Japan be diverted from the islands by giving her a "free hand in Asia," and that the Marshalls, Carolines, German New Guinea, and Samoa be internationalized. "Will it not be better to provide for the future expansion of Japan at the Peace Conference," the memorandum stated, "rather than exclude it and thereby leave in existence an immediate cause of future war in which Japan might attempt to expand in a direction opposed to the interests of the United States?" Far better, the Navy advised, "to turn Japan towards the continent of Asia."

Wilson's denial of Japan's claims disturbed the Japanese delegates at the Peace Conference. Privately, a delegate told Secretary of State Robert Lansing (who succeeded Bryan in June, 1915) that if their "rights" were denied, Japan would blame the United States. Lansing later stated that the delegate made "an indirect threat of what would happen to the friendly relations between the two countries" if Japan were rebuffed.

The President tried to uphold the Open Door, to maintain the territorial integrity of China with respect to Shantung, and to resist Japanese and British imperialism in the Pacific German islands. He expressed the hope that "by pooling their interest the several nations that had gained a foothold in China (a foothold that was to the detriment of China's position in the world) might forego the special position they had acquired and that China might be put on the same footing as other nations, as sooner or later she must certainly be." Lansing declared that Japan had not proved the justice of her claims and he doubted her ability to do so. But these arguments had no effect. They merely intensified hostility between Japan and America. The Japanese delegates intimated that unless her claims were fulfilled, Japan would not join the

League of Nations. This threat, and the fact that Britain, France, and Italy strongly supported the Japanese claims, weakened Wilson's position. By far, the thing that worried the President most was the possibility that the League might be destroyed before it was created. He finally conceded; but not in an outright fashion. Instead of annexation, he insisted that the north Pacific German islands be mandated only. Japan would thus be responsible for the development of this region under the supervision of the League of Nations. While permitting Japan to retain Germany's economic holdings in Shantung, he made it clear that the Shantung peninsula must ultimately be returned to China; and Japan did so in 1923.

Japan's diplomatic victory at Paris strengthened her position in Asia. It also convinced her that the major obstacle in her expansionist ambitions was the United States. Sooner or later, a showdown would be inevitable.

The mandate formula provided a solution not only to the German Pacific islands but also to her colonies in Africa. Britain had wanted to obtain these colonies without any strings attached; New Zealand and Australia likewise desired control of the German islands south of the equator to form a defensive ring around their waters. These colonies and islands—like the German Pacific islands mandated to Japan—were classified as "C" mandates, which meant that "establishment of fortifications of military and naval bases" and "military training of the natives for other than police purposes and the defense of territory" were prohibited. In the "C" mandate, also, nothing was said about independence or self-government. While Australia and New Zealand did respect the prohibitions, Japan did not. The Japanese armed their Pacific mandates and used them as bases for attack in World War II.

ITALY INSISTS ON HER SHARE

At the outbreak of World War I, Italy was an ally of Germany and Austria-Hungary, bound by a Triple Alliance. The alliance, however, did not commit Italy to join in an offensive war; nor was it understood to be directed against England. In 1914, therefore, Italy declared her neutrality. During the following year, Germany and Austria tried to persuade Italy to join them; but Italy obtained a better price from the Allies. Largely through the efforts of British Foreign Minister Grey, a secret Treaty of London was signed in April, 1915, by Britain, France, Russia, and Italy, in which the terms for Italy's joining the Allies were carefully spelled out. The treaty generously gave her territories then belonging to the Austro-Hungarian Empire but partly inhabited by

Italians. However, Italy's chief aim was to advance her frontier in the north to the Brenner Pass and to annex Trieste and a portion of the coast along the Adriatic in order to give her control of that sea. To make her control complete, she found at the end of the war that it was necessary for her to obtain Fiume, the most valuable sea outlet for the newly created state of Yugoslavia.

The secret Treaty of London perturbed Wilson just as the Japanese secret treaties with respect to the Pacific islands had done. He reluctantly agreed to support Italy's demands, but he refused to sanction Italy's claim to Fiume, which was not specifically awarded to her in the London Treaty. It would, he felt, conflict seriously with the principle of self-determination.

Divided opinion existed among the American "Inquiry" experts on the Italian question. One group opposed Italy's claim to Fiume, while a second favored it. Wilson hoped that a compromise might be worked out, but Prime Minister Vittorio Orlando became so incensed at the American attitude that he walked out of the Peace Conference. Orlando's action was definitely detrimental to Italy. Domination of the Paris meetings narrowed down to the Big Three; in so doing, Italy's claims were shunted aside. No colonial concessions or mandates were assigned to her. When Orlando returned to the Conference, it was too late for Italy to reassert her demands. A compromise was later worked out in 1925 between Italy and Yugoslavia on Fiume. But an unfortunate result of the Italian dispute was that it led to a serious break in the friendship between Woodrow Wilson and Colonel House. The President's confidant had sided with the American advisory group which favored Italy's claim; House felt that Fiume should definitely go to Italy. As a result, several flare-ups occurred and Wilson lost his confidence in Colonel House.

AMERICA AND WORLD AFFAIRS

The years between 1914 and 1920 saw many changes in the United States. America's attitude toward world politics was inevitably affected by her involvement in the conflict in Europe. She had entered this war in a great crusade "to make the world safe for democracy." The harsh realities of that war and the disillusion which accompanied the Paris Peace Conference in which each power selfishly sought to advance its own national ends made Wilson's idealism hollow and false. The advice of the Founding Fathers to avoid permanent "entangling alliances" and to have as little connection with Europe as possible seemed to be wiser than ever. This reaction manifested itself in the spirit of isolationism, and this was unfortunate indeed, for the United States was needed most vitally in restoring the stability of Europe so necessary to the maintenance of world peace.

Most Americans were largely unaware of the vast economic and social changes that were taking place during these years. The war built up a huge industrial machine and made the United States the greatest industrial power in the world. Overnight, America became a creditor instead of a debtor nation. American producers had little idea of what this change meant; what they noticed was that suddenly there was a pressing demand, not only for food products, but for manufactured goods as well. British and European competition, which before 1914 had been very great, virtually dried up. Export surpluses abroad also diminished, and markets for American goods opened up throughout the world.

The region that offered the most immediate opportunity for the United States was Latin America. Because of the war, European trade had declined drastically. American producers lost little time in making a triumphal entry into South America. With the expansion in trade, credit, and investment markets, America's merchant marine, long in the doldrums, began to build up mightily. The momentum of American industrial capitalism's crusade in Latin America continued without letup. The period witnessed an unprecedented capture of foreign markets on the part of the United States which extended into the decades of the twenties and thirties. Private capital after the war poured forth abundantly not only in South America but in Europe—where huge sums were invested to finance rehabilitation—in Middle East oil wells, in Southeast Asian rubber plantations, and in the development of public utilities in China and Japan.

A result of the growth of America's economic power was an awakening of a new pride in the country's achievements. By the 1920's, the image of America was painted in the glowing, Utopian colors of capitalism come of age. All of the former doubts about Big Business and about corporate leaders—pictured during the Progressive Era as evil "robber barons" bent on perverting American democracy into an economic oligarchy—soon disappeared. The war—with its full employment and good payrolls, with its expanding factories and markets—developed a confidence in the American system and the men who guided it.

America's desire was to consolidate and expand the enormous economic gains that had been built up during and after the war. This could be done, the nation's business leaders declared, by preserving for the United States the greatest freedom of action. And so America looked to America and ignored the power realities of the age.

4 · THE TROUBLED POSTWAR YEARS

> *We drove the Boche across the Rhine,*
> *The Kaiser from his throne.*
> *Oh, Lafayette, we've paid our debt,*
> *For Christ's sake, send us home.*
> WORLD WAR I DOUGHBOY SONG[1]

America's present need is not heroics but healing, not nostrums but
normalcy, not revolution but restoration, not agitation but adjustment
. . . not submergence in internationality but sustainment in triumphant
nationality.
WARREN GAMALIEL HARDING, *Speech, May 14, 1920*

The 1920's were a time of political reaction to Wilsonian idealism, of
buoyant economic optimism, and of a prohibition-crazed, jazz-age frenzy.
At the beginning of the decade, Ohio Senator Warren Gamaliel Harding came into the White House. He was, in every respect, the complete
antithesis of Woodrow Wilson. Devoid of Wilson's aristocratic coldness,
intellectual conceit, and self-assurance, Harding had modestly said during his campaign that he would rely on the "best minds" to advise him.
And he needed them badly! Unbelievably ill-informed, Harding nonetheless possessed certain distinct assets which made him extremely popular
in the country at the time. A former newspaper editor from the small
town of Marion, Ohio, easy-going, good-natured, a hard drinker and
sharp poker-player, strikingly handsome—his picture was frequently

[1] Quoted in Selig Adler, *The Isolationist Impulse* (London and New York,
1957), p. 99.

splashed across the rotogravure sections in the newspapers—Harding was just "plain folks" who liked people. His outstanding quality was that he seemed to have a certain Washington nobility and dignity, and as Harry Daugherty, Harding's political mentor, crony, and soon-to-be-appointed Attorney General, had remarked, "He'd make a great-looking President." No one was more aware of his own limitations than Harding himself. "I am a man of limited talents from a small town," he said. "I don't seem to grasp that I am President."

Whatever statesmanship existed in the Harding administration was supplied by three able individuals who charted the course of Republican policies: in the State Department, Charles Evans Hughes, the distinguished Supreme Court justice and 1916 Republican candidate, whom Wilson only narrowly defeated; in the Treasury Department, Andrew W. Mellon, one of the shrewdest and richest corporate leaders in the country; and in the Commerce Department, Herbert Hoover, successful engineering promoter, first-rate administrator, and head of Wilson's Food Relief program. While Mellon and Hoover became the architects of Republican economic policies—high tariffs, reduction of taxes, immigration restriction—Hughes piloted America through the rough waters of diplomacy. The Secretary of State was to be internationalist in his outlook, but he was circumscribed by the dominant mood of isolationism that prevailed in the country. The climate of opinion was such that the slightest move in the direction of international coöperation elicited a barrage of criticism. Harding's weakness increased Congressional influence, and Hughes had to proceed cautiously and timidly.

The campaign of 1920 had been a spiritless affair; only about half the eligible voters went to the polls. Nevertheless, more than twenty-six million votes were cast and Harding won by the largest plurality ever given to a President—sixteen million to nine. The Democratic party had tried to make the League of Nations the central issue; but Harding side-stepped this tactic by stating that if elected he would approve working out "an association of nations for the promotion of international peace." He avoided taking a clear-cut stand on America's participation in the League. Thus, some Republican leaders, including Hughes and Hoover, supported Harding because they were sure it would bring the country into the League, while others favored him because they were equally certain that it would not. Harding preferred to stress the domestic issues—the return of the country to "normalcy." What he actually meant was normality, but Harding who loved to "bloviate"—to make long-winded speeches bloated with clichés—helped to enrich the English language with some choice new words. Because of Harding's fence-straddling, it could not be said that the election results represented a mandate against America's participation in the League. However, a powerful minority group of Republican isolationists in Congress quickly interpreted the landslide victory in this light. Pressures were so great that the administration decided it would be best to shun the League like a plague; nor would it have anything to do with the newly created World Court, the independent, permanent body that was set up as a judicial arm of the League of Nations to settle international disputes.

Hughes recognized that America's interests—especially those of Big Business which looked toward Europe for markets—required international responsibility. But because of the climate of distrust of Europe and of the prevailing hostility to everything "foreign," he concluded that America's leadership should be demonstrated by acting alone, by showing the world that the United States could live up to its moral and ethical concepts, and by taking the initiative in a movement for world disarmament and a crusade to outlaw war. Unfortunately, Hughes's position contributed to a policy of drift. Europe, left to work out its own fate, felt bitterly that the United States had turned a cold shoulder to her.

After 1919, the basic problem of the world centered on the reconstruction of Europe—the need to remove the debris left by the war years so that peace and stability could be achieved. The task of reconstruction was unprecedented in scope—one which Europe could not undertake completely by herself without America's help. Psychological damage was irreparable; only time could heal the wounds. The social upheaval staggered the imagination. To people in some areas (Czechoslovakia, Poland, and Yugoslavia), the changes brought hope; but in others (Germany, Italy, Hungary, and Austria), it brought despair. Disillusioned, tired, and hungry, Europe after the war became a fertile breeding ground for communist revolutions.

The problem of reconstruction required boldness, perception, and political statesmanship of the highest order, together with a willingness to sacrifice crass national ends for the good of the world. But these virtues were almost completely nonexistent in both the United States and Europe. Distrust and suspicion took their place. Coöperation became a chimera. Meanwhile, during the twenties, the United States tried to insulate itself as much as possible from the revolutionary crises which existed in Russia and China.

Signs of future trouble lurked behind America's placid and complacent façade. But these signs, in domestic policies as well as in foreign affairs, were brushed aside or dealt with in an incompetent fashion. Many of these problems carried over from the Wilson era or developed as consequences of World War I. In world politics, they related mainly to the issues of reparations and war debts, to the problems raised by the Bolshevik Revolution, and to the conflicts between the United States and Japan.

"THEY HIRED THE MONEY, DIDN'T THEY?"

During the periods before and after the armistice, America had extended to its Allies, in cash and supplies, credits totaling more than $10 billion. This was the inter-Allied governmental war debt. No substantial collateral had been obtained for these loans, except the pledge that after victory the money would be repaid. But after the war, Britain and France argued that this debt should be canceled. They maintained that from 1914 to 1917 they had been fighting America's war as well as their own. Moreover, the money had been spent, not in Europe, but in the United States, where it had contributed to a booming wartime prosperity. America had thus been repaid amply; to insist on payment in gold would simply wreck all hope of economic recovery. The United States, however, would not hear of cancellation. Much of the funds for the Allied loans had been raised by the sale of Liberty Bonds; the treasury had used this money to advance credits. Cancellation would increase the public debt, and the American taxpayers would become the losers. No, the American government insisted, the loans had been made on a business basis, and it demanded that they be repaid.

The American attitude on war debts created a disturbing situation. The United States expected that all nations would abide by their sacred treaty and contractual obligations. If the Allies showed bad faith in honoring their pledges, what hope could there be for world peace? The debt had been contracted; it must be paid. As Calvin Coolidge later dryly remarked, "They hired the money, didn't they?"

The war debt hung like an albatross around the neck of Great Britain. Much of Britain's recovery depended on enlarging her world markets. The debt was considered an obstacle in the resumption of normal international trade. Lloyd George hesitated about bringing up this matter at the Paris peace meetings. In 1918, hints had been thrown out to the United States that it might be a good idea to cancel the war debt, but these suggestions were promptly discouraged. John Maynard Keynes, the British economist, proposed a plan to deal with the problem, but it did not meet with favor. Ray Stannard Baker observed:

In any event, it would not have worked if the other elements of the economic settlements had not been dealt with upon sound principles. For how expect a liberal solution of the debt problem with America ultimately assuming the chief burden when at the same time the British and French were demanding reparations that would practically make it impossible for Germany ever to pay those debts?[2]

Few, at that time, clearly recognized the interdependence of national economies.

The war-debt problem had direct repercussions on the question of reparations. For England, a number of dilemmas arose. On the one hand, to ease the burden of the debt she tried to transfer a large portion of it onto Germany by obtaining as much reparations as was possible; on the other hand, she was anxious to restore Germany to her prewar position, when Germany was Britain's good customer. It was obvious, though, that England could not have her cake and eat it too. By crippling Germany economically through heavy reparations, it was apparent that her potentialities as a customer would be necessarily reduced. Britain did hope that the lag would be taken up by the American market, and that it would be possible to reduce her indebtedness through the exchange of goods and services with the United States. But this outlet was to be closed to her. To eliminate foreign competition, including the British, from the American market, Congress began to enact high protective-tariff laws.

France was much less concerned about the debt than England. For her, there was no question that the burden had to be transferred to Germany. Clemenceau looked upon reparations as both an economic and political weapon. Her territory had been devastated, factories destroyed, and coal mines ruined. "The industries of France had been scientifically destroyed," Clemenceau told the Council of Ten at Paris on February 12, 1919, "not for military reasons, but in order to prevent France from recovering in peacetime." It was difficult for France to consider reparations rationally and soberly. With Germany's guilt clearly recognized and established by the Allies, France had no doubt that she was entitled to the heaviest possible indemnity and that her claims should be given first preference. "Make Germany Pay First" was the slogan which summed up the attitude of France.

By 1921, for different reasons, both Britain and France looked to Germany to recover their losses. Both expected that the Reparations Commission would come forth with a respectable figure for claims of damages. Meanwhile, they grabbed as much of Germany's tangible assets as they could. It was expected that $5 billion might be obtained in this way, a sort of down payment on the reparations bill. Actually, it was discovered when the total value of the assets was tabulated—ships, railway rolling stock, farm machinery, motors, etc.—that it amounted

[2] *Woodrow Wilson and World Settlement* (New York, 1923), Vol. II, p. 290.

to little more than $1 billion. The news was something of a shock. It was clear that more drastic measures had to be taken to obtain something substantial from Germany. When German Foreign Minister Walther Simons suggested at London in March, 1921, that the total German indemnity be reduced to $7 billion, Lloyd George declared the proposal was "an offense and an exasperation."

To make sure that Germany would not wiggle out of the payment of reparations, the Allies on March 8, 1921, occupied Düsseldorf, Duisburg, and Ruhrfort. On May 1, the Reparations Commission finally fixed the sum of reparations at about $33 billion, plus the payment of interest. Germany immediately accepted the figure; a first installment of $250 million was paid. However, because of severe inflation and the strain on her economy, Germany asked for a two-year moratorium to help her regain her economic stability. Raymond Poincaré, the Premier of France, immediately demanded French control of the Rhineland industries—which included more than 80 percent of Germany's heavy industry—in return for the moratorium.

The simple fact was that Germany could not meet her reparations payments and at the same time stabilize her economy. An uncontrolled inflation of currency inevitably set in. By 1923, price changes began to occur almost from hour to hour. Ordinary necessities of life were valued in the trillions of marks. The effect of the inflation virtually wiped out the lower middle class. Financial chaos produced violence and separatist movements, and gave rise to the Munich "Beer Hall" *putsch*—Hitler's first attempt to seize power in 1923.

Poincaré was unperturbed by the disturbances. He persisted in the collection of reparations payments. With Germany unable to comply, Poincaré ordered the French occupation of the Ruhr, Germany's richest industrial district. This move was quickly followed by an attempt by France to set up a separate Rhineland Republic. The occupation of the Ruhr proved very costly for France. Because of German passive resistance, the coal receipts from the Ruhr were cut by more than 75 percent. France also lost a large amount of governmental revenue from Lorraine, which was economically dependent on the Rhineland and the Ruhr. The Rhineland Republic was short-lived, and collapsed within six months. France held on to the Ruhr for a time, and then withdrew.

Frustrated and disappointed by the lack of returns from a bankrupt Germany, Britain and France turned to the United States to help them out of the economic mess. In 1922, Arthur J. Balfour, the British Foreign Minister, laid down the principle that the British government would try to collect only enough reparations to equal Britain's debt payments to the United States. This meant, in substance, that the war debt would be liquidated if Germany fulfilled her obligations on reparations. In the final analysis, therefore, to obtain collection on the war debt, the United States had to become the recipient of German reparations.

Secretary of State Charles Evans Hughes was quite upset at the general European situation and at the French occupation of the Ruhr. But he maintained a dignified silence and did not interfere. Nor did he interpose any serious objection to the principle set forth by Balfour. The United States did not care how the war debt was paid, as long as it was paid. However, the British recognized that the United States would have to assume some responsibility in helping England meet her obligations. In October, 1923, Stanley Baldwin, the British Prime Minister, invited the United States to participate in a conference of "competent and impartial" experts to investigate Germany's capacity to pay her reparations. Since German reparations were now closely linked to the war debt, Hughes responded favorably. The conference led to the creation of the Dawes Committee, which was given the job of trying to end the German inflation and balancing the German budget. If this was done, it was felt, Germany would be able to pay her reparations, and the United States could collect its war debt.

The Dawes Committee report favored the reduction of Germany's annual reparation payments, and to help Germany meet even these, it recommended that an effort should be made to improve the country's economy. The Dawes Plan stimulated the sale of German securities in the United States. About 180 German bond and stock issues were gobbled up by American buyers after 1923. The outpouring of American capital through stock purchases and bank loans helped finance the economic recovery of Germany, which made it possible for Germany to meet her reparations payments during the twenties and thus enabled the Allies to pay their war debt. "The transfer of these long-term 'investments,' " George Soule points out, "enabled Germany to fulfill the reparations payments, [but] the money that came to the United States from the Allies was only a rounding a circle to the point of its origin."[3]

The State Department tried to warn Americans against the excessive extension of credit. But it did so in a half-hearted manner, and American investors and bankers opposed all restraints which might mean that they would have to forego big profits and high interest rates. By 1929, the United States built up a financial relationship with Europe that was so unbalanced as to make disaster a certainty. German and European economic stability was largely sustained artificially by the flow of Amer-

[3] *Prosperity Decade* (New York, 1947), p. 264.

ican loans and investments. It might have been expected that the war debt would be liquidated, but this was not the case. During the twenties, the war debt was pared down by only about $3 billion. To obtain repayment of $10 billion, the United States—operating in a financial fairyland—managed by 1929 to increase the indebtedness to her by over $21 billion.

The end came in October, 1929. The Wall Street stock market crashed, and with it, the whole crazy patchwork of speculative financial structures collapsed. American loans ceased to flow, and the European economy went into a spin. The last straw was the passage of the Smoot-Hawley Tariff Act of 1930. Europe's economic retaliation for America's high protective tariffs produced sheer chaos. By 1930, the debt payments from abroad on both private obligations and war debts tapered off to almost nothing. When the depression in Europe reached panic proportions, President Herbert Hoover announced, in July, 1931, a year's moratorium on the payment of war debts; but he remained rigidly opposed to any cancellation or to any official linking of the war debts to reparations.

It is now clear that the war debt and reparations problems were badly bungled. Responsibility falls on the shoulders of both the United States and Europe. Had America canceled the war debt, and had Britain and France reduced their reparations bill to Germany, it is possible that the world-wide depression might have been avoided. Over and above the war debts and reparations, however, hung America's high protective tariffs. Had Europe been permitted, as she desired, to liquidate her debts by services, but especially through the sale of manufactured goods in the American market, the story of the 1920's again might have been different. But these things did not happen, and the war debts and reparations problems built a higher and higher wall separating the United States from Europe.

THE BOLSHEVIK REVOLUTION CREATES A THREAT

The aftermath of World War I gave rise not only to the war debts and reparations issues but to a more alarming problem: the establishment of the Soviet Union and the threat of Bolshevism. How to deal with the menace of Bolshevism had been discussed at length at the Paris Peace Conference. The prevailing opinion of the great powers, in Lansing's words, was that "Bolshevism must be suppressed." All the delegates, including Woodrow Wilson, agreed that there must be no compromise with any form of radicalism. But division arose on what should be done.

During the spring of 1918, the war had been going badly for the Allies. In March, the new, weak Soviet Union had signed the Brest-Litovsk Treaty with Germany, in which they surrendered a sizable portion of Russian territory and withdrew from the war. The Eastern Front then collapsed, and Germany began to arrange to transfer forty divisions to the Western Front. Demands arose in England to revive the Eastern Front in order to block the transfer of the German troops. Britain clamored for intervention and declared that the war would be indefinitely prolonged if Russian food resources fell into German hands. A series of incidents in April convinced Wilson that intervention would be necessary. In particular, he was most disturbed over the problem of the Czech legion in Siberia. These former draftees in the Austrian army had surrendered to the Russians; fifty thousand were now established as an independent army under the direction of the pro-Allied Czechoslovak nationalist movement. The Bolsheviks were preventing their transit across Siberia to Vladivostok, where they were to embark for the Western Front to fight for their newly established homeland, which Wilson had helped to create. He agreed to a limited intervention to "save the Czecho-Slovak armies" and "to steady any efforts of the Russians at self-defense" against the Bolsheviks. While Wilson's primary purpose was to encourage anti-Bolshevik elements in Russia, he was largely inspired to support a joint Allied intervention to block Japanese imperialists from seizing territory in Siberia and North Manchuria. Japan had indicated that if the Allies did not intervene, she would do so by herself. However, each of the powers involved in the intervention—Britain, France, America, and Japan—had different ideas about its purpose. The result led to a complete lack of coördination of strategy and hopeless confusion.

At the Paris Conference, Clemenceau argued that the limited military intervention that had been undertaken was not enough: Bolshevism had to be crushed by the full application of military force. Despite his support of the joint Allied intervention, Wilson had insisted that there must be no overt interference in the internal affairs of the Russian people. But he and Lloyd George opposed the French plans on other grounds. To them, it meant a continuance of the war, which was intolerable. What Lloyd George wanted was to set up a dike which would hold back the communist flood. This he felt could be done only if the economic and social structure of Europe was reënforced. Woodrow Wilson agreed that the use of military force was not the answer. "The way to cure this [Bolshevik] domination," he said, must be through "constant discussion and a slow process of reform."

Discussing the problem in January, 1919, Wilson pointed out that the French plan contained the sources of its own failure. Much of the Bolshevik strength, he said, derived from the threat of full-scale foreign intervention, which enabled the Bolsheviks to rally the people to their side. Wilson was convinced that "by opposing Bolshevism with arms they [the Allies] were in reality serving the cause of Bolshevism."

While Winston Churchill strongly seconded the French plan and supported a "definite war scheme," neither Prime Minister Lloyd George nor President Wilson was prepared to go that far. Both believed that whatever measures were taken had to be short of open war. How Bolshevism was to be suppressed, therefore, became an individual matter that was to be decided separately by the United States, Great Britain, France, and Japan. Without a unified, definite war scheme, it was evident that the most that could be expected was to try to contain the Bolshevik threat, with the hope that future developments would lead to a change in the Soviet political and economic system. This situation was strikingly apparent in the Siberian venture, which soon turned into a debacle. Wilson kept American troops in Russia long after the armistice was signed, mainly as a check on Japanese aspirations. The last contingent was finally withdrawn in April, 1920, and as it departed a Japanese band played Stephen Foster's "Hard Times Come Again No More." Japan stayed in eastern Siberia until the end of 1922, but her efforts to defeat the Bolsheviks and take sizable chunks of territory were unsuccessful.

The containment policy, nevertheless, attained a limited success. The major powers, each in its own way, supported the counterrevolutionary movements against the Bolsheviks. Wilson, for example, imposed an American economic embargo against the Soviets, and he tacitly approved Poland's efforts to obtain new territory in the Ukraine. Japan continued her military activities against the Bolsheviks. The effort to extend communist control to Germany, Central Europe, and China after the war was blocked. But Bolshevism in Russia was not destroyed. It managed to survive and tighten its grip upon the country.

The great powers still felt that the Soviet system could not endure the economic chaos of the war and revolution; communism, they were sure, would never "make a go of it." At the same time, the powers began to eye Russia for possible trade opportunities. Britain and France particularly desired to gain access to market areas to make up their wartime losses; the United States soon looked to Russia as a means of easing the agricultural depression which had hit the country in 1921.

THE RED SCARES

After World War I, America's relations with the Soviet Union, unlike those of Britain and France, were not rooted in any fundamental power conflict. Communism did not directly threaten any part of the American empire. The economic and political interests of the United States were largely concentrated in the Western Hemisphere. America was concerned about the communist revolutions in Asia and Europe, but not to the point where it felt that its own security was endangered. Its attitude toward the Soviet Union was one of cold aloofness, which was reflected in its refusal to grant recognition to Russia until 1933.

American policies toward the Soviet Union were influenced mainly by two things during the twenties: a domestic fear of communism, and the wishful hope that the Soviet Government would, as Herbert Hoover put it, "fall of its own weight." Some Americans at this time thought the United States could speed the inevitable collapse of the Soviet system by encouraging American economic penetration into Russia.

The domestic reaction to communism tended to set the pattern of American policies. Attitudes were largely conditioned by the wartime emotional atmosphere. Russia's withdrawal from the war and the belief on the part of many people that the Bolshevik movement was German-inspired aroused a great deal of hostility. But most disturbing were the bloody excesses of the Revolution. Here the newspapers did their part in feeding to the public a steady diet of atrocity stories. One story soberly reported that the Bolsheviks in Petrograd operated an electric guillotine that chopped off five hundred heads in an hour. Cartoonists seared into the American public mind the caricature of the Bolshevik as a blood-thirsty, bomb-throwing, bewhiskered revolutionist.

A great deal of stress was placed on the Communists' denial of religion and on the avowed intent of the Bolsheviks to destroy religion. Atheism, anarchy, and universal disorder were the things associated with Bolshevik rule. But what stiffened the backs of most Americans was the doctrine of world revolution. In 1919, a genuine fear arose that a huge radical conspiracy existed to overthrow the government and institutions of the United States. Many millions of Americans seriously believed that a Red revolution was going to be launched at any moment.

Domestic unrest played an important part in stirring up the Big Red Scare. Immediately after the war, organized labor intensified its demands for higher wages, shorter hours, and the right of collective bargaining. Employers resisted the wage increases and continued to insist on long hours of work. The result was a wave of strikes. Throughout the country—in the building trades, the stockyards, the shipyards, and in count-less factories—workers left their jobs. It was estimated that in a period of about eight months in 1919 close to two million people went on strike.

One of the more disturbing incidents occurred in the Seattle ship-yard strike. On January 21, 1919, thirty-five thousand workers struck for higher wages and shorter hours. The company directors refused to agree to collective bargaining. They demanded that the workers return to their jobs. The order was ignored. Labor leaders decided to enlist the support of the A.F.L. for a general strike. On February 3, procla-mation of a general strike was published in all the Seattle newspapers. The city panicked. The press warned that the Seattle labor unions were riddled with radicals; the general strike, they declared, was the first step toward revolution. In the frenzy of fear over the imminence of the gen-eral strike, people began to stock up on emergency supplies.

Ole Hanson, the mayor of Seattle, lost little time in crushing the strike. Federal troops poured into Seattle at his request. "The time has come," Hanson declared, "for the people in Seattle to show their Ameri-canism. . . . The anarchists in this community shall not rule its affairs." The A.F.L., realizing that it had made a mistake in supporting the gen-eral strike, and fearing the adverse affect it would have on the whole labor movement, exerted pressure to call off the strike, which ended on February 10. However, it was not soon forgotten. Newspaper editorials hammered away at the fact that the Seattle strike was a "revolutionary movement aimed at existing government," and the "stepping stone to a bolshevized America."

Mayor Ole Hanson suddenly found himself in the national limelight—the hero of the crowd. And he made the most of it. Shortly after the Seattle strike, Hanson resigned as mayor and went on a national lecture tour. By virtue of his experience in Seattle, he became the country's acknowledged expert on the dangers of domestic bolshevism. In seven months, this tour netted him $38,000, a tidy sum, considering that as mayor he received only $7,500 a year. One of the things that boosted Hanson's popularity was the fact that on April 28, 1919, a homemade bomb was discovered mailed to his residence. Fortunately, Hanson was in Colorado at the time, and the fluid in the package leaked so that it was detected before anyone was hurt. But hearing the news, Ole Hanson said: "If they have the courage why don't they attack me like men, instead of playing the part of cowardly assassins?"

What created a great deal of alarm was the fact that the Hanson bomb seemed to be part of a general bomb conspiracy. The press re-ported rumors of an ominous character. On the day following the mailing of the Hanson bomb, a similar package was delivered to the home of former Senator Thomas W. Hardwick of Atlanta. Apparently the bomb was sent because Senator Hardwick had proposed restricting immigration to keep out Bolsheviks. However, this time the package was opened by a maid, and she lost both of her hands in the explosion.

The most sensational incident occurred on April 30. Charles Kaplan, a clerk in the parcel-post division of the New York Post Office was riding the subway, reading the headline news about the bombs. "As his eye caught the description of the packages sent to Hanson and Hardwick," writes Robert K. Murray, "he was struck with terror. Just three days before, he had laid aside sixteen such packages for insufficient postage. Hurrying back to the post office, he found them piled neatly where he had left them and immediately notified post office inspectors who in turn called the police."[4] These packages, with a Gimbel Brothers return address, and marked "Novelty—A Sample," all contained homemade bombs. Another eighteen similar packages were intercepted by the Post Office, indicating thirty-six persons who were marked for death— high government officials and two of the country's leading capitalists: J. P. Morgan and John D. Rockefeller. Ole Hanson demanded that Washington take immediate action against the anarchists. "If the Government doesn't clean them up," he boasted, "I will."

Because the bomb scare coincided with May Day, the conviction arose that the bomb plots were part of an organized radical conspiracy to overthrow the American government, and not the work of isolated fanatics or lunatics. Attorney General A. Mitchell Palmer stepped in to take command of a compaign to eradicate the "human vermin" and clean up the Red menace. Mobilizing the resources of the government, Palmer directed a crackdown on all Reds throughout the country. But the bomb explosions continued.

About a month after the May Day scare, one of the more spectacular events took place when the front of Attorney General Palmer's home was demolished by a terrific explosion. As it happened, nobody in the house was hurt; Palmer had just gone to bed, and the rest of the family had already retired. Apparently the job was badly bungled; the anarchist —or anarchists—stumbled on the steps, it seems, and the bomb exploded prematurely. Palmer recalled hearing something hit the front door. Fragments of two left legs were found, which gave rise to the speculation that two men may have been responsible for the explosion. The Washington *Evening Star* commented that with such pedal equip-

[4] *Red Scare: A Study in National Hysteria, 1919–1920* (Minneapolis, 1955), p. 70.

ment it was no wonder that he stumbled. A copy of a radical pamphlet, *Plain Words,* was found near the Palmer house, which left little doubt that the incident was caused by anarchists.

The horror of the bomb plots and explosions created a mass hysteria in the country. Another sensational bomb explosion took place in September, 1920. This time a huge blast was set off during the noon hour in front of the Assay Office, directly opposite the House of Morgan in the Wall Street district of New York City. It appears that a TNT bomb went off in a horse-drawn wagon, while the driver left the scene. About thirty persons were killed outright by the explosion, and hundreds of others on their way to lunch were injured. The Morgan building was wrecked; windows were smashed for blocks around. The impact of the explosion was so terrific that it drove a slug through the window of the Bankers' Club on the thirty-fourth floor of the Equitable Building; the heat was so intense that people as high as the sixth floor who were near open windows were badly burned. The press and the American public, however, did not link this explosion to a revolutionary conspiracy as they had the earlier incidents. The general feeling was that a small group of insane anarchists was responsible. The culprit—or culprits— were never identified.

That there were justifiable reasons for a Red Scare is undeniable. All of the incidents which occurred during this period were shocking. But that they were the work of Bolsheviks or Bolshevik agents is doubtful. Nevertheless, the Red Scare was largely responsible for linking all shades of radicalism with Bolshevism. The labor movement was the first to come under a deep cloud of suspicion. But it was not long before school teachers and college professors, religious leaders, government employees, newspaper reporters, and judges on the bench were suspected. Politicians, superpatriots, and Big Business quickly found out they could crush those with unorthodox views by tarring them with the Bolshevist brush:

Big navy men, believers in compulsory military service, drys, anti-cigarette campaigners, anti-evolution Fundamentalists, defenders of the moral order, book censors, Jew-haters, Negro-haters, landlords, manufacturers, utility executives, upholders of every sort of cause, good, bad, and indifferent, all wrapped themselves in Old Glory and the mantle of the Founding Fathers and allied their opponents with Lenin.[5]

The effects of the Red Scare lingered on until 1924. Much of the excitement petered out when the government was unable to demonstrate that an organized Bolshevik conspiracy actually existed. Numerous

[5] Frederick Lewis Allen, *Only Yesterday: An Informal History of the Nineteen-Twenties* (New York, 1931), p. 59.

investigations were conducted, but their results were not impressive. Even the Attorney General, who operated in a high-handed fashion, made few arrests. Palmer later told the Senate Judiciary Committee:

I apologize for nothing that the Department of Justice has done in this matter. I glory in it. I point with pride and enthusiasm to the results of that work; and if . . . some of my agents out in the field . . . were a little rough and unkind, or short and curt, with these alien agitators, whom they observed seeking to destroy their homes, their religion and their country, I think it might be well overlooked in the general good to the country which has come from it.

But the American public soon lost interest and tired of the Red Scare. The general attitude became one of apathy and indifference, while attention shifted to other things less worrisome—tinkering with crystal radio sets, baseball, and the latest homemade gin recipes.

While the Red Scare may be viewed primarily as a domestic reaction to the Bolshevik Revolution and the overwrought emotionalism of the postwar climate, its consequence on American policies toward Russia was considerable. For more than a decade, these policies were put into a strait jacket. Even when the panic subsided after Germany and other European nations failed to be engulfed by the Bolshevist tide, and the idea that communism would sweep irresistibly across the Atlantic became less plausible, the United States refused to have any official dealings with the Soviet Union. The policy of nonrecognition was a negative response which reflected the repulsion and hatred which most Americans felt toward communism.

AMERICA TRIES TO HELP THE RUSSIAN PEOPLE

The official policies of the administrations from Woodrow Wilson's to Franklin D. Roosevelt's tried to make a clear distinction between the Soviet system and the Russian people. The Communists, it was asserted on frequent occasions, were not the real representatives of the Russians. They were a minority gangster clique that would eventually be thrown out of power. The United States, it was felt, should help in this task, but not by direct interference. The problem posed to the American people was presented in a somewhat rhetorical manner: How could the United States weaken the Soviet system to assure its collapse, and at the same time win the support of the Russian people to democracy and free enterprise?

Wilson believed strongly that Bolshevism fed on ignorance and hunger. "The real thing with which to stop Bolshevism is food," he said, writing to Lansing in 1919. Contradictions in American policies were apparent throughout the period from 1917 to 1933. To weaken the Soviet government, the United States adopted the policies of nonrecognition and the imposition of an economic blockade. The State Department refused to license shipments to the Soviet Union, and this action was supplemented by pressures on neutrals to prohibit all trade with Russia. On the other hand, the United States tried to obtain the confidence of the Russian people. To this end, it relaxed its economic blockade and offered to help Russia in its reconstruction. When Moscow promised a "gigantic role" to American Big Business to aid the reconstruction of Russian economic life, the offer was too good to ignore. The prospect of changing the Soviet economic system by American economic penetration was viewed by many as an excellent complement to the hostile policy of economic restrictions. Business interests especially favored this line of approach, and in the early 1920's a small group of American businessmen organized the American Commercial Association to Promote Trade with Russia. They campaigned vigorously to force Washington to relax its regulations.

The postwar recession in 1921 had much to do with the demands which arose to open up Russia to trade. The International Association of Machinists bluntly advised the State Department that, since industry was "stagnated," something should be done. With an acute agricultural depression, with unemployment mounting, many agreed with the declaration of the United Mine Workers that the "opening of trade relations with Russia would materially relieve the situation." George W. Morris, a manufacturer, aptly described the business sentiment in the country at the time. He said that since business was "on the blink," he wanted "a crack at the Russian market right away." While some people in the State Department did favor American friendship with Russia, Secretary of State Hughes maintained that the first essential for recognition and free-trade relations was the "abandonment of their [the Soviet Union's] present economic system."

When a terrible famine occurred in Russia in the spring and summer of 1921, threatening thirty million people with starvation and death, a number of Americans immediately expressed the belief that this was a heaven-sent opportunity to help the Russian people, to put them on the road to capitalism and democracy. "I ask all honest European and American people for prompt aid to the Russian people," Maxim Gorki pleaded in July, 1921. "Give bread and medicine." The response in the United States was overwhelming. Congress quickly approved an appropriation of $20 million for an American Relief Administration, headed by Herbert Hoover. The American farm bloc supported the relief program enthusiastically. All told, about $66 million was raised, mostly through private contributions.

The famine-relief program was undoubtedly a great, positive achievement of the United States. It has been estimated that the lives of some 10,500,000 persons were saved, many of them children. Unfortunately, it also provided another source of suspicion in American-Soviet relations. Hoover's open admission that the relief program was an important phase of his broad plan at the ultimate Americanization of the Russian economy created distrust. Hughes's declaration, moreover, that he saw in the American Relief Administration a substitute for international negotiation also aroused suspicion. "Full information will be obtained in this way," explained the Secretary of State, "without the risk of complication through government action"—namely, recognition.

Soviet officials eyed the relief program dubiously from its very beginning. They later attributed it mainly to an effort to bolster the sagging American domestic economy by exporting surpluses. The United States, on its part, was angered when the Soviet government began to export considerable supplies of grain from the famine-stricken Volga region. Typical "double-dealing" by the Bolsheviks, cried the American press.

The famine-relief program did help, however, to remove the roadblock in the State Department against American economic penetration and, ultimately, recognition.

THE WASHINGTON CONFERENCE

The tremendous business expansion during the 1920's required for the United States a stable international world: one in which peace would be the supreme goal for all nations. How was it to be achieved? Wilson's idea of a League of Nations had been rejected. "Balance of power" and "spheres of interest" were regarded as equally repugnant. The best way to assure the attainment of world peace, it was thought, would be to remove the instruments of war, to achieve disarmament. If all nations, acting in good faith, disarmed—so the argument ran—there would not and could not be war.

The idea was most attractive. It fitted in neatly with the desire of the great powers to relax the crushing burden of heavy armament expenses and with the distaste of the American people and American Big Business interests for an unbalanced war budget, mounting public debt, and heavy taxes on personal and corporate incomes. The largest items in the national budget were military and naval costs. Here was a logical place where drastic reductions might be made. But could America sacrifice its own military and naval strength unless other nations were prepared to do the same thing at the same time? Obviously not! It could be done only through world disarmament.

After the Paris Peace Conference, pressures for disarmament and a settlement of issues in the Far East became extremely great. The ambitious postwar naval programs of Japan, Britain, and the United States had developed into a full-fledged race that, once started, was difficult to stop. Wilson's determination to thwart Japan's designs in Asia had contributed to the launching in 1920-21 of the armaments race between America and Japan. Wilson's challenge to Japan had been fully disclosed in the joint Allied intervention in Russia, in his opposition at Paris to Japan's claims to Shantung, and in his revival of the Bankers' Consortium. However, Japan agreed to participate in the new consortium, signed in October, 1920, only after she obtained recognition of her "special position" in South Manchuria. The consortium, nevertheless, was designed to check further Japanese encroachments.

At the beginning of the 1920's, the threat of war with Japan seemed to be quite serious. America was flooded with books and magazine articles with such provocative titles as "The Menace of Japan," "The New Japanese Peril," "Rising Japan," and "Must We Fight Japan?" The Hearst press took up the cry of the "yellow peril." The situation in Japan was equally hostile.

The war scare led to one of the most notorious scandals during the Harding period. Three government oil reserves—among them Teapot Dome in Wyoming and Elks Hill in California—were secretly transferred in 1921, without competitive bidding, to two prominent oil men, Harry F. Sinclair and Edward F. Doheny. To effect the deal, Secretary of the Interior Albert B. Fall accepted bribes—$260,000 in Liberty Bonds from Sinclair for the rights to Teapot Dome, and $100,000 in cash from Doheny for the Elks Hill reserve. Secrecy, Fall later explained, was necessary because of the threat of war with Japan and because certain military arrangments had to be made. The purpose of the transfer was to encourage the building up of fuel-oil storage depots at Pearl Harbor and other strategic points in case of trouble. Fall believed that this could be done better by private oil men than by the government. But Sinclair and Doheny had no genuine intention of building these depots; they were primarily interested in their own private profit. Indeed, while the transfer was taking place, the two were actually selling oil to Japan.

When the story came to light in 1924, an investigation was undertaken. In 1927, the Supreme Court ordered the oil reserves returned, and in unusually sharp language, branded Sinclair, Doheny, and Fall guilty of "fraud, conspiracy, and corruption." Fall was eventually found guilty of accepting a bribe; he was fined $100,000 and sentenced to a year in jail. Sinclair and Doheny were both acquitted in criminal prosecution for conspiracy; but Sinclair was forced to serve a short prison term for contempt of the Senate and for hiring private detectives to shadow members of the jury sitting on his case.

The tension between the United States and Japan in the early 1920's was reflected in the Yap controversy. The island of Yap in the Carolines, which had formerly belonged to Germany, was awarded to Japan as a mandate by the League of Nations. America considered it important because it provided the best cable connections with the Dutch East Indies and China. Wilson had insisted at Paris that Yap be internationalized. But the Japanese held firm that it be included in their mandate, and they were backed in this claim by the British. Since the United States did not ratify the Versailles Treaty, the transfer of the former German islands to Japan on a mandated basis was technically effected without America's consent. One of the last acts of the Wilson administration was the dispatch of a note to Japan stating that America would have to be consulted in regard to Yap's final disposition. Japan brusquely refused to consider the matter. Early in the Harding administration, Secretary of State Hughes raised the issue of Japan's right to a mandate not only to Yap, but to the other German Pacific islands. While the controversy was of relatively little importance in itself, it was a portent of the mounting tension between America and Japan in the Far East.

By 1921, the two problems—disarmament and the crisis in the Far East—converged. America was more deeply concerned about the issue of disarmament; but Britain was much more perturbed about the situation in the Far East. A great debate arose in Britain and the Dominions over renewing once again the Anglo-Japanese alliance, originally entered into in 1902 to counteract the expansion of Russia in Asia. Since Russia was no longer an immediate threat because of the internal chaos of the Bolshevik Revolution, many feared that the renewal of the alliance could be used by Japan against the United States. In the event of war, it was said, Britain would be obligated to support Japan. A modification or abrogation of the alliance therefore appeared necessary.

In her desire to find a working substitute for the Anglo-Japanese alliance, Britain suggested calling a conference with America, China, and Japan to discuss the problems of the Far East and to seek a general understanding. The United States, at precisely the same time, endorsed an international conference to discuss the limitation of armaments, but made no reference to the Far East. While America made preparations for such a conference, George Harvey, the American ambassador in London, reported early in July, 1921, that Lloyd George was about to make an announcement in the House of Commons of a plan for an international conference to consider all matters touching upon the Far East and the Pacific Ocean. Secretary Hughes, disturbed that Britain would get the entire credit for the idea of an international conference, jumped the gun, and on July 11 publicly announced that the United States had addressed "informal but definite inquiries" to the powers concerned for a conference on armament limitation. He added that it would also take up questions relating to the Far East. Britain had hoped that the discussion on the Far East would take place in England; then one would be held in Washington on disarmament. But Hughes refused to consider this; in view of the sharp criticism directed against Wilson on his trip to Paris, he opposed a meeting abroad. Britain finally consented to a Washington conference to deal with both the disarmament and Far Eastern issues.

Hughes sent invitations to Britain, France, Italy, and Japan. So that the nations with interests in the Far East would be represented, he later included, at Britain's suggestion, China, Belgium, the Netherlands, and Portugal. Thus nine powers were invited to participate in the conference, which was scheduled for November, 1921. Japan was reluctant to attend; as far as she was concerned, there were no general outstanding problems in the Pacific. But she was interested in peace and disarmament; she wanted a renewal of the Anglo-Japanese alliance; and, above all, she desired to retain the status quo of 1921. Unwilling to take a chance that her position might be jeopardized, Japan, accordingly, accepted Hughes's invitation unenthusiastically. The Secretary of State brushed aside Japan's qualified reply and announced that all the interested parties had accepted the conference proposals.

On November 12, with the opening of the Washington Conference, Hughes stepped into the world spotlight. In an unexpected, dramatic speech, the Secretary of State laid America's cards on the table. He called for the adoption, without delay, of a naval-disarmament program and a ten-year holiday in the construction of capital ships. "The world looks to this Conference to relieve humanity of the crushing burden created by competition in armament," declared Hughes. "If there is to be economic rehabilitation, if the longings for reasonable progress are not to be denied, if we are to be spared the uprisings of peoples made desperate in the desire to shake off burdens no longer endurable, competition in armaments must stop."

Hughes then calmly proceeded to scuttle capital ships of the American, British, and Japanese navies. He pledged that the United States would scrap at once thirty of its own capital ships. Turning to the British, he sent to the bottom four new capital ships and nineteen older ones. One observer at the Conference lamented that Hughes in one breath had managed to destroy more British ships than all of her enemies had succeeded in doing in centuries. Japan was asked to scrap seven partly built ships and ten others. The aggregate total of capital ships which Hughes recommended for destruction by the three nations came to nearly two million tons.

Japan protested Hughes's drastic program. The Japanese delegates stated that to comply with the Secretary of State's proposals would seriously endanger Japan's security. They made it clear that Japan could not consent to naval reductions unless Britain and America stopped further construction of naval bases and fortifications in their Far East insular possessions. Specifically, Japan demanded that the Philippines, Wake, Guam, the Aleutian Islands, and Hong Kong not be fortified. On her part, she agreed that she would not fortify Formosa and the Loo Choos (later called the Ryukyus Islands). With this understanding—to which the United States and Britain consented—a Five-Power Naval Treaty was signed. It ostensibly established the relative naval strengths of Britain, the United States, Japan, France, and Italy at a ratio of 5–5–3–1.7–1.7. The treaty was to remain in effect until 1936, at which time any of the signatories might terminate their adherence by giving a two-year notice. The Five-Power Treaty also pledged the powers to a ten-year holiday with respect to the construction of capital ships; no limitation, however, was placed on submarines, destroyers, and cruisers, except insofar as cruisers were not to exceed ten thousand tons or be equipped with guns larger than eight-inch caliber. Actually the American Navy had reached a point where it had begun to consider large capital ships obsolete for strategic purposes; the exceptions of submarines, destroyers, and cruisers—which were then considered much more necessary for naval defense—in effect nullified the whole noble intention of the Five-Power Treaty to achieve naval disarmament. Because of the pledge on nonfortification of insular possessions, Japan immeasurably strengthened her relative position, and despite her smaller ship ratio, she secured naval supremacy in the Far East. However, the Five-Power Naval Treaty, hailed as a great American diplomatic triumph, temporarily ended all talk of war between the United States and Japan.

After the Five-Power Treaty was concluded, the Conference turned its attention to the abrogation of the Anglo-Japanese alliance. Originally, Britain had merely wanted to modify her treaty with Japan in such a way so as to include the United States; thus it could never be used against America. This was agreeable to Japan, whose main concern was to make sure that the United States would not interfere with Japanese interests in Manchuria or China. Hughes, however, objected. He feared the possibility of America being dragged into an "entangling alliance." The Secretary of State, moreover, insisted on the inclusion of France. Her pride had been seriously wounded in the Five-Power Naval Treaty, which placed her on a naval par with Italy. Before World War I, she had been a first-rank naval power, and despite the new limitation agreement, she intended in the future to regain this rank. To assure France that the United States still regarded her as a leading world power, Hughes persuaded her to enter the discussions on a Far East pact. In addition, the Secretary wanted to head off the charge that Britain and Japan could outvote the United States in case some controversial issues arose; France could serve as an effective balance. The result was the signing of the second important treaty at the Washington Conference—the Four-Power Pact, abrogating the Anglo-Japanese alliance and substituting an innocuous consultative agreement. A specific pledge was given by the powers to respect each other's "rights in relation to their insular possessions and insular dominions in the region of the Pacific Ocean." If disputes arose among the four signatories, or if an outside power threatened the rights of the pact members, the decision as to what to do was to be worked out at a joint conference.

The most far-reaching agreement concluded at the Washington Conference was the Nine-Power Treaty. Each nation—including Japan—pledged herself to respect the sovereignty and independence of China and its territorial and administrative integrity. The treaty also provided for free access of all nations to Chinese markets; to the United States, this represented a clear affirmation of John Hay's original Open Door notes. Each of the signatory powers agreed to refrain from taking advantage of conditions in China in order to seek special rights or privileges. While the parties agreed to respect the Open Door, none bound themselves to defend it by force. The treaty simply rested on the good faith of the nine powers. As such, it proved to be a weak reed.

The Washington Conference, in the final analysis, represented a setback for Japan despite her apparent gains in the Five-Power Treaty. The status quo was established, not on the basis of 1921, but as it existed before 1914. Because of the pressures of America, Britain, and France, Japan was forced to make a full-scale retreat. She agreed to certain modifications of her special privileges in Manchuria and officially withdrew the portion of the Twenty-One Demands in which she had claimed control of Chinese government policy. Japan also consented to evacuate her troops from Shantung, to sell to China the former German-owned railroad there, and to give up her special economic privileges in the province. Japan further agreed to evacuate her troops from Siberia and to restore Sakhalin Island to Russia. In addition, she conceded free access to Yap's cable facilities and agreed not to establish a naval or military base on the island.

Why did the Japanese delegates consent to these concessions, which were later so sharply criticized by the imperialists in Japan as humiliating submission to the Western powers? Part of the reason lay in the fact that the Japanese liberals, then in control of governmental policy, sincerely desired to end the friction with the United States. They hoped that Japan's goals of control in China might be achieved by a peaceful economic penetration, rather than by aggression. The liberals believed that a close partnership with Britain and America would be helpful toward this end.

For two years, cordial relations were maintained between Japan and the United States. It appeared that the promise of the Washington Conference would be fulfilled. And then the bottom dropped out! America's blundering policies on immigration and tariffs created disaster. Overnight, Japan's friendly attitude turned to burning hostility. The igniting factor was the passage by Congress of the Johnson Immigration Act of 1924. This law barred from immigration "aliens ineligible to citizenship." Pacific Coast pressures were largely responsible for the exclusion of Orientals. While the act as phrased applied to China as well, and intense nationalist agitation against the United States arose in that country, it was the Japanese who felt especially affronted since it represented a sudden abrogation of the Gentlemen's Agreement. Secretary of State Hughes and Masanao Hanihara, the Japanese ambassador in Washington, were partly responsible for the mess that occurred. Realizing how sensitive the Japanese were toward the slightest sign of discrimination, Hughes had suggested that the ambassador set forth an explanation of Japan's position. In this way, the Secretary hoped that Congress would be persuaded to include Japan in the quota system. However, in his statement Ambassador Hanihara most unwisely referred to the "grave consequences" which would ensue if exclusion were adopted. With a chip-on-the-shoulder attitude, Congress promptly approved the exclusion feature. Charles Evans Hughes wrote:

It is a sorry business and I am greatly depressed. It has undone the work of the Washington Conference and implanted the seeds of an antagonism which are sure to bear fruit in the future. . . . Our friends in the Senate have in a few minutes spoiled the work of years and done a lasting injury to [the] country.

The protective tariff laws enacted by Congress during the 1920's were equally disruptive of hopes for establishing more amicable relations with Japan. Especially injurious and therefore offensive was the Smoot-Hawley Tariff, which came at the end of the decade, in 1930. Although enacted as a measure to help ease the Great Depression in the United States, it had most unfortunate repercussions in the Far East. Japan's foreign trade, on which her existence depended, was hit very badly.

But the collapse of the peace-treaty foundations of the Washington Conference stemmed not only from the worsening of Japanese-American relations; it was also due to the fact that the great powers—with the exception of the United States—actually did not wish to reduce their naval power drastically, nor were they willing—and here the United States was no exception—to enforce the provisions of the Washington treaties.

DISARMAMENT HITS A SNAG

Outwardly, the Washington Conference treaty on naval limitations seemed to be a success. Britain, America, and Japan scrapped about 40 percent of their strength in capital ships. But the big loophole lay in the unrestricted categories of the Five-Power Naval Treaty. No slow-down occurred in the building of cruisers, destroyers, and submarines: during the years from 1922 to 1930, Britain constructed or appropriated money to build 74 naval vessels; Japan, 125; France, 119; Italy, 82; and the United States, 11. A new rivalry had developed, especially in building of cruisers. In 1927, President Calvin Coolidge—that "odd fish" in the White House, who disliked spending money, even that of other people—issued a call for another conference to halt the incipient naval race. Britain and Japan accepted the invitation, but France and Italy declined. Coolidge's efforts led to the fruitless Geneva Conference, largely dominated by naval, rather than diplomatic, experts. Wrangling arose on the questions of parity and large versus small cruisers, and no agreement could be reached. One result of the conference was a flurry of bitter American antagonism toward Great Britain. The conviction grew strong that Britain was not really willing to concede full naval parity to the United States. Congress, in a huff, authorized, in February, 1929, the building of fifteen of the largest size cruisers possible under the Washington Naval Treaty.

Disillusion over the deterioration in arms reduction led to an insistent demand on the part of idealistic advocates of peace through the 1920's that something more be done to "outlaw war." Senator Borah was won over to a plan to call all war, except war in self-defense, illegal. A peace-crusade movement suddenly built up momentum. It was abetted in the spring of 1927 by French Foreign Minister Aristide Briand, who was persuaded by Professor James T. Shotwell of Columbia University to make an impassioned appeal for a treaty between France and the United States renouncing war. Coolidge and Secretary of State Frank B. Kellogg were cool to the proposal. But the idea caught fire. Sensing the strong popular sentiment, Kellogg enthusiastically joined the peace crusade and declared that he would support a treaty to "outlaw war," provided it was endorsed by many nations, not simply the United States and France. This was not what Briand had in mind, but he agreed to accept the Secretary of State's suggestion. In August, 1928, representatives of fifteen countries agreed to the Kellogg-Briand Pact, and it was eventually signed and ratified by nearly all the nations of the world.

The pact was a noble gesture, but little more. Because of its great promise, the fact that the Kellogg-Briand Pact was virtually meaningless deepened, rather than dispelled, the disillusion. All the nations were pledged to "condemn recourse to war for the solution of international controversies, and renounce it as an instrument of national policy in their relations with one another." The pact did not "outlaw war"; it merely condemned and renounced it. There was not a country in the world that did not condemn and renounce war, but each—including the United States—recognized that wars were necessary and justified in "self-defense." Since all nations claimed that they waged war only for "self-defense," the Kellogg-Briand Pact did not advance by one iota the abolition of war, which was what was implied in the treaty's aim of "outlawing war."

Efforts to achieve disarmament continued. President Herbert Hoover, deeply devoted to peace, returned to the problem of naval limitations, and sought to clear up the misunderstandings in Anglo-American relations. In May, 1929, the Labor party came to power in Britain. Prime Minister Ramsay MacDonald replaced the Conservatives' Stanley Baldwin, and out with Baldwin went Winston Churchill, the most outspoken fighter for British naval supremacy. A good-will tour by MacDonald to the United States in October, 1929, helped to thaw Anglo-American coolness. An amiable meeting between Hoover and MacDonald at the President's summer fishing camp at Rapidan, Virginia, led to the London Naval Disarmament Conference in 1930. After three months' negotiation, agreement was reached on fixing a tonnage limit for cruisers, destroyers, and submarines. In addition, Britain, Japan, and the United States pledged to scrap nine battleships then in commission, and a five-year holiday was proclaimed in laying down new ones. A new over-all ratio was set at 10–10–7. However, the London Treaty gave the United States the right to maintain larger cruisers than Britain, and Japan obtained equality in submarines. France and Italy did not sign the agreement, Italy demanding parity with France, which the latter refused to acknowledge. The London Treaty applied therefore only to the three great powers—Britain, America, and Japan. An "escalator clause" was inserted which made it possible for any of the three nations to exceed the tonnage allotment if a nonsignatory power engaged in construction that threatened its national security.

By 1930, no progress whatsoever had as yet been made on disarmament with respect to land and air forces, and the naval reductions had made little significant effect on the national distribution of world power. The Great Depression quashed hopes that genuine world disarmament could become a reality. Japan and Germany began to press ahead on an aggressive course. The rising threat of Germany convinced France that security arrangement had to precede disarmament. The changing world conditions doomed the one great effort of the League of Nations to achieve a general limitation on all national armaments. The League's Geneva Conference of 1932 was valuable for the minute, exhaustive, and realistic manner in which it approached the problem of world disarmament. But it was an academic exercise. After twenty-eight months of discussion, the conference had to confess failure.

After the collapse of the Geneva World Disarmament Conference— the last conference undertaken by the League on this problem—the end of disarmament efforts was in sight. Japan, in December, 1934, announced its termination of the Five-Power Naval Treaty, effective at the end of 1936. The last conference on naval limitations took place in London in 1935. Japan insisted on full naval parity with Britain and the United States. When this was refused, she walked out. A treaty was concluded which merely limited the tonnage and guns of war vessels; but Japan and Italy would not sign it. By 1936, the pretense of even partial restrictions of naval armaments came to an end. In that year, the United States had lagged so far behind the other powers in naval construction that it would have had to build 102 new ships at a cost of $380 million simply to restore its position to a basis originally permitted in the Five-Power Naval Treaty. "The letters of FAILURE, written large over the portals of successive disarmament conferences during the two decades after Versailles, became letters of impending catastrophe for the Western world."[6]

⁶ Frederick L. Schuman, *International Politics* (New York, 1948), p. 351.

THE MANCHURIAN CRISIS

For almost ten years after the Washington Conference, relative peace existed in the Far East. The test as to whether the great powers would enforce the Nine-Power Treaty to protect the territorial and administrative integrity of China and uphold the Open Door came suddenly in 1931 as a result of the crisis in Manchuria. During the 1920's, Japan's domestic policies were on the whole directed by the liberal faction in the country. Except for the stresses and strains created by the passage of the Immigration Act of 1924, her attitude was one of conciliation toward the great powers. Nevertheless, the military element in Japan, which advocated an aggressive and imperialistic policy, remained openly hostile to the United States.

Japan's major problem centered on China. Since the outbreak of Sun Yat-sen's revolution in 1911, China continued to be divided, weak, and almost helpless. In the early 1920's, three separate factions existed: the Kuomintang (Nationalist) party, whose headquarters were at Canton, controlled the southern provinces; a military clique at Peking—the old northern capital—dominated Central China; and Chang Tso-lin, an independent war lord, ruled in Manchuria. The Chinese Nationalists, the dynamic force in China's revolution, aimed at the reunification of the country, recovery of its full independence, and the elimination of foreign domination. The Soviet Union offered to help the Nationalists to achieve these objectives, and this aid was heartily welcomed, especially when the great powers refused to extend any of the assistance which the Chinese Nationalists desired. Russian agents worked closely with the Chinese revolutionaries, and under the whiplash of Soviet propaganda, intense antiforeign agitation arose. A Chinese boycott was launched against British, American, and Japanese goods. However, the introduction of communism threatened to split the country further apart. By 1926, the Nationalists came under the leadership of Chiang Kai-shek, the successor of Sun Yat-sen. A drive developed against the Peking military clique in an effort to extend Nationalist control into Central China, and a civil war erupted in 1927. Fearful of communist influence, Chiang Kai-shek, in the midst of the civil war, suddenly turned against his Red supporters. In a nightmarish blood bath, Bolsheviks were ruthlessly exterminated, and reprisals were taken on their native followers. Thus began the fierce struggle between the Chinese Communists and the Nationalists which continued for more than two decades.

Chiang Kai-shek emerged triumphant in the civil war. In June, 1928, the Kuomintang defeated the rulers at Peking and established a new capital at Nanking. After consolidating his power, Chiang Kai-shek looked toward Manchuria and at the same time embarked on a campaign to annihilate completely the Chinese Communists throughout the country. Chang Tso-lin in Manchuria, who had been sympathetic to Japan, decided to support the Nationalists; his sudden conversion was, no doubt, responsible for his assassination in June, 1928. Chang Hsueh-liang, his son and successor, swung even further away from the Japanese.

In 1929, Chiang Kai-shek attempted to extend Nationalist control into Manchuria and thus complete the reunification of China. A two-pronged attack was directed against the Russians and Japanese, who had long since divided North and South Manchuria into their respective spheres of influence. A Russo-Chinese clash occurred when China seized some Russian property and arrested Soviet agents. The Soviet Union launched a full-fledged invasion and quickly brought the Chinese to terms. The incident, however, alarmed Japan. She feared that her own interests in South Manchuria were endangered. What worried the Japanese especially was the steady Chinese immigration into Manchuria that was greatly encouraged by the Nationalists. By 1931, approximately thirty million people lived in Manchuria; all but two million were Chinese. Most of the Chinese were farmers who had streamed into the region during the late 1920's from the overcrowded provinces immediately south of the Great Wall. Efforts by Japan to stimulate Japanese migration to the province had been unsuccessful. Only a bare two hundred thousand Japanese—most of them employees of the South Manchuria Railway and huddled along its lines—were in Manchuria.

Hard hit by the depression, Japanese imperialists, fearful that Japan's Manchurian economic life line would be cut, denounced the conciliatory policy of the liberals and demanded a more aggressive policy. In 1931, the tension between the Chinese Nationalists and Japanese militarists reached a breaking point. A crisis occurred when a Japanese army officer on an intelligence mission in central Manchuria was reported secretly executed by Chinese soldiers. In September, 1931, the inevitable "incident" took place: a skirmish arose between Japanese and Chinese soldiers along the South Manchurian Railway. The fight was followed by a full-scale Japanese invasion.

STIMSON'S SHIRT-SLEEVE DIPLOMACY FAILS

The 1931 outbreak of hostilities in Manchuria came as a shock to the United States, much more so, in fact, than to Europe. Japan's role at the London Conference held the previous year and her conciliatory attitude had lulled the Western powers into a false sense of security. She was regarded in 1930 as the guardian of peace in the Pacific. All causes of conflict seemed to be liquidated.

The United States was convinced that the action in Manchuria was not spontaneous. Four days after the Japanese invasion, the American minister to China wired:

According to all information available to me here, I am driven to the conclusion that the forceful occupation of all strategic points in South Manchuria . . . is an aggressive act by Japan apparently long planned and when decided upon most carefully and systematically put into effect. I find no evidence that these events were the result of accident nor were they the acts of minor and irresponsible officials.

It was Secretary of State Henry L. Stimson's belief, however, that the Manchurian incident was not initiated by the Foreign Office, but by the Army, which had done so without the consent of the Premier. Nevertheless, both President Herbert Hoover and Stimson recognized that if the Japanese militarists were not checked the entire security program in the Pacific established by the Washington Conference treaties would be destroyed.

During the first few weeks, Stimson followed a policy of caution. He obtained assurances from the Japanese ambassador in Washington that Japan harbored "no territorial designs in Manchuria"; that it was anxious "to cooperate with the Chinese government in order to prevent the present incident from developing into a disastrous situation." But that matters no longer were in the hands of the Foreign Office and were effectively controlled by the Army, became evident early in October when Japanese planes bombed Chinchow in southwestern Manchuria. The attack induced Stimson, with Hoover's approval, to send an American delegate to sit with the League of Nations Council when it discussed the Manchurian problem. He likewise indicated that the United States would support the League in creating a commission to study the situation. In October, the League Council passed a resolution which called upon Japan to withdraw her troops into their legitimate zone by November 16. But two days after the announced deadline, Japanese forces launched another offensive campaign.

Stimson was angered. He had avoided taking a firm stand and had hoped that the Japanese liberals in government would coöperate with the League. When this failed to happen, Stimson threatened that unless steps were taken to liquidate the Manchurian affair, he would publish all of the confidential papers and documents on the subject that had passed between the two governments. "I told Debuchi [the Japanese ambassador in Washington] that as he knew for two months I had been preserving these papers in confidence in the hope of a settlement," recorded the Secretary, "so that it might not embarrass the Japanese government or the chance of such a settlement." Japan, quite disturbed, advised Stimson against such drastic action and reiterated her desire to settle the matter amicably. The Secretary of State insisted that in order for this to be done Japan had to cease hostilities, withdraw her troops, and permit a neutral League commission to investigate the controversy between China and Japan. To make American pressures more effective, Stimson also recommended the possibility of the United States joining with the League in imposing sanctions. President Hoover, however, who believed that economic sanctions might involve the United States in war, promptly vetoed this idea. He would go no further than moral pressure, but agreed to support the League of Nations if it imposed sanctions.

Japan accepted in principle the proposal for a neutral League investigating commission. However, she refused to withdraw her troops, maintaining that they were necessary to guarantee the safety of Japanese lives and property. Without the withdrawal of troops and the cessation of hostilities, Stimson felt that the proposed League investigation "would be quite futile for accomplishing the intended beneficent purpose and for winning the support of world opinion." The blunt demands of the Secretary of State incensed the Japanese Foreign Office. They were especially furious at Stimson's remark that the Japanese armies were running amuck, and asked "if he considered the meaning of his words before using them."

In a tense atmosphere, the League of Nations set up in December, 1931, the Lytton Commission, headed by Britain's Earl of Lytton. The Japanese liberal government accepted the commission. It was its last act. On December 10, the day the government approved the League resolution, the Japanese Army took control in Tokyo and in Manchuria. The conquest of Manchuria was completed in January, 1932, and the militarists retained domination over the Japanese government until the end of World War II.

Stimson refused to give up the fight against Japanese aggression. A war was clearly out of the question; the Quaker President would not consider it, and it would have met with vigorous public opposition. Talk of war, in fact, led to the charge that the Hoover administration was seeking a diversion from the agonies of the domestic depression. But the administration had other weapons, and Hoover and Stimson did not hesitate to use them. Two tactics were employed. The first invoked the declaration of "nonrecognition," which Secretary of State Bryan had first set forth in 1915 in connection with the Twenty-One Demands. The second aimed at rallying world opinion against Japan and branding her an aggressor.

In January, 1932, the Hoover-Stimson doctrine was laid down. In effect, it declared that the United States would not recognize "the legality of any situation de facto" or any treaty or agreement between Japan and China which impaired "the sovereignty, the independence, or the territorial and administrative integrity of the Republic of China, or . . . the open door policy" that was contrary to the Kellogg-Briand Pact to which China, Japan, and the United States were parties. However, the weapon of nonrecognition proved to be useless. France simply ignored Stimson's note; the British, responding to it in a press communiqué, stated that they would rely on Japan's publicly announced promise to respect the Open Door. Apparently, Britain did not object to the absorption of Japanese energies in Manchuria—an area where Japan's "special rights" had been well defined—for otherwise, she thought, it might be spent in the Yangtse Valley, where her chief interests lay, or in Australasia, or along the Indian frontier.

Late in the month, however, Britain had something of a change of heart when Japan suddenly attacked Shanghai. The attack against the Chinese section of the city was partly in retaliation for a boycott that seriously undermined Japanese trade. Stimson once again demanded the cessation of hostilities, and he urged Britain to apply economic sanctions. While the British stressed the need for a policy of caution and moderation, she nevertheless joined the Americans in sending naval vessels and marines to Shanghai. This step, combined with the unexpected opposition of the Chinese Nineteenth Route Army, quickly induced Japan to put an end to the "Shanghai Incident." An armistice was signed in May, but Japan refused to suspend her war preparations or agree to a settlement of her controversies with China "with the aid of neutral observers" until all her demands were met. Meanwhile, she consolidated her position in Manchuria, proclaimed the independence of the region, and created the puppet state of "Manchukuo."

The establishment of Manchukuo was a red flag to Stimson; it flagrantly disregarded the Hoover-Stimson doctrine. Angered, he decided to mobilize world public opinion against Japan through the device of an open letter to Senator Borah, chairman of the Senate Committee on Foreign Relations. This blistering letter he released to the press late in February, 1932, shortly after Japan proclaimed the new state of Manchukuo. In it he castigated Japan for her violation of the Nine-Power Treaty of 1922, declared that the United States would insist on her treaty rights in the Far East, and called upon the other nations of the world to adhere to the policy of nonrecognition. The letter was effective; Stimson's clear recitation of the dangers of Japan's actions blackened her as an aggressor power. But without European support to enforce the Nine-Power Treaty—either through effective economic sanctions or, if necessary, through the use of force—the implied threats of the Secretary of State were worthless. Japan did not budge.

During the next six months, the Lytton Commission carried on its investigation of the Manchurian crisis. It submitted an exhaustive and carefully prepared report to the League of Nations in September. The Commission did not fix responsibility for the original outbreak of hostilities in Manchuria a year earlier. It noted that the Chinese had given serious provocation for the incident, but concluded that Japan's military operations in Manchuria could not be regarded as measures of legitimate self-defense. The report stated further that the puppet state of Manchukuo disregarded the wishes of the people and was not compatible with the principles of existing international obligations. The Commission, in effect, supported Stimson's position and branded Japan as an aggressor. The Secretary of State won a belated victory for the Hoover-Stimson doctrine when the League members passed a resolution approving the Lytton Commission's recommendation that Manchuria remain autonomous under Chinese sovereignty, and that no League member recognize Manchukuo "either *de jure* or *de facto*." On the same day the resolution was passed, Japan walked out of the League Assembly, and one month later, submitted a two-year notice of her intention to withdraw from the League of Nations.

Despite Stimson's protests and diplomatic pressure, Japan proceeded to consolidate her military victories. The League action came too late. Without the coöperation of Britain and France, the United States was powerless to check Japan short of the use of force; and war was ruled out as an instrument of policy throughout the crisis. Had the great powers and the League taken effective action to curb Japan, it is probable that the onward rush of subsequent events toward World War II might have been averted. On the basis of hindsight, it is clear that the Manchurian crisis sounded the death knell of the foundations for peace and of the League of Nations itself.

AN ERA DRAWS TO A CLOSE

The postwar years saw the United States essentially pursuing a policy of drift in world affairs. America's attention focused primarily on the promotion of foreign trade and overseas investments. Foreign policy was little more than an offshoot of international business. The impact of America's economic power, indeed, was felt very strongly in the countries throughout the world, particularly as manufactured goods poured into the markets abroad. The impressive achievement of mass-production technology exerted a powerful influence in Europe and especially in Japan and the Soviet Union. But it also produced a negative reaction. Resentment, envy, and distrust of America's wealth and power were widespread. The hard, cold, business practicality of America's dealings with other nations widened the gap of international misunderstanding. This was particularly evident in the handling of the war-debt and reparations problems.

After World War I, the United States had the capacity to assume a leadership to guide the world—in coöperation with all other nations—toward constructive political and economic goals. "The financial leadership will be ours," Woodrow Wilson declared. "The industrial primacy will be ours. The commercial advantage will be ours. The other countries of the world are looking to us for leadership and direction." But the necessary ingredient of executive leadership was to be lacking tragically during the 1920's. Harding was devoid of it; Coolidge abdicated it in favor of the business class; and Hoover, confronted by the Great Depression and coping with domestic economic problems, could not demonstrate it.

The damage caused by America's policy of drift reflected in the regression to isolationism could not easily be repaired. The Great Depression marked the turn in the tide. The world, without a rudder, found itself out of control.

5 · DIPLOMACY OF THE

NEW DEAL ERA:

FIRST PHASE (1933-1937)

*We believe in democracy; we believe in freedom; we believe in peace.
We offer to every nation of the world the handclasp of the good
neighbor. Let those who wish our friendship look us in the eye and take
our hand.*
PRESIDENT FRANKLIN D. ROOSEVELT, *Speech at Chautauqua,
New York, August 14, 1936*

The myopia of America's policies toward Europe carried over into
President Franklin D. Roosevelt's first administration. The Great Depression profoundly intensified isolationist sentiment. In the troubled,
disillusioned postwar years, emphasis had largely focused on political
separation—"Keep out of the League"—but after 1929, political separation became strongly and directly linked to economic isolation. The
keynote of Roosevelt's foreign policy during the first phase of the New
Deal Era was retreat—retreat in Europe, in Latin America, and in the
Far East.

The campaign of 1932 was chiefly concerned with the issue of the depression. Economic distress was acute. Industrial production and national income plunged downward, while unemployment climbed steadily
upward, reaching somewhere between thirteen and seventeen million.
America was a country in crisis—a nation paralyzed by economic collapse. With breadlines, farm-foreclosure riots, apple venders in the cities,

debt and tax burdens, crime waves, and veterans clamoring for bonuses and marching on Washington, the American people could not seriously concern themselves with foreign affairs—there was so much to be done at home. At first, President Hoover had thought the depression would "iron" itself out through the natural workings of the business cycle— "Prosperity was just around the corner"—and he resisted governmental interference. When the crisis deepened, however, he recognized that the government had to assume a moral responsibility to prevent total disaster. Valiantly, Hoover strove to save the top structure of the economy, but despite his efforts, the downward spiral continued. In 1932, recovery was nowhere in sight.

Democratic candidate Franklin D. Roosevelt argued that the causes of the depression were largely domestic in origin; solutions had to be sought in bold, persistent experimentation. "It is common sense to take a method and try it," he declared. "If it fails, admit it frankly and try another. But above all, try something." The basic trouble, Roosevelt maintained, was not "an insufficiency of capital." Instead it stemmed from the imbalance in the economic structure: between production and consumption, between agriculture and industry, between capital and labor, and between investments and savings. The goal, said Roosevelt, must be to restore the balance.

But President Hoover saw the depression in a different light. He felt equally strongly that it was part of the long-range aftermath of World War I, and the product of world-wide conditions over which the United States had little if any control:

Nowhere do I find the slightest reference in all the statements of the opposition party to the part played by the greatest war in history, the inheritances from it, the fears and panics and dreadful economic catastrophes which have developed from these causes in foreign countries, or the idea that they may have had the remotest thing to do with the calamity against which this administration is fighting day and night.

Roosevelt's optimism that something had to be done and could be done to end the depression—he was somewhat vague on exactly *what* would be done—contrasted sharply at the time with the pessimistic and negative approach implied by Hoover's observations that the depression could be solved only when world conditions were righted.

Roosevelt won the election in 1932 handsomely; he carried all but six states, and the Democratic party won majorities in both houses of Congress. In his nomination acceptance speech, Roosevelt had told the Democratic convention in Chicago, "I pledge you, I pledge myself, to a new deal for the American people." The phrase "new deal," tacked on without any special significance at the end of a long, rambling speech, was quickly picked up to identify Roosevelt's bold new program.

During the election campaign, the impression which Roosevelt had made upon the country was mixed. His appeal to the interests of the "forgotten man," his thrusts against Big Business, and his stabs at a "do-nothing" President were effective and won widespread support. Many people also admired Roosevelt's courage in overcoming his crippled condition (due to poliomyelitis, contracted in 1921). Eager to prove that he was not an invalid, he stumped the country, traveling some 25,000 miles and in high-spirited fashion ripped into the Republican party. Roosevelt also used the radio—then coming into its own in popularity—to great advantage. His smooth, precise, "magic" voice contrasted with the somber, dolorous tones of Hoover. At fifty-one, Roosevelt was robust, jaunty, and in bubbling spirits. His confidence and self-assurance were a tonic in the depressing atmosphere pervading the country. Hoover appeared old and tired, weighed down by the burdens of his office.

But many Americans were somewhat uncertain as to whether Roosevelt would make a "good" President. The liberals especially were a bit skeptical. Some saw him as a Democratic Harding—cheerful, friendly, impressionable, immature, a politician rather than a statesman, without any of the qualities of "greatness." Columnist Walter Lippmann summed up the general reaction of liberals when he described Roosevelt as "a pleasant man who, without any important qualifications for the office, would very much like to be President." The hesitation of liberals, however, struck deeper than outward appearances. During the campaign, Roosevelt had, like his Republican predecessors, stressed the fact that the United States must retain its freedom of action in world affairs. In this respect, he was completely in tune with the isolationist feelings in the country. Roosevelt did not feel that the League of Nations was an effective instrument for peace. It no longer was the League of Woodrow Wilson, he said, but had become "a mere meeting place for the political discussions of strictly European national difficulties." America, he thought, had no place in it. Liberal doubts were further reënforced when Roosevelt, newly installed as President, declared that Europe's war debts were sacred "debts of honor." As Selig Adler, has put it, "Sometimes, in the manner of Calvin Coolidge, he would offer the foreigners gratuitous advice on how to pare down their expenses in order to square themselves with their creditor."[1]

No doubt existed that Roosevelt was a politician par excellence. Like

[1] *The Isolationist Impulse* (New York and London, 1957), p. 253.

his distant cousin Theodore Roosevelt, much of his life had been groomed to attain the office of the presidency. Brought up on the family estate at Hyde Park in rich and comfortable circumstances, Roosevelt went to Groton, Harvard, and Columbia Law School. He then began a law career in New York, specializing in admiralty law, which reflected his enthusiasm for ships and the navy.

In 1910, F.D.R. entered politics and ran for state senator. Campaigning as a Democrat in a strongly entrenched Republican district, he toured around Dutchess County in a bright red Maxwell car—"The Red Peril"—wearing riding pants to political meetings, and making it clear that he was having a grand time. To the surprise of the professionals— the district had not elected a Democrat in thirty-two years—Roosevelt won. His personal charm and name quickly convinced the state Democratic leaders that he was a vote-getter. But a Tammany boss jokingly exclaimed, "You know these Roosevelts—this fellow is still young. Wouldn't it be safer to drown him before he grows up? If you don't he'll cause trouble sure as shootin' before he's much older."

Roosevelt did not stay at Albany long. After getting his feet wet in state politics, he moved into the national arena and campaigned fervently for Woodrow Wilson in 1912. The following year F.D.R. was appointed Assistant Secretary of the Navy, a position which had been a stepping stone to the presidency for his fifth cousin Theodore Roosevelt. As Assistant Secretary, Roosevelt became known as a brilliant young man "with a flashing mind." The war years brought him into close association with President Wilson, and he became an ardent advocate for a League of Nations. Hailed as Wilson's disciple, F.D.R. was chosen as the Democratic vice-presidential candidate in the 1920 election which saw the Harding-Coolidge victory over the Cox-Roosevelt ticket.

Back in action in 1924, after his crippling attack of infantile paralysis, Roosevelt made the speech at the Democratic National Convention nominating Alfred E. Smith—the "Happy Warrior"—for the presidency. His good record as a liberal and progressive governor of New York beginning in 1929 and his landslide reëlection victory in 1930 made him a natural Democratic presidential candidate.

Roosevelt came into the White House in March, 1933, at a time when capitalism was in crisis. As President, Roosevelt tried to combine Jeffersonian idealism with Theodore Roosevelt's practicality and Woodrow Wilson's vision, giving to the United States "enlightened administration." But during his first administration, Roosevelt's primary attention centered on domestic economic recovery. To achieve this goal, he did not hesitate to foster an American economic nationalism.

The Great Depression had a devastating impact not only in the United

States but throughout the world. In Germany, it gave rise to Adolf Hitler and his Nazi party; in Japan, to the militarist, imperialist faction. Benito Mussolini, whose conversion of Italy into a fascist state had begun in the early 1920's—but who, on the international scene, was not taken too seriously before 1933—suddenly burst forth in an increasingly belligerent fashion. Totalitarianism, emboldened by the collapse of capitalism and feeding on hunger and distress, came forward strongly to challenge the leadership of the Western democracies. "I am convinced that Germany has a world mission to fulfill," declared Paul Joseph Goebbels, Hitler's propaganda mouthpiece. "Hitler's declaration of war on the democratic state is only the prelude. The end of the development will be a Europe organized along National Socialist lines."

In January, 1933, President Paul von Hindenburg invited Hitler— after a year of turmoil, bitter unrest, Communist threats, street brawls and assassinations—to become Germany's chancellor. By the end of the year, Germany withdrew from the League of Nations. Ominous signs of future trouble had arisen at the League Disarmament Conference when Germany insisted upon her right to "equality" in armaments, and demanded, in effect, that the Versailles Treaty be scrapped. In 1934, after Hindenburg's death, Hitler liquidated his enemies, consolidated his power, and established himself as *Der Fuehrer*. He promptly suppressed opposition parties, invoked anti-Semitic measures depriving Jews of citizenship, and destroyed civil liberties.

With a fanatical, pathological zeal, Hitler set to work to revive the dying body of Germany. In his unbalanced mind, this could be done in only one way: by pumping the lifeblood of power into its veins. Power meant the revival of militarism, the expansion of German industrialism, and the harnessing of the rich raw materials and minerals of the European continent. It meant uniting the German people, instilling in them confidence in their superiority, and creating a new ideology and a new spirit. The Master Race, *Lebensraum, Drang Nach Osten!*—all of the formulas had been set down in *Mein Kampf,* a chaotic book written by Hitler while in jail in 1923. To a beaten, crippled, frustrated nation hit hard by the depression, Hitler's frenzied and hysterical cries seemed to awaken a new hope for the future.

The depression not only broke Germany's back; it dealt a severe blow to France and Britain. Both countries pleaded with the United States to make some adjustments on their war debts. The Hoover moratorium had offered only temporary relief. When it expired, the debtor nations met at Lausanne, Switzerland, in June, 1932. A settlement was made which reduced German reparations to only $714 million—this amounted to a reduction of nine-tenths of her remaining reparations, almost outright cancellation—but ratification of the agreement was made dependent on a corresponding reduction of the war debt by the United States. In effect, it meant that America would be footing the bill for Germany's reparations. After the November election, Hoover tried to consult with President-elect Roosevelt about the matter, but Roosevelt, unwilling to commit himself until he was installed in the White House and more concerned about domestic problems, is reported to have said that the war-debt headache was "not my baby." In December, 1932, France and five other nations defaulted outright on their payments. When Roosevelt became President, he refused to discuss revision of the Allied war debts. "That stays with Poppa," he said, "right here." While Britain and Italy made token payments, the forfeiture and general evasion of the Allies on war debts angered the new Democratic Congress and set the stage for retaliation.

More disruptive than the war debts were the trade problems which arose in the wake of the depression. The Smoot-Hawley Tariff Act had already erected barriers to eliminate European competition in the American market. In an effort to bolster her own tottering economy, Britain went off the gold standard to lower the prices of her manufactured goods in foreign markets. She also reversed her free-trade policy and set up protective tariffs to shut out the entry into England of American goods. The erection of tariff walls in other countries quickly followed. Stagnation of trade began to stultify the hope for world-wide recovery.

Shortly after Roosevelt came into office, a movement arose to break down the tariff barriers and to establish an international stabilization of currency by making foreign currencies freely interchangeable. In the summer of 1933, sixty-three nations gathered together at the London Economic Conference to achieve these objectives. Secretary of State Cordell Hull, who firmly believed that foreign-trade stimulation and monetary reforms were necessary to alleviate the depression, brought to the conference a plan for tariff reciprocity—a program close to his heart. Roosevelt, at first, also seemed to agree that reforms in the international economy were essential. However, after the Secretary of State sailed for England, F.D.R. suddenly changed his mind and instructed Hull to oppose tariff reductions and currency stabilization. Roosevelt's message destroyed the London Conference. It was a staggering blow which many internationalists found hard to explain. The President's precipitate action, it appears, was inspired by his fear that tariff reductions might wreck the New Deal program. The move was unfortunate. It strengthened the forces of economic nationalism in the United States and deprived

America of leadership in a field where her guidance was crucial. For the next four years, Roosevelt's foreign economic policies with respect to Europe did not differ greatly from the isolationist course charted by his Republican predecessors.

Ironically, Roosevelt broke with past Republican policies in connection with the recognition of the Soviet Union. Pressures for a change in America's position had developed in the 1920's. Economic ties with the Soviet Union had multiplied rapidly after 1924. When Stalin came to power in 1927, he welcomed the help that America's great corporations could contribute to Russia's economic progress. Millions of dollars worth of electrical equipment was sold by General Electric to the Soviet Union. Henry Ford, in 1929, signed a contract to build a plant at Nizhni Novgorod that would turn out 100,000 automobiles annually. Du Pont, Standard Oil, Vacuum Oil, the Radio Corporation of America, the American Locomotive Company, and numerous other American firms concluded agreements with Russia. In 1928, Colonel Hugh L. Cooper, an American engineer who helped to construct the great Dneprostroi Dam, said: "We have their confidence and unless this confidence is abused, and if it is encouraged in a practical way, we can do more to advance peace and create happiness in Russia and Europe than can any other nation or group of nations."

When the Great Depression set in, the refusal to grant recognition was viewed as unrealistic by many groups, especially by farming and business interests. The possibility that a closer collaboration might help ease the depression and foster a less doctrinaire Communist attitude toward the West encouraged in part a change in America's nonrecognition policy. By 1933, the conviction also arose that the Soviet Union did not constitute a threat to the security of the United States. Communism was temporarily shunted aside as America fixed its vision on the golden opportunities in Russia. "If America would recognize Russia," wrote William White, the *New York Times* Moscow reporter, "$500,000,000 of Russian orders would immediately appear on the desks of American industry."

By 1933, many of the obstacles to recognition were brushed aside. Convinced that the establishment of friendlier relations with the Soviet Union would open Russian markets to American agricultural and manufactured goods, President Roosevelt extended recognition in November, 1933, after protracted discussion and exchange of a series of letters had taken place with Soviet Foreign Minister Maxim Litvinov. In these letters, agreement was reached on a number of points. These included assurances that the Soviet Union would not interfere in America's internal affairs; that it would refrain and restrain Communist organizations under its control from engaging in agitation and propaganda against the United States government; that it would grant religious liberty to American citizens in the Soviet Union, and guarantee to them the right of a fair trial if accused of crimes in Russia; and that it would negotiate a settlement of claims.

These solemn pledges were not fulfilled by the Soviet Union after 1933. The promise to discontinue Communist propaganda proved to be a farce. Americans were still imprisoned on trumped-up charges. While trade increased slightly, it never reached the high point of 1930. Nor did the expectation that the Roosevelt-Litvinov agreement would mean new jobs for tens of thousands of persons on government relief materialize. The knottiest diplomatic problem centered on the "debt issue." The Soviet government had repudiated some $650 million of American public and private claims after its seizure of power. This matter had remained a sore point since 1917. In his talks with Litvinov, Roosevelt had indicated that Congress might be willing to settle the debt for as little as $150 million. But no final agreement was made; nor was one ever forthcoming. Misunderstandings on the debt and "credit" or "loan terms" to the Soviet Union complicated relations between the two countries throughout the 1930's.

Instead of fostering coöperation, recognition sharpened distrust and hostility. An accumulation of grievances arose between 1933 and 1937 which provided powerful ammunition to Roosevelt's enemies in the United States who charged that recognition had been a dangerous mistake and should never have been granted in the first place. However, while recognition did not serve its immediate intended purpose, the non-recognition policy had been even more fruitless and unsuccessful. The problem that remained was to remove the climate of suspicion and distrust, not only in the Soviet Union but throughout the world, and this could not be done by a head-in-the-sand attitude.

THE GOOD NEIGHBOR POLICY

The impact of the Great Depression was chiefly responsible for a strategic retreat of the United States in world affairs during Roosevelt's first administration. While the retreat was disastrous in Europe and Asia, it had a most beneficial effect in Latin America. The essence of America's retreat lay in its expressed desire to restrain the use of its power. In a speech devoted primarily to domestic matters, Roosevelt inserted in his first inaugural address a call for the adoption of a new international approach. "In the field of world policy," he said, "I would dedicate this nation to the policy of the good neighbor—the neighbor who resolutely respects himself and, because he does so, respects the rights of others—the neighbor who respects his obligations and respects the sanctity of his agreements in and with a world of neighbors." This appeal was directed toward putting an end to the dangerous power rivalries which then existed. Roosevelt hoped that America might set an example and show that mutual trust could be the basis of relations among nations.

In its original expression, the "Good Neighbor" idea was intended to be universal in its application, and not limited to Latin America, with which it was later so completely identified. However, as a method to cope with the powerful aggressive forces arising in Europe and Asia, it was vague and elusive and totally inadequate. Its main virtue lay in its stress on the need to cultivate friendly coöperation with all nations. This required, Roosevelt later said, that countries must put aside "all thought of domination, of selfish coalitions, or of balances of power. These false gods have no place among American neighbors." But none of the great powers was prepared to follow the President's advice.

In the United States, the Good Neighbor Policy came to be regarded as a "half-policy"—one which did not adequately come to grips with the principles of collective security or satisfy isolationists who demanded more complete independence in America's political and economic affairs. Considering the climate of opinion in the United States in the early thirties, a "half-policy" was probably all that Roosevelt could set forth.

The test of America's good-neighbor intentions came in Latin America in 1933. Here the United States enjoyed political and economic supremacy. For more than thirty years, the Latin-American republics had tried to thwart the right of American intervention in their internal affairs. In 1902, Argentine Foreign Minister Luis M. Drago had argued that when foreigners invested abroad they should do so at their own risk. The use of armed forces to collect public debts, he declared, was not justified. Although the United States supported a modified form of the so-called Drago Doctrine in 1907, it maintained its right of intervention under the Roosevelt Corollary to the Monroe Doctrine to prevent "chronic wrongdoing" and to protect the lives and property of its nationals. At each meeting of the Pan American Union, Latin-American delegates tried to raise the issue of American intervention; but before 1933, it was quashed by the United States, which refused to discuss the matter. At the Havana Conference in 1928, the controversial question threatened to destroy the inter-American movement. "The right of intervention," declared the delegate from El Salvador, "is the right of might," and should be put at an end; but Charles Evans Hughes, the American delegate, once again side-stepped a pledge committing the United States to non-intervention.

Despite the reluctance of the United States to support in an outright fashion the principle of nonintervention, a definite reorientation of America's Latin-American policy began in the 1920's. The United States showed a greater willingness to withdraw its troops from the Caribbean and Central American areas. This was partly due to the fact that the threats to the security of these regions lessened after World War I, when the prospects of European intervention no longer appeared to be great. A greater confidence, moreover, arose that the Latin-American republics might be able to govern themselves without endangering American interests. In 1922, a provisional government was set up in the Dominican Republic, and two years later American troops were withdrawn from the island, although control over customs receipts continued until 1941. American marines likewise were pulled out of Nicaragua in 1925; but because of disorders, Calvin Coolidge promptly ordered them back the following year. Difficulties were quickly straightened out by Colonel Henry L. Stimson, America's special representative, who managed in 1927 to persuade the opposing political faction to agree to the supervision of elections by the United States. When peace was finally restored, President Hoover announced that the marines would gradually be withdrawn, with final evacuation after the 1932 elections. Despite a new outbreak of guerrilla warfare, the American intervention ended in January, 1933.

Three outstanding indications of the change in America's attitude toward Latin America were Dwight W. Morrow's mission to Mexico, President-elect Herbert Hoover's good-will tour to South America in 1928, and the official acceptance in 1930 of the J. Reuben Clark *Memorandum,* which repudiated the Roosevelt Corollary to the Monroe Doctrine.

Calvin Coolidge appointed his Amherst classmate Dwight W. Morrow, an associate partner of the House of Morgan, as ambassador to Mexico in 1927. The Wall Street banker faced an unusually difficult assignment. Relations between the United States and Mexico had deteriorated badly since Mexico's Constitution of 1917, especially as a result of controversies in connection with America's oil rights, land confiscations of American citizens, claims for damages caused by the Mexican Revolution, and the Church problem. The United States refused to recognize the regime of Álvaro Obregón, which succeeded the Carranza government in 1920, for three years, until an agreement was reached on oil matters. The so-called "Bucareli agreements," however, proved to be temporary, and ugly quarrels arose once again after 1925 when a new petroleum law was passed imposing virtually confiscatory taxation on the oil industry. The action of President Plutarco Calles coincided with a renewal of seizures of agricultural lands belonging to Americans and with an intensified anti-Catholic campaign. Mexico was accused of fostering Bolshevism, and demands were loudly voiced in the United States for American intervention, if not outright war.

It was in this tense atmosphere that Morrow arrived in Mexico. Coolidge's admonition to the new American ambassador was typically crisp. "The situation in Mexico is grave," he said. "Keep us out of war." Morrow threw aside all protocol and quickly demonstrated his sympathies for Mexico's problems. He calmed Mexico's fears that a Wall Street banker was representing the United States by saying that he was not going to the country as a bill-collector, but as a friend, respecting the dignity of the Mexican people. What was unusual was that Dwight Morrow genuinely liked Mexico and everything about the country; moreover, he was determined to be friendly, to promote understanding, and to show that the United States could be a "good neighbor." The little man with untidy clothes, baggy trousers, and warm personality was not at all what the Mexicans had expected. Morrow quickly won over Calles by his "ham-and-egg" diplomacy, frequently settling problems over the breakfast table. His greatest coup came when he persuaded the hero-of-the-hour, Charles A. Lindbergh (who later married his daughter, Anne Morrow), to make a nonstop flight from Washington to Mexico City. The Mexicans gave the famed aviator a tumultuous fiesta-welcome; the holiday spirit continued for a week. Ambassador Morrow also invited the great American humorist, Will Rogers, to the country, and his wry witticisms delighted Calles. While Morrow did not succeed in achieving any final solutions to American-Mexican problems, he managed to obtain important concessions on oil rights and to slow down land confiscations and the anti-Catholic drive. But no significant progress was made on the matter of claims.

President-elect Herbert Hoover's South American trip contributed further to Morrow's good-neighbor program. On his tour, during which the Latin-American countries, with the exception of Uruguay and Argentina, received him with warmth and courtesy, Hoover made pointed reference to the need of the United States to pursue such a policy; he used the phrase "good neighbor" in several speeches. This policy may properly be considered to have originated during his administration.

Hoover's trip was responsible for the settlement of the long-outstanding Tacna-Arica boundary dispute between Chile and Peru. He suggested a formula that led to a peaceful compromise. The most important feature of the "new" Latin-American policy was reflected in Hoover's determination when he took office to avoid intervention in the internal affairs of the countries south of the border. In this respect, he abandoned Wilson's practice of withholding recognition from revolutionary governments, if power was obtained unconstitutionally, and returned to the traditional American policy of granting de facto recognition when the new government demonstrated that it was in control and agreed to fulfill its international obligations.

The final turn in the reorientation of America's Latin-American policy came with Hoover's official acceptance of the J. Reuben Clark *Memorandum*. Clark had been an Under Secretary of State and a special adviser to Ambassador Morrow in Mexico. In 1928, he prepared a *Memorandum on the Monroe Doctrine*, but it was not released for publication until 1930. In a 236-page document, Clark argued that the Roosevelt Corollary was not in accord with the original Monroe Doctrine, and that America's intervention in the Caribbean could not be justified on the basis of the principles established in 1823. The *Memorandum* repudiated the Roosevelt Corollary, but it did not surrender the right to intervene for purposes of defense or in the event America's interests were endangered. While intervention for defensive reasons was legitimate, Clark declared, it did not carry with it the corresponding right of domination. It was this latter admission that was so important—the implication that the Roosevelt Corollary, indeed, had contributed to domination. The publication of the Clark *Memorandum* and Hoover's endorsement of it breathed new life into the Pan-American movement.

The showdown came at the Montevideo Pan-American Conference in 1933. President Franklin D. Roosevelt had announced America's desire to adopt a "good neighbor" program. To Latin America this clearly meant a continuance of Herbert Hoover's policies. Would the United States agree to permit the delegates to debate the issue of American intervention and support a binding pledge that "No state has the right to intervene in the internal or external affairs of another"? The skepticism of the delegates was reflected in the billboard signs which greeted the Secretary of State when he arrived in Montevideo—"Down with Hull." While Cordell Hull had some qualms about unequivocally supporting the Latin-American position, he agreed to permit discussion, and more important, he pledged the United States to the Montevideo Declaration of Nonintervention. This step was a landmark in America's Latin-

American policy, and was interpreted as a reaffirmation of the original Monroe Doctrine. Roosevelt's support of the Montevideo Declaration meant, in effect, that henceforth the United States would follow a "hands-off" policy. It was the "hands-off" idea that became the cornerstone of the Good Neighbor Policy.

From 1933 to 1937, President Roosevelt went far in carrying forward the Good Neighbor Policy. In 1934, the United States abrogated the Platt Amendment, bringing to an end the quasi-protectorate status over Cuba. To the island's people and to all the Latin-American countries, it was an epochal event. The Platt Amendment had been a constant reminder of America's imperialism early in the century. "The definite policy of the United States from now on," Roosevelt declared, "is one opposed to armed intervention." American marines that same year were evacuated from Haiti—the last troops to leave an independent Latin-American republic. Two years later, a treaty was signed with Panama; protectorate control here, too, was relinquished.

Political retreat was accompanied by economic coöperation. The reciprocal trade program was most fruitful in building up good will. The Latin-American countries, like nations throughout the world, had been jolted by the Smoot-Hawley Tariff of 1930. Roosevelt did not obtain the repeal of this law, but the Trade Agreements Act of June, 1934, authorized the President to make adjustments in tariff schedules up to 50 percent of those specified in the schedules of 1930. The reciprocal trade program was a momentous victory for Cordell Hull, and it contributed to Roosevelt's unprecedented popularity in Latin America. Although a full liberalization of trade was not achieved—the reciprocal treaties were limited to specific commodities—the opening up of the American market to many Latin-American products was most welcome. At the same time, the United States benefited by the expansion of its own trade.

Roosevelt's actions were largely responsible for strengthening a Pan-American solidarity. After 1933, the United States became increasingly concerned with the problems of hemispheric security. The menacing clouds of European aggression grew larger. Equally serious was the fact that the Latin-American republics, knee deep in the depression, showed an attraction toward German Nazism and Italian Fascism. Black shirts, brown shirts, green shirts made their appearance. The encroachments of Germany were especially alarming to the United States. In 1936, Roosevelt took the initiative and suggested calling an extraordinary inter-American conference—the next conference was not scheduled to meet until 1938—for the purpose of determining how the peace in the Americas might best be safeguarded. The response was favorable, and the result led to the Inter-American Conference for the Maintenance of Peace held in December at Buenos Aires, Argentina.

The Buenos Aires conference was noteworthy for three reasons. First, the United States clearly found itself in a dilemma. The right of American intervention had been firmly disavowed, but it was recognized that circumstances might arise in which intervention was essential to maintain peace, either as a result of disputes within Latin America or threats of external aggression. No machinery existed to handle such situations. To overcome this problem, the United States decided that joint consultation was imperative to provide for coöperative action. Secondly, the acceptance of the principle of joint consultation established a clear recognition of the juridical equality of the Latin-American states. Each nation was thus placed on an equal par with the Great Colossus of the North. Finally, the United States reasserted its pledge to adhere to the Montevideo Declaration of Nonintervention, and accepted without qualification the Drago Doctrine that there would be no forcible collection of pecuniary debts.

To emphasize the importance that America attached to these matters, President Roosevelt attended the Buenos Aires conference in person. He did so at a time when he had emerged overwhelmingly victorious in the presidential election of 1936, which greatly strengthened his leadership. Roosevelt's opening speech was forceful and dramatic. He convinced the Latin-American republics that the United States had at last completely abandoned the principle of intervention. The only country that still remained skeptical was Argentina. Because of the intense rivalry between the two countries, she challenged America's leadership in South America and declared that the Latin-American republics still had more to fear from the encroachments of the United States than from those of the European powers. Argentina's opposition made it difficult for the American delegates to obtain their entire program. Compromises were necessary; nevertheless, substantial gains were achieved which proved enormously valuable during World War II. Agreement was reached on the adoption of a consultative pact, and a Declaration of Solidarity was proclaimed. But one major thing was lacking: no permanent organization was created for consultation in the event that peace in the hemisphere was threatened. Roosevelt continued to look toward this goal—in effect, the establishment of a league of nations in the Western Hemisphere.

As a result of the Good Neighbor Policy, the United States by 1937 found itself moving away from the old economic nationalism and drifting toward collective security.

THE MARCH OF EUROPE'S DICTATORS

While Roosevelt concentrated on the New Deal program and on cementing closer relations with Latin America, he was not oblivious to the dangers which arose in Europe. A warning had already been sounded by the American consul-general in Berlin as early as June, 1933. Some of the men running the German government were "psychopathic cases," he reported. Others were "in a state of exaltation and in a frame of mind that knew no reason." The leaders of Germany, he said, had "no desire for peace unless it was a peace in complete compliance with German ambitions." While Hitler and his associates wanted peace for the moment, it was "only to have a chance to prepare for the use of force if it were found essential." Ominous rumblings also echoed from Italy, where Mussolini made no pretense of his desire to turn the Mediterranean Sea into a *Mare Nostrum* and, at the same time, covetously eyed Africa for colonies.

Britain and France watched the stirrings in Germany and Italy with misgivings. The Roosevelt administration, mired by the depression, clung steadfastly to a policy of noninvolvement. France's greatest fear was the possibility of the creation of a German-Soviet bloc. To prevent such a rapprochement, she tried to draw closer to the Soviet Union; opposing ideologies were overlooked. But her biggest problem was to maintain her ties with the eastern European countries: Poland, Czechoslovakia, and Rumania. When France moved more closely to the Soviet Union, it tended to push these countries into the German orbit. The French aim was directed toward creating a new balance of forces in Europe. After protracted negotiation, a Polish-Soviet Nonaggression Pact was signed in January, 1934; Rumania could not be persuaded to be a party to the treaty. Nevertheless, France, anxious to draw the Soviet Union to the side of the Western democracies, supported her admission into the League of Nations in 1934 and the following year concluded a Franco-Soviet Mutual Assistance Pact. At the same time, France sought to drive a wedge between Italy and Germany, and an understanding on colonial matters was reached with Mussolini in January, 1935.

Britain was much less concerned than France about the menace of Germany. She had little interest in the countries of eastern Europe or in supporting France's efforts of political encirclement. Britain wanted to bring about a better and more stable order on the European continent. She conceived of this state of affairs, however, not in terms of isolating

Germany and Russia, but rather of making Germany a major bulwark east of the Rhine and of adjusting the Versailles Treaty. Unlike France, Britain did not feel that the status quo of Versailles should be rigidly maintained; nor did she think that Germany's efforts to revise the treaty were necessarily harmful. By placating Germany, Britain hoped that the way might be cleared for a new comprehensive European settlement which would take the place of the Versailles system. The British were far more concerned about the menace of Bolshevism than that of Nazism.

Britain's attitude after Hitler's rise to power reflected mixed emotions. On the whole, the British people regarded Hitler as a curiosity, Nazism as evil, and the racist doctrines as abominable. But from a detached point of view, many Britishers favored a strong and dynamic Germany, one which might provide a secure base for Europe. Germany's economic recovery was held to be essential to European stability, and such stability, it was felt, was necessary if England were to get back on her feet. Many in the Conservative party's right wing, in fact, were convinced that a strong Germany was necessary as a bulwark against Bolshevism, and they frankly expressed the opinion that Germany ought to become the master of the European continent. The influence of this group in Britain during the thirties was considerable. British foreign policy, one finds, tended tacitly to support the revival of Germany. To the extent that this was so, therefore, Hitler found a strange ally.

The basic assumption of British foreign policy proved to be ill-founded. Germany did not become a strong economic base in Europe, mainly because her programs of economic nationalism starved inter-country trade. After 1933, Hitler's fixed goal was to make Germany as self-sufficient as possible. While Germany had to import certain raw materials for her industries, these imports were largely paid for in blocked marks. Later, Hitler turned to reclaiming all kinds of scrap, and relying on *ersatz* (manufactured substitute) materials. The German dictator, moreover, organized the whole country's economy on maintaining a large standing army and building munitions factories. These activities took the place of developing legitimate industries. While they alleviated mass unemployment, they provided at the same time an unhealthy outlet for the energies of the German people. Hitler's aim was not to establish a sound European economy, but to create out of the wreckage of Europe a great German Colossus—the "thousand-year Reich."

From 1933 to 1937, Hitler shrewdly played Britain against France and worked to isolate the Soviet Union. He put his finger on the most vulnerable point of the Versailles system: the disunity and lack of solidarity among the Allied powers. He hammered hard on the "mistakes" and "injustices" of the Versailles Treaty and constantly appealed to the conscience of the West to redress the wrongs that had been committed. These appeals rallied the German people to his cause, while they infuriated the French. The more Hitler blustered, the harder France worked on constructing the Maginot Line of fortifications along the eastern frontier—the impregnable line that was intended to prevent any future German invasion of France. This feverish defensive activity merely convinced Hitler that France had no intention of adopting an aggressive policy against Germany. Hitler's ace card was his constant threat of war. Whenever Germany's sabers rattled, Britain, France, and the United States got a bad case of the jitters. The horrors of World War I were still too fresh in the minds of people.

During this period, a pattern neither of general war nor of true peace developed. The European nations remained partially mobilized, partially on a war footing, constantly alerted, and dreading the outbreak of war. American newspaper columnists, radio commentators, and experts on foreign affairs repeatedly predicted that a war would surely break out next month, or next year, or certainly within two or three years at the most. The conviction arose that it was only the clear memory of the Great War holocaust that was keeping things in check in Europe. The response of the American people to these crisis years was an increased determination, no matter what happened, to keep out of the next war that might break out.

Events in 1935 and 1936 foreshadowed the complete collapse of the Versailles system. Mussolini, late in 1935, sent his Italian legions plunging across the borders of Ethiopia. Beginning in 1933, the Italian dictator had begun to make preparations for a military campaign in East Africa. Quietly and secretly, these plans were pushed ahead in 1934. A border clash between Ethiopian and Italian troops at Walwal in December gave Mussolini a moral pretext for his act of aggression; actually, Italy had long been casting envious eyes on Ethiopia from the vantage point of its adjoining colonies, Eritrea and Somaliland. Emperor Haile Selassie of Ethiopia offered to submit the new dispute to arbitration, but Mussolini refused. As a member, Ethiopia then appealed to the League of Nations. The issue quickly became a test of the League's ability to maintain world peace.

Unfortunately, the efforts of the League to take effective action were undermined by France and Britain. The Franco-Italian agreement of January, 1935, virtually assured Mussolini that in return for Italy's coöperation in Europe, France would not interfere in the dictator's colonial affairs. Equally serious was the abortive Hoare-Laval plan. The Foreign Ministers of Britain and France, Sir Samuel Hoare and Pierre Laval, secretly came to an understanding that in the event of Italian aggression, brakes would be put on the imposition of sanctions by the League; these would be limited to financial and economic measures. They also agreed that Italy could keep most of the territory she had already conquered, while Ethiopia would be given "in exchange" a narrow corridor to the Red Sea. Laval, ungraciously, published this plan before it was approved by the British Cabinet. Widespread public condemnation in Britain led to Hoare's resignation and the appointment of Anthony Eden.

Despite British and French attempts to sabotage collective action, the League branded Italy an aggressor and voted for economic sanctions, which proved totally ineffective. Sanctions were to be imposed in successive stages, and during the first stage no restrictions were placed on oil, iron and steel, and coal and coke—items which greased Mussolini's war machine. Moreover, each of the coöperating states was required to enact necessary legislation to enforce the sanctions. None of the powers was anxious to move speedily. This was the first time that sanctions had been applied, and because of the depression, few were willing to sacrifice good business. Vigorous action, moreover, was discouraged since the United States and Germany were excluded as participants in the embargoes. America did place an embargo on shipments of munitions, but not on oil, aviation gasoline, or other military supplies. Oil shipments to Italy were six times greater in 1935 than they had been the previous year. Mussolini, therefore, successfully defied the League "sanctions," and after seven months of warfare, he annexed Ethiopia to Italy.

The Ethiopian crisis provided Hitler with an opportunity to tear up the Versailles Treaty. In March, 1935, he announced the resumption of compulsory military training in Germany, and increased the size of the army to half a million men—five times the Versailles limit. These actions were condemned by the League Council. However, in June, 1935, Britain indirectly condoned Hitler's action by approving the building of a German navy which would be 35 percent the size of Britain's—again a limit which far exceeded that set by the Versailles Treaty. The boldest move came in 1936, when Hitler reoccupied the Rhineland over the frantic objections of his general staff. Unprepared to risk war, the military experts obtained a promise from Der Fuehrer that he would resign if France resisted. But France retreated; only sharp diplomatic protests were made. The remilitarization of the Rhineland—which later bristled with fortifications of the Siegfried Line—was a devastating setback to the Western powers and increased Hitler's power enormously in Germany.

The impotence of the Western democracies was fully revealed in the Spanish Civil War. In 1931, the Spanish Bourbon monarchy was overthrown by revolution and a "Popular Front" republican government was established. Economic reforms and anticlerical measures aroused bitter opposition on the part of the Church, the army, and the landholding aristocracy. General Francisco Franco soon became the leader of a military rebellion, whose supporters embraced most conservative and monarchist elements and the Falange, an organization inspired by Italian and German fascism. In 1936, with 90 percent of the army officers and the bulk of the army behind him, General Franco led the uprising. After taking over Spanish Morocco, Franco and his forces pushed into continental Spain. He was, however, unable to gain control of the air force or navy. But secret promises of counsel and help had been obtained from Rome and Berlin before the military revolt. Mussolini dispatched whole divisions of Italian troops to Spain, and Hitler supplied his Nazi air corps and German navy. The so-called Loyalist Government lacked a disciplined military force, but it rallied against the insurrection and for the next three years a terrible civil war raged. While Britain and France adopted a policy of nonintervention and the United States clamped an arms embargo on Spain, the Soviet Union, fearful that a Franco victory would strengthen the forces of fascism and thus increase danger to her, supported the Loyalists; late in October, 1936, she began to send men and materials. This aid came in time to help with the defense of Madrid. Soviet support, however, never matched that of Germany and Italy, and by the end of the year, it was almost completely cut off. The Loyalists also obtained help from foreign volunteers, including Americans, who were convinced that the battle for "democracy" was being waged on the Spanish battlefields. This fighting force was partly equipped with Soviet tanks and airplanes.

In the United States, the Spanish Civil War aroused strong emotional sentiments. Most Americans were disinterested or ignorant about Spanish affairs and desired to avoid involvement. But determined minorities of liberals and Catholics clashed over the issues. Liberals and left-wingers saw the Spanish Civil War as the struggle against the victory of fascism and the collapse of Western democracy; American Catholics, on the other hand, shocked by anticlerical excesses, including atrocities inflicted on priests and nuns, and fearful of the possible victory of communism, supported the rebels. Meanwhile, the Spanish Civil War became an invaluable laboratory for training Nazi airmen and Italian troops, and with the help of Hitler and Mussolini, Franco established in 1939 a dictatorship in Spain.

The years from 1935 to 1937 saw the step-by-step retreat of Britain, France, and the United States in the face of Italian and German aggression. The symbol of retreat was reflected in the policy of nonintervention in the Spanish Civil War. Later, in March, 1939, Stalin prophetically stated:

Far be it for me to moralize on the policy of non-intervention, to talk of treason, treachery, and so on. It would be naive to preach morals to people who recognize no human morality. Politics is politics, as the old case-hardened bourgeois diplomats say. It must be remarked, however, that the big and dangerous political game started by the supporters of the policy of nonintervention may end in a serious fiasco for them.

CONGRESS SHIELDS AMERICA FROM WAR: THE NEUTRALITY ACTS

The mood of the United States during Roosevelt's first administration was profoundly influenced by the Great Depression and the crises in Europe. Disillusion after World War I was inchoate; it arose principally as a reaction to Wilsonian idealism, the bitter aftertaste of the horrors of war, and the difficulties of adjusting to a new America, an America that had left behind the swaddling clothes of the well-ordered, quiet, small-town, agrarian society. As America moved into a prosperity era, however, it was willing to forget the past. It had learned its lesson, and it would see to it that in the future the country would stay out of Europe's wars. But the depression added a new dimension to the attitude of isolationism. Disillusion sharpened and became more pinpointed. "Revisionist" historians gave it form and substance. Guilt for the outbreak of World War I, it was shown, was not simply on the German side. America was sucked into the war by British propaganda, by bankers, by munitions makers, and the "mistakes" of Woodrow Wilson. Anxious to find a scapegoat for the calamities of the depression, the American people, especially in the Middle and Far West, seized upon the Eastern financiers and industrialists. It was these men who had led the country into war, who had failed the United States by bringing on the Great Depression. The confidence in Big Business leadership of the 1920's collapsed, especially after the investigations of 1933 disclosed the shoddy conduct of many bankers and corporate figures.

By 1935, isolationism was no longer passive; it was militantly aggressive. Internationalists—now in a small minority—continued to argue that the best method of avoiding involvement in future wars was the support of the principles of collective security. But many Americans agreed with isolationist Senator William E. Borah when he said, "I [can] not subscribe to the theory that collective action against the supposed aggressor means peace. It inevitably means war unless the nation is too weak to resist, and then it means oppression." Aggressor nations had a legitimate right to object to the "oppressive" policy of collective action, Borah declared, and if war resulted the "morality" would be on their side, not on America's.

Hostility in the United States was directed not only against Big Business, but against the "chiselers" of Europe who refused to pay their war debts. In 1934, after the Allied nations had defaulted on their payments, Congress passed the Johnson Act. Nations which had defaulted on the interest payments of their war debts were to be denied the right to float public securities in the American money market. The law, reflecting America's resentment of the Allies' refusal to honor their financial obligations, had unfortunate repercussions. It increased the economic difficulties of Britain and France, and it indirectly benefited Nazi Germany since it enabled Hitler to exploit to fuller advantage the weaknesses of the Western powers.

The Senate added more fuel to the fire by setting up a committee in 1934 to examine the reasons for American intervention in World War I. Vice-President John N. Garner selected the Republican isolationist Senator Gerald P. Nye as chairman. Selig Adler has given us this description of Nye:

The senator, a rough-hewn Solon from the North Dakota back country, had the advantages of a high school education, journalistic experience as editor of the Griggs County *Sentinel-Courier,* and nine years of give-and-take on the floor of the Senate. He was hardly equipped to winnow the mass of evidence, nor was he aware of the dangers of over-simplified interpretations of the complex workings of history.[2]

For about two years, the Nye Committee remained in the glare of the public spotlight. A spectacular show was put on. Avid interest was created by the parade of bankers and armament manufacturers, including four Du Pont brothers, who appeared before the Committee. J. P. Morgan's command performance, in which news photographers flashed a picture of the giant financier with a female midget in his lap, produced a sensation in the country. The disclosures of Big Business lobbying activities in Congress and at international conferences, of the existence of an international armaments cartel, and of Morgan's role as the purchasing agent for the Allies strengthened isolationist and antiwar sentiment. By

[2] *The Isolationist Impulse: Its Twentieth-Century Reaction* (London and New York, 1957), p. 257.

personalizing the issues, the Nye Committee achieved a powerful impact on the nation, even beyond the spate of books and articles that was published at the time. Two of the most popular debunking books were Walter Millis' *Road to War* and Helmuth C. Engelbrecht's *Merchants of Death*. The high peak of antiwar sentiment was reached when a newspaper advertisement appeared, showing a veteran in a wheel chair, with the caption *"Hello, Sucker."*

Much of the information compiled in the 1,400-page Committee report had much substance of truth. Nye's preconceived hypothesis—then fairly well accepted—implied that only "bankers, arms makers, and profiteers" were responsible for America's entry into World War I. Senator Nye told an audience at New York's Carnegie Hall in May, 1935:

Let us know that it is sales and shipments of munitions and contraband, and the lure of profits in them, that will get us into another war, and that when the proper time comes and we talk about national honor, let us know that simply means the right to go on making money out of war. Let us have done with all the fraud, and we will have done with all the post-war friction. . . . It is useless to pretend that our isolation from foreign political entanglements means anything if we open wide the gates to foreign loans and credits for munitions and spread out a network of munition ships that will be ignition points of another war.

But Nye and the Committee's report did not tell the whole story. Specifically, it completely glossed over the actions of Germany, especially its decision to resume unrestricted submarine warfare in January, 1917. For, in the final analysis, as many historians have pointed out, the decision of America's entrance into the war was not made by Wilson, but by Germany. Ignored, too, were Wilson's abortive peace efforts. While these efforts failed, they nevertheless disclosed that the President desired to avoid American participation and to bring an end to the war. Economic factors were important in shaping Wilson's final decision, but they were not an exclusive influence.

In the spring of 1935, with the Italo-Ethiopian crisis shaking the world's uneasy calm and isolationism gathering momentum, Roosevelt offered little leadership or guidance. The President drifted with the popular tide in America. He not only denounced the arms trade, but permitted Senator Nye to have access to executive papers and encouraged the Committee in its work. However, Roosevelt indicated that while he opposed the export of arms and munitions to aggressor nations, he felt the President should be authorized to sell arms to their victims. The State Department drafted a bill to this effect. But Congress would have none of this; it refused to give the President such discriminatory authority. Roosevelt was warned that he was riding for a fall. The administration bill, in fact, was set aside by the Senate, and a joint resolution—the First Neutrality Act—was passed instead in August, 1935. In the event of war, the President, at his discretion, could declare its existence and impose an arms embargo on *all* belligerents. He could also warn Americans that they would travel on belligerent ships at their own risk. Ships were to be prohibited from carrying arms to warring nations, and a National Munitions Board was established to provide for federal regulation of the armament industry. Roosevelt signed the First Neutrality Act "reluctantly." He did not object to the purpose of the law, but he felt that the inflexibility of the mandatory arms embargo might drag America into war instead of keeping the country out. He suggested that Congress might reconsider the embargo sections; but on the whole, he was satisfied with the law.

The First Neutrality Act was promptly applied in the Italo-Ethiopian incident. No war had been declared by either side; the Kellogg-Briand Pact of 1928 had made declarations of war unfashionable—countries that had "renounced" and "condemned" war were unwilling to admit that they were involved in "war." Conflicts therefore became "clashes" or "incidents." Roosevelt proclaimed in October, 1935, however, that war existed. But the practical effects of the mandatory embargo were nullified, largely because the thing that Italy needed most was oil, and oil was not classified as ammunition or as an implement of war.

In February, 1936, Congress passed a Second Neutrality Act. It extended the original provisions for fourteen months, and in addition, prohibited loans to belligerent powers. The President was also directed to extend the arms embargo in the event that a new belligerent entered an existing war. In effect, this meant that if a power became involved in a conflict in which it opposed an aggressor, the mandatory embargo would have to be applied against her regardless of the circumstances. In other words, the United States would not pass any moral judgment on the matter, but would remain aloof.

With the world situation deteriorating badly, Congress decided in 1937 to enact a permanent neutrality policy. The arms embargo and the prohibition against loans were extended indefinitely. The Third Neutrality Act specified that Americans were no longer to be simply warned against traveling on belligerent ships; they were to be expressly forbidden from doing so. Arming of American ships was also to be prohibited. The new feature of the neutrality law was the inclusion of a temporary "cash-and-carry" provision. It stated that non-embargoed shipments could not be carried in American ships, nor could they leave the United States until the cargo had been paid for in advance. This provision was never put into effect, although it was hotly debated at the time. The "cash-and-carry" clause was to remain in force only until May 1, 1939; it expired before the outbreak of World War II.

The purpose of the Neutrality Acts was to guarantee peace for the United States by legislation. This, it was felt, could only be done by effective insulation. A few voices were raised to question the wisdom and omniscience of Congress to "legislate peace." Walter Lippmann warned:

> In case of a possible great war in the future nobody knows today, nobody in the Senate, nobody in any country anywhere, when it will break out. Nobody knows where it will break out. Nobody knows who will be fighting. Nobody knows who will be neutral. . . . Nobody can look into the future and predict the character of the war which Congress is to make laws about. How under these circumstances, can any Senator pretend that he knows enough, that he is sufficiently a prophet, to write a law which fixes in advance the correct policy of the United States.

But the neutrality laws were passed. While it is true that what Congress can do, it can undo—despite the "permanence" of the legislation—the effect of the policies was to immobilize the United States at a most crucial moment in world history. Although few realized it at the time, the result was bitter tragedy.

AMERICA TURNS ITS BACK ON JAPAN

The Great Depression had a paralyzing effect on America's policies not only in Europe but also in the Far East. The Hoover-Stimson doctrine of nonrecognition had not thwarted Japan in her conquest of Manchuria, and Japan's expansionist drive in China, it appeared, could only be checked by counterforce. When Roosevelt came into the White House, the United States found itself in a position where it could either "put up" (apply effective sanctions and risk the outbreak of war) or "shut up" (retreat and limit its actions to diplomatic protests). The Roosevelt administration decided to pull back. In contrast to its attitude toward Europe, Congress had seriously contemplated opposing Japan, and a bill was introduced imposing an arms embargo against her. Secretary of State Cordell Hull blocked the measure. He did not feel that any kind of embargo should be levied, against either both belligerents or Japan alone. An embargo applied to both sides, Hull told the Senate Foreign Affairs Committee in May, 1933, would benefit Japan, since China was more dependent on importing war supplies. If applied only to Japan, he said, she would probably seize the arms intended for China. Unless an arms-embargo policy was supported by other powers—and there was no evidence that such would be the case—Hull urged that an arms embargo act not be passed, and the measure was defeated by Congress.

The retreat of the United States was evident in the desire which arose in the early 1930's to grant independence to the Philippine Islands. The effect of the depression and a belief that the islands were militarily indefensible were largely responsible for support of this move. In 1932, Congress passed a bill which provided for a ten-year transition period for Philippine independence. Hoover vetoed it, largely because he felt that freedom would unsettle conditions in the Pacific and Far East. While the measure was passed over the President's veto, the Filipinos themselves rejected the Hawes-Cutting Act because it did not provide for economic assistance and because it was felt the proposed retention of American naval and military bases would infringe too greatly on their sovereignty. In line with its anticolonial policy, the Roosevelt administration championed Philippine independence. In 1934, the Tydings-McDuffie Act—which modified some but not all of the objectionable features of the previous law—was passed with the President's approval. It was endorsed by the Philippine legislature. The new law provided for full liberation after a ten-year transition period, at which time the United States pledged to withdraw from all military bases. The granting of independence was delayed by World War II. In 1946, however, the Philippine Commonwealth was established and the islands became free and independent. To the Filipinos, independence appeared to be a mixed blessing, mainly because the economy of the islands had grown so dependent on the United States. Many fears had been voiced that more might be lost than gained by freedom. During the first difficult years, however, America extended economic help through tariff privileges, and the early forebodings gradually disappeared.

With respect to Asia, Roosevelt pursued a cautious, passive course. Japan proceeded to ride roughshod over the Open Door policy. From 1933 to 1935, she consolidated her position in Manchuria and began a systematic encroachment upon China. Japan declared that her aim was to establish a close political and economic union embracing China, Japan, and Manchukuo. This was elaborated in 1934 in a proclamation announcing, in effect, an Asiatic Monroe Doctrine. Later, Japan spoke of creating a "New Order" for China and establishing a "Greater East Asia Co-Prosperity Sphere." The intent of Japan, however, was the complete subjugation of China.

Weak and disunited, Chiang Kai-shek's China was compelled to submit to Japanese pressures. Favorable tariff concessions were granted, and steps were taken to discourage popular opposition to Japan. Meanwhile, Chiang Kai-shek renewed his offensive against the Chinese Communist forces. During 1935-36, with the Western powers absorbed by the Ethiopian crisis, Hitler's occupation of the Rhineland, and the Spanish Civil War, Japanese militarists demanded a program that would lead to the conquest of China. Despite Chiang Kai-shek's collaboration with Japan and repressive measures, popular opposition had not been quelled. Japanese provocations had led to a boycott of Japanese goods. In 1935, widespread demonstrations took place: students' movements, monster meetings, and parades clamored loudly for an end to concessions to Japan and for united action against the aggressor. Chinese students were in the forefront of the agitation, mobilizing the hostility against Japan into a powerful force. Chiang Kai-shek bowed to the mass pressure, and in 1936 promised to develop national solidarity, but he refused to agree to a union of Nationalist and Communist armies to resist the Japanese invasion. However, his Manchurian followers disagreed with him, and when Chiang Kai-shek went to Sian to organize an offensive against the Communists, he was arrested. Some of the Manchurian leaders wanted to execute him, but they were dissuaded by the fear that China might be plunged into hopeless confusion. Suspicion arose that Moscow had a hand in the plot, but Max Beloff points out that "the extreme perplexity of the Soviet press at the news of the Sian *coup* and its expressions of suspicion as to its motives, strongly suggest that neither the Chinese Communists nor the Russians were privy to the plot."[3] The Generalissimo was set free after two weeks' imprisonment. While he did not make any definite commitments, he decided to call off the civil war.

As the crisis mounted, the Japanese war lords decided to take political matters into their own hands. Strong sentiment existed in Japan against any adventures that might precipitate war with the Western powers. Parliamentary elections in February, 1936, had resulted in a definite setback to the right-wing, promilitary candidates, many of whom were defeated. The militarists were faced with the choice of giving up their plans for military conquest in China or driving the moderates out of government. They decided on the latter alternative. Shortly after the election, a mass purge took place in which the prominent moderates were assassinated. The Army retained its influence in government, and embarked on a program which called for increased military appropriations and the establishment of a controlled economy to fit military needs.

[3] *The Foreign Policy of Soviet Russia, 1929-1941* (New York, 1949), Vol. II, p. 173.

Japan was ready to take to the road of military conquest once again and push forward a "positive" foreign policy. In July, 1937, the inevitable incident occurred which led to the outbreak of the second Sino-Japanese war.

Roosevelt did not invoke the Neutrality Act of 1937 in the "China Incident." He refrained on the grounds that the mandatory embargo would be much more detrimental to China in her efforts to resist the Japanese aggression. Although no pretense was made of America's sympathies for China, Roosevelt's policies were those of "hands off."

The negative attitude of the United States was brought home glaringly when the American gunboat *Panay* was sunk by Japanese aviators in December, 1937. The State Department had announced that Americans should leave Nanking, an area where fighting was intense. It reported that the *Luzon* and the *Panay,* gunboats on the Yangtze River Patrol, would help in the evacuation. On the morning of December 12, the *Panay* proceeded upriver and escorted several Standard Oil tankers. At about 11 A.M., the ships anchored at a point about twenty-eight miles above Nanking; the American flags were prominently displayed. They were spotted by some Japanese bombing planes, which suddenly attacked the vessels. The *Panay* was sunk and the Standard Oil tankers severely damaged. While survivors attempted to get to shore, the Japanese planes dive-bombed and machine-gunned them. In the attack, two American crew members were killed and some thirty persons were injured.

Ordinarily, in past periods of America's history, such an incident which appeared to be deliberately provocative would have resulted in loud clamors for war. This, however, was not the case in 1937. Newspapers demanded to know why Americans were still in China, and why the *Panay* was escorting Standard Oil vessels. The response to the incident resulted in increased pressures for the withdrawal of American forces from dangerous areas in China. The Japanese ambassador promptly expressed his government's official regret and apology, adding that the bombing was a "very grave blunder." It was intimated that the attack was an accident; because of the poor visibility, the ships were mistaken for Chinese vessels. However, on board the *Panay* was a newsreel photographer. He managed to swim ashore and bury his film in the mud on the banks of the Yangtze River. It was later recovered, processed, and showed that the visibility was perfect. There could be no mistake about the identity of the ships. The Japanese Foreign office later said that irresponsible military officials had committed the blunder. They offered to pay reparations for those who had been killed and injured. The American government accepted Japan's apologies, and the incident was quickly settled. The Japanese people tried to make amends by contributing generously to a reparations fund. In April, 1938, more than two million dollars was given to the United States. With this payment, the *Panay* affair was regarded as closed.

AMERICA BUILDS ITS STORM CELLARS

During Roosevelt's first administration, foreign affairs distinctly took a back seat to domestic policies. The theory which underlay the New Deal program was that once the United States solved its economic problems and found its way toward recovery, then America's prosperity would flow outward to the shores of the countries throughout the world. Roosevelt's desire was to avoid distraction. He had no wish to become involved in crises outside the United States. There was enough trouble at home. The keynote of his foreign policy before 1937, therefore, was the contraction of America's commitments. This fitted in ideally with the isolationist temper in the country.

Unfortunately, the first phase of the New Deal program did not bring the expected recovery or prosperity. Roosevelt's bold experimentation did ease the agonies of the depression. Psychologically, the fact that the government accepted full moral responsibility to help those crushed by the economic crisis was enormously important. It marked an end to the old laissez-faire attitude. But, it was clear that the depression could not be solved on a national basis to the exclusion of a revival of worldwide trade. A vicious cycle ensued in which tariff restrictions bred retaliation and economic nationalism intensified in each country. The world's skies grew darker and darker, and the American people took to their storm cellar to wait out the big blow. The neutrality laws brought no calm; indeed, they indirectly helped the aggressor powers.

By 1937, it became evident that the policy of drift in foreign affairs could not continue indefinitely. The crisis would come, and the United States might be in the middle of it. America, whether it wanted to or not, would have to face up to the threatening storm.

6 · DIPLOMACY OF THE NEW DEAL ERA: SECOND PHASE (1937-1939)

When an epidemic of physical disease starts to spread, the community approves and joins in a quarantine of the patients in order to protect the health of the community against the spread of the disease.
PRESIDENT FRANKLIN D. ROOSEVELT, *"Quarantine Speech" at Chicago, October 5, 1937*

Franklin D. Roosevelt's official policies during his first administration were oriented in an isolationist direction that was broadened to include an identity of America's security interests with the whole of the Western Hemisphere. As late as August, 1936, the President could say in his Chautauqua speech, "We shun political commitments which might entangle us in foreign wars; we avoid connection with political activities of the League of Nations." Though Roosevelt drifted with the isolationist tide, privately he remained an internationalist at heart, firmly believing in the necessity of coöperation among nations and the uniting of America with the world's democracies against aggressor nations to meet the danger of war. Political reasons were chiefly responsible for the President's split personality before 1937. Anxious to assure his renomination and a Democratic victory in 1936, Roosevelt did not want to widen the breach in the party—badly divided on international issues—or alienate popular support. He was primarily intent on the success of the New Deal, and did not wish to risk the slightest chance of repudiation.

After the election returns showed a smashing victory for the New

Deal, Roosevelt breathed more easily. With the worst of the slump over, the exuberant newly reëlected President now felt that he could turn his attention more directly toward removing the major obstacles to complete recovery and that he could also concentrate on foreign affairs. Roosevelt pinpointed two obstacles to full recovery: the "reactionary" Supreme Court, which in 1935 suddenly began to block New Deal legislation by declaring many programs unconstitutional—among them one of the cornerstones of New Deal policy, the National Industrial Recovery Act—and Big Business, whose lack of coöperation and hostility were disturbingly irritating to the President. Roosevelt's attempt to reorganize the federal judiciary and to "pack" the Supreme Court with liberal justices occupied most of his time early in 1937. It became the burning issue in the country, while the crises in Europe were temporarily shunted aside. In the Supreme Court "fight," Roosevelt suffered an immediate and serious personal defeat. A result of the struggle was the end of the generally harmonious relationship between the President and Congress. Angered by the fierce opposition to the New Deal, Roosevelt sought in the following year to "purge" Democratic members of Congress who had refused to support his policies. The whole situation had a dampening effect on Roosevelt's efforts to develop a stronger foreign policy. Nor were the attempts successful to whip Big Business into line by threats of vigorous antitrust action. The war clouds in Europe soon nullified the antimonopoly crusade as a closer partnership between government and business became necessary.

In the area of foreign affairs, the outbreak of the Sino-Japanese War in the summer of 1937 was largely responsible for the beginning of a shift in Roosevelt's policies. The previous year had witnessed the drawing together of the Axis bloc. An accord had been signed between Hitler and Mussolini in October, 1936, in which each had pledged mutual coöperation in the policies toward Spain and against Communism in Europe. Mussolini's Ethiopian empire was recognized by Hitler, in return for which he obtained economic privileges in Italy's colonies. The following month, Germany and Japan signed an Anti-Comintern Pact, ostensibly aimed against Communism but actually directed against the Soviet Union. A secret clause provided for political, and if necessary military, coöperation in opposing Russia. Thus, the Berlin-Rome-Tokyo Axis was forged.

Roosevelt was acutely conscious of the danger which this entente represented to world peace. In some way, he felt, it had to be counteracted. Yet, while Roosevelt hesitated over active opposition to the European dictators or interference in the Spanish Civil War, Japan's case, he thought, was different. She was trampling on the Open Door policy and violating international agreements to which the United States was a party, particularly the Nine-Power Treaty of 1922. America's sympathies for China, moreover, were very strong. Dislike of Japan, on the other hand, intensified by her aggression in China, was great. Since Japanese power was not highly rated in America, a firm attitude toward her seemed far less risky than standing up to Hitler and Mussolini.

In the fall of 1937, Roosevelt groped for a constructive approach to maintain peace in the face of the organized assault against the democracies. He seriously considered calling a world conference to bring together the conflicting nations to see if some sort of agreement, upholding the principles of international law, could be reached; but the plan never materialized. The conference idea, of course, was not new, and it is doubtful that it would have brought any fruitful results. Its chief virtue might have been its demonstration of America's desire to assume an initiative in world affairs.

While Roosevelt side-stepped any outright move in the direction of collective action against the aggressor powers, the grave situation in the Far East persuaded him of the need to take a strong stand. The prevalent isolationism, it seemed to him and Secretary of State Hull, had to be blunted. Hull was largely responsible for suggesting to Roosevelt that he speak about the problems confronting the United States in the course of a planned visit to the Middle West. The State Department, in fact, prepared the text for an address. F.D.R., deciding that the time had come for greater forthrightness, revised the somewhat cautious draft into the famous "Quarantine Speech."

Speaking of the rampant "reign of terror and lawlessness," Roosevelt told his Chicago audience in October, 1937, "Let no one imagine that America will escape, that America may expect mercy, that this Western Hemisphere will not be attacked and that it will continue tranquilly and peacefully to carry on the ethics and arts of civilization." He called upon the peace-loving nations to make a concerted effort against the growing international anarchy "from which there is no escape through mere isolation or neutrality." To prevent the spread of the epidemic of world lawlessness, he asked for a quarantine of the aggressors, since war was contagious, whether declared or undeclared. "We are determined to keep out of war," Roosevelt said, "yet we cannot insure ourselves against the disastrous effects of war and the dangers of involvement." Concluding, he affirmed, "America hates war. America hopes for peace. Therefore, America actively engages in the search for peace."

Reaction to the Quarantine Speech was mixed; there was no middle ground. American newspapers generally divided between those that took an enthusiastic stand in support of the President, and those that were blatantly hostile. Many thought that Roosevelt had chosen a very inopportune time to call for a vigorous American foreign policy. The country was in the midst of a severe business recession, anger was still widespread over the Supreme Court fight, and the feeling arose that Roosevelt was seeking a diversion from the failures of the New Deal. Greatest confusion centered on the President's use of the word "quarantine." What did quarantine mean, and against whom was it to be applied? Roosevelt never clarified what he meant. Later, well-informed writers said that the idea the President had in mind was that when a clear act of aggression had taken place, such as Japan's in China, then all peace-loving nations should pledge nonintercourse with it. Generally, nonintercourse was interpreted in terms of applying severe sanctions. This was the meaning which many isolationists attached to the word "quarantine." Senator Borah, however, declared that imposing sanctions against Japan would be "just the same as initiating war." This line was picked up by the Hearst press, which declared that America had become a puppet of Britain and that Roosevelt was being manipulated to save the British Empire in the Far East.

The day after Roosevelt delivered his Quarantine Speech, the League of Nations Assembly in Geneva held that Japan's invasion of China had violated the Nine-Power Treaty and the Kellogg-Briand Pact. The United States officially concurred with the League Assembly. Joseph C. Grew, American ambassador at Tokyo, who had urged a policy of noninvolvement in the Sino-Japanese conflict, was disheartened by the openly expressed position of the State Department. Moral judgments, he was convinced, could not deter aggression, and he lamented that America had chosen the road to war "in the Far Eastern mess."

In October, the League of Nations also suggested that the original signers of the Nine-Power Treaty meet to see if they could settle the dispute between China and Japan. The Belgian government took the initiative, and a conference was arranged at Brussels. Besides the original signatories, invitations were sent to Germany and the Soviet Union. Japan and Germany, however, declined to attend. The Japanese insisted that their quarrel with China was purely between the two countries, and she opposed interference by the other Nine-Power Treaty nations. The Brussels Conference turned out to be a wake; it disclosed the complete impotence of the Western democratic countries to cope with aggression. With Japan absent, the delegates found it impossible to consider a settlement of the conflict. Nor was the conference willing to impose sanctions. It merely contented itself with a restatement of the principles of the

Nine-Power Treaty and urged China and Japan to resolve their disputes in accordance with these principles. The polite advice was ignored by Japan.

The Quarantine Speech and the dismal failure of the Brussels Conference led to a turning point in Roosevelt's foreign policies. Heretofore, he had been willing to bow to public pressures and to avoid engaging in any open battle with the isolationists. By the beginning of 1938, however, he was convinced that America's security was being seriously endangered by the growing threats of war. The crucial question hinged on the neutrality laws. Did they adequately protect the security of the United States? Could they keep America out of war? Isolationists were sure that they would, provided the provisions were strictly enforced. Roosevelt no longer believed so. He accepted the neutrality legislation as the law of the land and coöperated with the policy as far as it would go. It was not, however, invoked in the Sino-Japanese War; Congress, openly favorable to China, did not raise any major objections. What bothered Roosevelt was the possibility that the United States might not "escape" from war. Japan had formally renounced the Five-Power Naval Treaty of 1922; all attempts to work out programs for armament limitations had been woefully unsuccessful. The American Army in 1938, antiquated in material, was smaller than that of a third-rate European power. Could the United States predict what the future course of events might be? Surely it was wiser to prepare for the storm—if one should come—than to do nothing.

In January, 1938, Roosevelt asked Congress for a billion-dollar naval appropriation. He emphasized the necessity for building up a two-ocean Navy, one which would equal the combined fleets of three "have-not" nations. In the spring of 1938, the crises in Europe and Asia mounted. Congress, alarmed by rumors that the Japanese were pressing for an outright military alliance with Germany, approved the appropriation. The President signed the bill in May, 1938.

Japan briskly pushed ahead with the war in China. Every effort was made to liquidate the "China Incident" by compelling Chiang Kai-shek to accept peace on Japan's terms. But the Chinese maintained their resistance, with moral support from the United States and material help from the Soviet Union. Nevertheless Japan captured Nanking, the Nationalists' capital. Chiang Kai-shek removed the government to Hankow. When Hankow and Canton were occupied in October, 1938, the Nationalists retreated deep into the interior of China, to Chungking on the upper Yangtze. Despite Japan's control of all principal ports, the coast cities, and the main railway lines, the Nationalists stubbornly refused to admit defeat, and Japan had difficulty in maintaining her control. Nevertheless, the Japanese Foreign Office proclaimed the establishment of a "New Order" in November, 1938, creating "a tripartite relationship of mutual aid and coordination between Japan, Manchukuo and China in political, economic, cutural and other fields." The "New Order" was promptly rejected by the United States.

Gradually, Roosevelt adopted in 1938 a firmer policy in the Far East. America's retreat was halted, and an active program of naval construction got under way. The United States, however, was so far behind in its naval-building program that it did not expect to catch up to the limits allowed in the Five-Power Naval Treaty until 1942. And while the United States watched with anxiety the developments in China, the storm center moved from the Far East to Europe.

MUNICH: PROLOGUE TO DISASTER

Adolf Hitler, much more than Franklin Roosevelt, was responsible for ultimately breaking down isolationist sentiment in the United States. Many Americans had been perturbed by the German dictator's belligerence, by the miltarization of the Rhineland, by the Nazi intervention in the Spanish Civil War, and by the attempted grab of Austria through *Anschluss* (union with Germany). But these events were viewed with detachment. They were primarily European problems which only remotely affected the United States. The thing that appalled most Americans was Nazi brutality, the ruthless persecution of religious groups, and the horrors of genocide. When the hideous policy of mass extermination of the Jews came to the forefront in Germany in 1938, it shocked the nation and began to reawaken the American conscience. America's role in world affairs no longer became a matter of whether the United States would or would not join the League of Nations and support collective security, but rather whether America would or would not defend freedom and democracy.

Though Americans bemoaned Nazi atrocities, the majority of people still believed strongly that the United States must not become involved in the horrors of war. The strength of ultraisolationist feeling was dramatically disclosed in the support of the Ludlow Amendment. Indiana Democratic Representative Louis Ludlow proposed in 1938 a constitutional amendment which would require a national referendum on a declaration of war, except in the event of an actual invasion. Passage was blocked in Congress only after an extraordinary appeal from President Roosevelt. While isolationism retained the allegiance of millions of Americans, nevertheless, after 1938 a subtle transformation took place.

It was reflected in the idea—put forward hesitantly at first—that America should become an active and aggressive champion of the principles of freedom. As a new internationalist movement gained momentum, the antiwar sentiment gradually began to lessen.

The climax came in Europe in the spring of 1938. Hitler was on the move. Since his rise to power, the German dictator had directed his attention on a drive to the East. In 1934, he had tried to annex Austria, his native land; but the move was abortive. Mussolini, fearful of a powerful Germany at the Brenner Pass, mobilized his troops on the Austrian frontier and declared that he would defend the independence of the country. By 1938, however, a complete rapprochement had been achieved between Germany and Italy, and Hitler felt strong enough to cast aside his promise to Mussolini to respect Austrian independence. After a Nazi coup, the new Austrian Chancellor invited German troops into the country to suppress disorders. The next day, Hitler proclaimed Austria annexed to the German Reich, and then on March 12 triumphantly entered Vienna. Britain and France protested, but they stood by as Hitler completed the *Anschluss*.

Immediately after taking over Austria, Hitler turned to Czechoslovakia. Like Austria, the democratic Czechoslovakian state contained several million ethnic Germans, most of whom lived in the Sudeten area in the western part of the country, close to Germany's borders. Hitler declared that it was his intention to "rescue" the Sudeten Germans from their "torture and oppression." Both France and the Soviet Union had mutual-assistance pacts with Czechoslovakia; but the Soviet Union made it clear that her support of Czechoslovakia's independence would depend on the actions of France. French policy, however, had become closely tied to Britain, which did not have any treaty of guarantee with Czechoslovakia. The role of Britain in the Czechoslovakian crisis was therefore pivotal.

The British Foreign Office in 1938 was prepared to make certain concessions to Hitler with respect to the Sudetenland. At the time, the feeling was quite strong that in this case a violation of the principle of self-determination had been made in the Versailles Treaty and that a legitimate correction of borders might be effected. Britain's policy of "appeasement" was not the result of weakness or a surrender to Hitler's blackmail threats of war or to a paralysis of the will to act. It was instead a deliberately calculated policy in which British statesmen played a gambit—and lost.

During the critical months from January to September, 1938, Britain had hoped to restore a balance of power on the European continent by strengthening Germany as a bulwark against the Soviet Union. As a result, Prime Minister Neville Chamberlain did not strenuously object to the absorption of Hitler's energies in the East. American Ambassador Joseph E. Davies in Moscow was quite concerned about the attitude of both Britain and France, who were suspected of trying to stir up discord, especially between Germany and Russia, so that Hitler would leave the West alone. Rather prophetically, he warned in March that both England and France were playing into the hands of the Nazis. "The Soviet Union is rapidly being driven into a complete isolation and even hostility to England and indifference to France," he wrote. "This may extend to the point where there might be developed a realistic union of these forces with Germany in the not distant future."

Stalin was greatly alarmed about Britain's tendency to sympathize with Hitler's demands for the incorporation of the Sudetenland into Germany. Equally disturbing was the signing of the Anglo-Italian agreement in April, 1938, which in substance recognized Italy's sovereignty over Ethiopia. The Soviet Union was worried about the growing close accord between Britain and the fascist countries. "The only thing that would prevent complete fascist domination of Europe," said Soviet Foreign Minister Maxim Litvinov, "was a change in government or policy in Britain."

At the outset of the crisis, Stalin indicated his willingness to coöperate with England and France in calling Hitler's bluff. But at the time a great deal of skepticism was voiced in British and French circles about Soviet military strength. Stalin's "purges" of the Red Army and reports of serious setbacks in Soviet industrial production strengthened the conviction that the Soviet Union could not offer really effective support in the event of war. Moreover, Chamberlain believed that Stalin would like nothing better than to embroil Germany in conflict with the West. Distrust and suspicion led to the fear that the Soviet Union was trying to set a trap. Once committed in Czechoslovakia, Chamberlain thought, Stalin might pull out and leave Britain and France in the lurch. "Such [joint] action as is proposed by the Soviet Government," he told the House of Commons, would "in the view of His Majesty's Government be inimical to the prospects of European peace."

In his personal letters, Prime Minister Chamberlain frankly expressed his suspicions of the Soviet Union. The Russians, he told his sister in March, 1938, were "stealthily and cunningly pulling all the strings behind the scenes to get us involved in war with Germany." Again, he wrote later, "I must confess to the most profound distrust of Russia. . . . I distrust her motives, which seem to me to have little connéction with our ideas of liberty and to be concerned only with getting everybody else by the ears."

Tension steadily mounted between Germany and Czechoslovakia. At the end of April, Britain and France each assured Hitler that they were urging the Czechs to make the utmost concessions possible to the Sudeten Germans. Chamberlain had already made up his mind about the Sudeten issue. "You have only to look at the map to see that nothing that France or we could do could possibly save Czechoslovakia from being overrun by the Germans, if they wanted to do it," he had written his sister. "I have, therefore, abandoned any idea of giving guarantee to Czechoslovakia, or to the French in connection with her obligations to that country." To make sure that the Czechs would be amenable to the British and French pressures, Hitler massed twelve German divisions along the Czech frontiers, ready to march on twelve hours' notice.

The Czechs suddenly disrupted Hitler's plans on May 20. Fearful of a sudden German attack, and not consulting Britain and France, the Czech government ordered a partial mobilization of its forces. This move precipitated a chain reaction that had unfortunate consequences. Actually, at the time, evidence indicates that Hitler did not plan a German attack, "unless," as the directive for "Operation Green"—the campaign against Czechoslovakia—stated, "an unavoidable development of the political conditions within Czechoslovakia forces the issue, or political events in Europe create a particularly favorable opportunity which may never recur." The British and French tried to control the situation to prevent any rash action on the part of the Czechs or Hitler. But the German dictator, angered that Czechoslovakia had dared to stand up against Germany, altered his plans. His general staff warned him against undertaking any aggressive move in the face of the demonstrated solidarity of Britain and France. Hitler brusquely rejected all suggestions that it would be wiser to retreat. On May 28, 1938, his military directive for Operation Green declared: "It is my unalterable decision to smash Czechoslovakia by military action in the immediate future without provocation. . . ." That same day, the dictator ordered that preparations for the attack were to be completed by October 2. Work was immediately speeded up on the western defenses of the Reich.

The weeks which followed were fraught with anxiety. Would Britain and France stand by Czechoslovakia? Stalin did not think so. "The reactionary elements in England and represented by the Chamberlain government [are] determined upon a policy of making Germany strong against Russia," he told Ambassador Davies. The Soviet Union, he said, "had every confidence that it could defend itself."

Conversations were carried on continuously between Litvinov and French Foreign Minister Georges Bonnet. Litvinov tried to convince Bonnet that, in the event of war, the Soviet Union would support France;

she had nothing to fear. However, Litvinov did point out that France would have to remove a serious obstacle—the refusal of Poland and Rumania to permit the passage of Russian troops through their countries. The Soviet Union's efforts to obtain such consent had been unsuccessful. Since France had treaty relations with both of these countries, Litvinov pointed out, France would have to secure their coöperation. Bonnet found it no easy task. Rumania vehemently opposed the suggestion. Under the circumstances, Soviet help for France in a war against Germany was dubious.

Throughout the crisis, France showed an inclination to abide by her treaty commitments with Czechoslovakia. But she could not act alone. On September 10, Bonnet asked the British ambassador, Sir Eric Phipps, "Tomorrow Germany may attack Czechoslovakia. In this case France will mobilize at once. She will turn to you saying: 'We march. Do you march with us?' What will Great Britain's answer be?" The British reply two days later was equivocal. "So far as I am in a position to give any answer at this stage to M. Bonnet's question," Lord Halifax stated, "it would have to be that while His Majesty's Government would never allow the security of France to be threatened, they are unable to make precise statements of the character of their future action or the time at which it would be taken, in circumstances that they cannot at present foresee."

Indeed, Britain's dilemma was acute. The last thing the British wanted was an open war with Germany with the possibility of the Soviet Union remaining on the side lines. The British had counted on a policy of diversion, shifting Hitler's pressures from the West to the East. If a war occurred, Britain hoped that it would be she who would stand on the side lines, conserving her energies while Germany and the Soviet Union became exhausted in a long conflict. For Britain, a war in defense of Czechoslovakia seemed to be the wrong war, in the wrong place, at the wrong time.

Since the end of August, Chamberlain had thought that if he held a private conference with Hitler the whole Sudeten question might be quickly settled. On September 13, he decided to delay no longer. He wrote to Hitler and proposed a conference to try to find a peaceful solution to the Czechoslovakian crisis. Hitler was delighted. The British *Schweinhund* at last was coming to talk directly to him. The French were apprehensive; but they, too, were pleased that the British had finally decided to take some positive action.

The first talks were held at Berchtesgaden on September 15. Chamberlain saw Hitler alone (except for an interpreter), and spoke to him for about three hours. Hitler, Chamberlain told his sister, "spoke quietly and in low tones. I did not see any trace of insanity, but occasionally he became very excited and poured out his indignation against the Czechs in a torrent of words, so that several times I had to stop him and ask that I might have a chance to hear what he was talking about."

Hitler suggested quite innocently that the Sudeten question might be solved by means of the principle of self-determination. Chamberlain told him that he "didn't care two hoots whether the Sudetens were in the Reich, or out of it, according to their own wishes." But he did feel that a plebiscite might entail certain "practical difficulties." Nevertheless, he said, he would be perfectly willing to accept Hitler's suggestion as a basis for settlement. Chamberlain told Hitler that he would recommend it to his Cabinet, and to the French and Czech governments. Meanwhile, Hitler promised not to give any orders to march, unless an outrageous incident forced his hand. This pledge could be readily given, since the military directive for a German attack against Czechoslovakia was not intended to go into operation before October 1. Actually, Hitler did not expect Chamberlain to meet with much success.

The British Prime Minister, on the whole, was quite pleased with the talk. "I had established a certain confidence," Chamberlain wrote, "which was my aim, and on my side, in spite of the hardness and ruthlessness I thought I saw in his face, I got the impression that here was a man who could be relied upon when he had given his word."

With great difficulty, Chamberlain obtained French and Czech consent to Hitler's proposals. Czechoslovakia at first rebuffed the offer, but on sober second thought, realizing her isolation, she succumbed. On September 21, Czechoslovakia announced that because of the "severe duress and extreme pressure of the French and British governments," she decided to accept "with bitterness the Anglo-French proposals."

Chamberlain thought that now only the technical details of the plebiscite and the inevitable transfer had to be worked out. But when he arrived at Godesberg, where the second meeting was to be held, he found that Hitler was no longer interested in negotiations. He wanted surrender —surrender at once. No agreement! No plebiscite! Chamberlain was shocked; angrily he told Hitler that he had taken his political life in his hands, that he had been booed on his departure. Hitler shouted that he had never thought a peaceful solution could be reached. He had never believed that the Prime Minister could have achieved what he had. Military preparations, he stormed, had already been undertaken, and Germany was ready to move at once. Surrender—or war! Deeply disturbed, Chamberlain returned to London. The British press reported the breakdown of negotiations.

The Western world girded for the outbreak of war. Frantic, last-ditch efforts were made to try to preserve the peace. Roosevelt sent a personal appeal to Hitler and Mussolini on September 27. He warned that the use of force might lead to a general war, and suggested an immediate meeting in some neutral European city, which "would offer the opportunity for this and correlated questions to be solved in a spirit of justice, of fair dealing, and, in all human probability, with greater permanence." Chamberlain asked Mussolini to intervene on behalf of peace. There is no indication that these and other appeals had any effect on Hitler, but he did agree to hold another conference.

Chamberlain was addressing the House of Commons on the gravity of the situation when a note was handed to him. He interrupted his speech and read the message silently; then he told the waiting Commons, "I have something further to say to the House yet. I have been informed by Herr Hitler that he invites me to meet him at Munich tomorrow morning. He has also invited Signor Mussolini and M. Daladier. Signor Mussolini has accepted, and I have no doubt M. Daladier will accept. I need not say what my answer will be." Shortly after this dramatic moment in Parliament, Roosevelt instructed his ambassador in London to transmit a two-word message for him to the Prime Minister. It said, "Good man."

The Four-Power Conference convened at Munich on the afternoon of September 29, and an agreement was signed in the early hours of the next day. The Czechs were allowed to complete the evacuation of the Sudeten area in ten days, "without any existing installations having been destroyed." The same day an Anglo-German pact was signed in which Hitler and Chamberlain renounced war in the settlement of their national differences. "This is the last territorial claim I shall make in Europe," Hitler had declared three days before the Munich agreement. Britain and France pledged to guarantee the new Czechoslovak frontiers. Later, England gave Czechoslovakia a large loan to help her overcome the disruptive effect on her economic life created by the surrender of the Sudetenland.

THE AFTERMATH OF MUNICH

The initial reaction to the Munich agreement was one of relief: war had been avoided. Chamberlain returned to London, umbrella in hand, and told a tensely waiting crowd that it would mean "peace in our time."

Although he was then campaigning actively in the Congressional elections, Roosevelt followed the course of events in Europe closely. Indeed, it was impossible to do otherwise at the time, as newscasters breathlessly alerted the American public with hourly reports. Roosevelt told a friend that he had had a strenuous two weeks, but managed to come through—"except for a stupid and continuing runny nose"— because of a relaxing cruise he had taken during the summer. "A few days ago I wanted to kill Hitler and amputate the nose," he wrote after the news broke about the signing of the Munich agreement. "Today, I have really friendly feelings for the latter and no longer wish to assassinate the Fuehrer."

But relief was tinged with doubt and worry. Warnings were posted that the Munich agreement had merely postponed the prospects of war. "We have sustained a total and unmitigated defeat," said Winston Churchill, a vigorous opponent of the appeasement policy. Ambassador William C. Bullitt in France reported that this feeling was shared by high officials in Paris. "Unless France can recover a united national spirit to confront the future," the French Foreign Minister told him, "a fatal situation will arise within a year." Disillusion was swift; as pessimism deepened, the Western powers stepped up their armament programs. Two weeks after the Munich conference, Roosevelt called for an increase of $300 million for national defense. By the end of the year, war in Europe appeared to be certain.

With war clouds on the horizon, America focused its attention on the security of the Western Hemisphere. German and Italian penetration in Latin America had grown fearfully alarming. Two years earlier, the Buenos Aires Conference had provided for consultation in case of the threat of war, but no machinery had been set up to bring it about. Secretary of State Hull felt that the gap had to be closed, and he achieved a notable diplomatic victory for the United States by securing agreement at the Eighth International Conference of American States, at Lima, Peru, in December, 1938, that common dangers to the Hemisphere were to be met by common action. To cope with such threats, the Lima Declaration provided that a conference of Foreign Ministers could be scheduled upon the call of any one of them. Thus a firm basis was established for Pan-American solidarity.

In his annual message to Congress in January, 1939, Roosevelt for the first time took off his gloves. America, he said, could no longer ignore the aggressions in Europe and Asia. He did not urge the use of force to counteract them, but he said, "There are many methods short of war, but stronger and more effective than mere words, of bringing home to aggressor governments the aggregate sentiments of our own people." Of one thing he was sure—the inadequacy of the existing neutrality laws. "We have learned that when we deliberately try to legislate neutrality, our neutrality laws may operate unevenly and unfairly—may actually give aid to the aggressor and deny it to the victim," F.D.R. declared. "The instinct of self-preservation should warn us that we ought not to let that happen any more."

The turning point in the steadily deteriorating international situation came in the spring of 1939, when Hitler suddenly absorbed all of Czechoslovakia; the Western powers again looked on with protests but with no call to action. This move enormously enhanced Hitler's military position. In March, 1939, all of the resources of Czechslovakia became the property of Germany. Germans were surprised at the size, output, and advanced techniques of the Skoda and Bruenn armament works. By taking over these plants, Germany acquired tremendously important technical secrets. Amazed at the military stores found, Hitler exclaimed that they were "truly gigantic!"

The greatest coup was the seizure of Czech tanks, which were far superior to Germany's. Most of Hitler's tanks were all below ten tons (Mark II) and were armed with machine guns, except for a handful of eighteen-ton tanks (Mark III). These were armed with a 37-mm. gun. The Czechs had hundreds of thirty-eight-ton tanks armed with 75-mm. cannon. When Germany overran Czechoslovakia, it captured 469 of these superior tanks, along with 1,500 planes, 43,500 machine guns, and over a million rifles. Hitler ordered all war matériel found in Czechoslovakia transported to Germany within four weeks after occupation. He thus came into possession of a formidable war machine; within six months, it was to spearhead the Nazi *Blitzkrieg* against Poland.

The annexation of Czechoslovakia provided Hitler with the opportunity to press forward his aggressive plans. But one thing was lacking. In 1939, there was grave doubt that Germany, despite her enhanced military position, could overcome the combined might of Britain, France, and the Soviet Union, which in all likelihood would be lined up against her. The national-defense program of England had been built up considerably. In 1938, Britain had produced less than three thousand military planes; it was increased the following year to eight thousand—and British planes were far superior to those of Germany. While France had not mobilized completely, the French infantry divisions and the Maginot Line were on a war basis. The questionable factor was Russia, with more than one hundred divisions mobilized. A coalition of Britain, France, and Russia, it was clear, could break Germany's military back, even with the Czech tanks and munitions. Hitler recognized as he built up his pressures upon Poland, in his demands for the Polish Corridor and Danzig, that he could not risk war unless either the Soviet Union or the West was immobilized.

THE NAZI-SOVIET PACT

Early in 1939, Britain and France tried to work out an understanding with the Soviet Union with respect to guaranteeing the security of Poland and Rumania. Protracted negotiations ensued. Russia was willing to agree to the Anglo-French proposal, provided it also included a "guarantee of protection of Soviet security." In effect, the Soviet Union insisted that in the event of German aggression she was to receive the tacit consent of Britain and France to occupy Estonia, Latvia, Lithuania, and southeastern Finland. The Western powers found Stalin's price too high. They realized that it would mean the Soviet Union would be in a position to carve out for herself a sphere of influence in Eastern Europe. If Moscow restored her influence in the Baltic states, the British Foreign office feared that the Reich would be driven back toward the West again, and the Soviet Union would have a free hand in the East.

Hitler moved into the breach between Russia and the West. Early in April, he issued his first general directive for Operation White—the attack on Poland. "We cannot expect a repetition of the Czech affair," Hitler said. "There will be war. Our task is to isolate Poland. The success of this isolation will be decisive. . . . There must be no simultaneous conflict with the Western Powers."

The decisive question which arose was whether Poland could be isolated, and war with Russia and the West avoided. Hitler's primary concern was the Soviet Union. If Stalin did not interfere directly, the possibility existed that Britain and France might accept the *fait accompli*. "It is not impossible," Hitler told his general staff, "that Russia will show herself to be disinterested in the destruction of Poland."

In May, 1939, Germany undertook her first overtures to see if a deal could not be worked out for closer Soviet coöperation. Russia was to be sounded out in a casual way. For some time, the two countries had been discussing trade problems; but the talks had been broken off. It was now suggested that they might be resumed. After the breakdown in Anglo-French negotiations, Russia agreed late in June to renew her trade talks with Germany through her chargé d'affaires in Berlin. At a dinner on July 26, the German representative—under orders to raise political, as well as economic, issues in his discussions—turned the conversation to the advantages of a broad agreement between the Soviet Union and Germany. "What could England offer Russia?" he asked his Russian guests. "At best, participation in a European war and the hostility of Germany, but not a single desirable end for Russia. But what could we offer, on the other hand?" he went on. "Neutrality and staying out of a possible European conflict, and, if Moscow wished, a German-Russian understanding on mutual interests which would work out to the advantage of both countries."

This line of conversation was followed up by the German ambassador in Moscow. Two things were stressed: that Germany was prepared to come to a positive understanding on the Baltic question, and that in Asia steps would be taken to decrease Japanese hostility to the Soviets. Border clashes had been going on between Japanese and Russian forces since 1931, and in the summer of 1939, German Foreign Minister Joachim Ribbentrop's reminder to Russia that his "influence on the Japanese government was certainly not slight" and his offer to neutralize Japan undoubtedly pleased Stalin. It certainly was in sharp contrast with the attitude of Britain and France, both of whom had rejected any arrangement with the Soviet Union which would extend to Asia.

The German overtures brought results. Russia showed obvious interest. The immediate prize which both countries sought was in Eastern Europe: the Soviet Union desired control over the Baltic countries and a return of Polish territories lost after World War I; Hitler wanted the Polish Corridor and Danzig. Poland could be divided between the two countries. In the short run, no conflicts of interest existed; in a certain sense, a common bond of unity could be found, since Germany and Russia both wished to restore their pre-World War I territorial positions. In the long run, it was a different matter, and neither Hitler nor Stalin harbored any illusions on this score.

Ribbentrop had foreseen the possibilities of a Russo-German deal in May, when Stalin suddenly dismissed Maxim Litvinov. The Soviet Foreign Minister had been identified with a policy of coöperation with the Western powers. His ouster came shortly after Stalin had delivered a speech in which he denounced the West for its attempt to "incense the Soviet Union against Germany, to poison the atmosphere and to provoke a conflict with Germany without any visible grounds." He had warned that Russia would not "be drawn into conflicts by war-mongers who are accustomed to have others pull the chestnuts out of the fire for them." When Vyacheslav Molotov was chosen as Litvinov's successor, the move was interpreted by Ribbentrop as indicating a Soviet desire for a rapprochement with Germany.

Molotov was aware of Germany's eagerness to conclude a nonaggression pact. He therefore bided his time to obtain the maximum advantage for the Soviet Union. What, he asked, would be the specific provisions for a Nazi-Soviet pact? The matter, he felt, called for a great deal of discussion. As the summer of 1939 progressed, Ribbentrop showed his impatience. He told Molotov that everything could be settled quickly. The Soviet Union need not worry. But, he said, an agreement had to be concluded immediately. The reason for the haste was that Hitler had fixed August 26 as X-day for the invasion of Poland (Operation White); Y-time—the signal for the attack—was set at 04:30. Time began to run out while Molotov dawdled in making definite commitments. Hitler sent a direct appeal to Stalin. He asked the Soviet dictator if Ribbentrop could not see him on August 22, or at the latest on the twenty-third. For two days, Hitler waited anxiously for Stalin's reply. Would the Russians back down at the last minute and make a deal with the British and French? Before Hitler had time to decide what he would do in this eventuality, Stalin telegraphed a reply: "The Soviet Government has authorized me to inform you that it agrees to Herr von Ribbentrop's arriving in Moscow on 23 August."

The exultation of Hitler and his Nazi cohorts at the prospect of signing a Nazi-Soviet pact was boundless. With the Soviet Union immobilized, he no longer feared the possibility of war with Britain and France. "Our enemies are men below average, not men of action, not masters," he said after Stalin's telegram arrived. "They are little worms. I saw them at Munich." Hitler told his general staff, "My only fear is that at the last moment some *Schweinhund* will make a proposal for mediation." On August 22, he dispatched orders to put Operation White into effect.

Two days later, the Nazi-Soviet pact was signed. Each country pledged that it would adopt a strict policy of nonaggression. In the event of war, they agreed not to give help to the other's enemies nor to join any grouping of powers aimed directly or indirectly at the other. After World War II, a secret protocol appended to the treaty came to light. Hitler's price for Soviet "coöperation" was disclosed. It was a price that he could easily afford to pay—much more so than the Western powers—since it was based on a division of future spoils. The two countries agreed to divide Poland between them, and the Soviet Union was given a free hand in the Baltic regions north of Lithuania and in Bessarabia in the Balkan region. To Stalin, the most important thing that had been gained was time—time to build up Russia's defenses for a future attack that might come from Germany, Japan, or the Western powers. While Stalin could drink a toast to Hitler, "to the revival of the traditional German-Russian friendship," more than mere words were necessary to obtain a genuine basis for coöperation. Ideological differences and conflicting ambitions were still great. The Nazi-Soviet Pact was useful, but only up to the point that it furthered the *immediate* aims of each country.

To the rest of the world, the new partnership created a feeling of great consternation and disbelief. Hostilities, it was recognized, would now be inevitable, and they came swiftly. Hitler invaded Poland on September 1, and two days later, Britain and France formally announced their declaration of war against Germany. With the anxiety which arose that the Nazi dictator would not be fighting a war on two fronts, there also arose some relief that the "war of nerves"—which had been going on for two years—had now come to an end. The die had been cast on the battlefield.

ROOSEVELT SEEKS TO REPEAL THE ARMS EMBARGO

Because of its isolationism and neutrality laws, the United States had dealt itself out of the game of power politics in Europe. Hitler did not have to pay a price to immobilize the United States; she had voluntarily and gladly remained immobile. After the German absorption of Czechoslovakia in the spring of 1939, the European crisis reached an acute stage. Roosevelt realized that the United States had to have a greater freedom of action, and he specifically requested the repeal of the arms-embargo provision of the Neutrality Act.

In July, the President sent a special message to Congress, enclosing a statement by the Secretary of State which had his "full approval." Hull told Congress, "I profoundly believe that the first great step towards safeguarding this nation from being drawn into war is to use whatever influence it can, compatible with the traditional policy of our country of noninvolvement, so as to make less likely the outbreak of a major war." And he went on to say, "It must be clear to every one of us that the outbreak of a general war increases the dangers confronting the United States. This fact cannot be ignored." In blunter fashion, Hull privately remarked that the next war in Europe was not going to be just "another goddam piddling dispute over a boundary line." The existing Neutrality Act, he said, "substituted a wretched little bobtailed, sawed-off domestic statute for the established rules of international law" and gratuitously benefited "the probable aggressors."

The Congressional isolationist bloc was solidly opposed to the arms-embargo repeal. Convinced that revision of the Neutrality Act was essential, Roosevelt invited some of the leading Senate isolationists to the White House on July 18 to try to win their support. But Senator William E. Borah refused to be moved by the President's appeal to lift the arms embargo. Hull carefully reviewed for the group the cables and dispatches from abroad that convinced him that war was certain and close. "No one can foretell what may happen," interrupted Borah, "but my feeling and belief is that we are not going to have a war. Germany isn't ready for it." Hull asked him, almost tearfully—as he had many times in the past—to come down to the State Department and read the cables that were coming in. "So far as the reports in your department are concerned," replied Borah, "I wouldn't be bound by them. I have my own sources of information . . . and on several occasions I've found them more reliable than the State Department." These "sources of information," it was later discovered, amounted to an obscure press service in London that was favorable to the Axis cause.

Borah's opposition made the administration's case hopeless.

"Well, Captain," Vice-President John Garner told Roosevelt. "We may as well face the facts. You haven't got the votes, and that's all there is to it." The President replied that he had done his best, and the Senate would have to accept the responsibility. Borah assured him, as he left the meeting, that there would be "no difficulty about that."

About a month and a half later, the Nazi-Soviet Pact was signed. Hitler was ready to launch a German invasion into Poland. Senator Borah was unable to stem the tide of world events. Poland, unwilling to surrender bloodlessly, resisted Hitler's demands. And this time, Britain and France pledged their support. There would be no more Munich surrender. Unable to obtain his ends by bluff, Hitler gave the fateful order on September 1 to the German armies to cross the Polish frontiers. The mechanized Nazi *Blitzkrieg* began. Within hours, German bomber planes rained their cargo of death on Poland's cities. Britain and France declared war on Germany two days later. World War II had begun. Roosevelt promptly invoked the Neutrality Act and soon obtained repeal of the arms-embargo provision. The declaration of war in Europe was a blow from which the isolationists never effectively recovered. After September, 1939, they found themselves increasingly on the defensive.

JAPAN AND THE OUTBREAK OF WORLD WAR II

Japan was stunned by the signing of the Nazi-Soviet Pact and the swift outbreak of war in Europe. Ribbentrop had hinted that Germany might enter into an accord with Russia; warnings had been posted, but Japan did not take them seriously. The first official inkling of a Nazi-Soviet Pact came on the night of August 22. Ribbentrop told the Japanese ambassador in Berlin, Hiroshi Oshima, that he was going to Moscow to sign an agreement with Stalin. Oshima predicted that an accord with Russia would disrupt the friendly relations between Germany and Japan and create a "certain shock" in Tokyo. But he realized that it was too late and useless to interfere.

Germany's nonaggression pact with the Soviet Union led to a change in Japan's policies. After the liquidation of the "China Incident," Japanese militarists had hoped to turn northward to obtain mastery over Siberia. Since the invasion of Manchuria, border clashes had regularly taken place with Soviet forces in the north. Tensions had steadily increased as a result of Russia's support of the Nationalists, aid which had contributed greatly to the frustration of the Japanese.

Before 1939, Germany and Japan had been drawn together by their common hostility toward Communism and the Soviet Union. Both Axis nations were imbued with a desire to create New Orders: Germany in Europe, and Japan in Asia. Japan had counted heavily on Hitler's coöperation as she pushed ahead with her expansion in China. Her partnership, she thought, had been firmly established in the Anti-Comintern Pact of 1936. In the event of a threat of attack, it was understood that both countries would consult with one another. But more important, the Anti-Comintern Pact clearly stipulated that no political treaties were to be concluded with the Soviet Union without mutual consent, and no Axis power would take measures "of a kind which would have the effect of relieving the position of the U.S.S.R." The provision for consultation had been completely ignored in the signing of the Nazi-Soviet Pact. Nothing that Germany could say or do could assuage Japan's feeling that she had been cast aside by Hitler. The Anti-Comintern Pact became worthless. What was worse, Japan was made to look ridiculous; the humiliation struck deep.

The outward façade of unity had concealed the great differences which existed between Germany and Japan. Although Hitler publicly declared that the Far East, including China, should be the exclusive property of Japan, privately he refused to acknowledge the loss of Germany's rights in China to the "lacquered half-monkeys" of Japan. Once the decision was made to attack Poland in 1939, he did not hesitate to ignore Japan. Hitler explained to Mussolini that his reason for doing so was that while Japan would certainly agree to an alliance against Russia, he knew that she would not "undertake such definite obligations against England, and this, from the standpoint not only of Germany, but also of Italy, [is] of decisive importance."

The swift turn of events in 1939 temporarily threw Japan off balance. But she quickly recovered. Her Siberian dream shattered, Japan turned her eyes to Southeast Asia, Indochina, the Dutch East Indies, the Philippines, Thailand, and even to Australia. She shifted her expansionist drive southward. An opportunity seemed to present itself to acquire the colonial possessions of France, England, the Netherlands, and possibly the United States without the obligation of becoming involved in the European war. Japanese Foreign Minister Yosuke Matsuoka declared that there was no reason why Japan could not pursue "an independent parallel policy, similar to that of the Soviet Union."

Japan's decision to capitalize on the changed conditions in Europe and use them to her advantage was fateful to America. For one thing, it posed an immediate threat to the interests of the United States in the Philippines. Moreover, it directly menaced the Open Door in the Far East. The lines of conflict, therefore, were to be sharply drawn.

AMERICA IN A WORLD OF CRISES

While the whole structure of European peace crumbled between 1937 and 1939, Roosevelt's policies reflected caution and moderation. He frequently appealed to Mussolini and Hitler to halt the onward rush to war. But he made it clear that the United States would accept no political involvements in Europe. During this period, the striking thing which occurred, however, was Roosevelt's growing resistance to the isolationist forces in the country. Stronger sympathies were expressed to America's European allies, and doubts were raised about the wisdom of the neutrality laws which appeared to work to the benefit of the aggressor powers.

Roosevelt's Quarantine Speech, on the whole, had met with a negative reaction throughout the country. It showed that popular opposition to any program of common action with other nations was still very great. Hull had been shocked that the President had departed so rashly from the State Department's prepared text for the speech. Later, in his memoirs, the Secretary of State noted that the "quarantine" reference had set back by at least six months the building up of support for the principles of collective security.

It was the year 1938 which saw the beginning of a change of sentiment in the United States. The Munich surrender, the irresponsibility of Hitler, the brash arrogance of Japan's New Order, and Mussolini's belligerence pointed to a world running amuck. Freedom and democracy clearly seemed to be endangered by the assault of the Axis powers. The United States could not remain indifferent. While the crises in Europe and Asia reënforced the isolationist belief that America must keep out of the imminent war, an equally strong sentiment arose that the neutrality laws should be modified. By the time of the outbreak of World War II, most Americans, although determined to avoid involvement in the conflict, clearly identified the United States with the cause of the Western European democracies.

Frustration and confusion were great as the Nazi armed columns plunged across the Polish borders. Whatever happened in Europe, Roosevelt assured the country that there would be "no black-out of peace in the United States." The prevailing mood on the eve of World War II, therefore, was one of anxiety, an anxiety nurtured by uncertainty as to whether America's allies could survive without America's help.

7 · AMERICA EDGES
TOWARD WAR

It is for you to decide whether it is in your interest to give us whatever assistance may be necessary to make certain Britain shall not fail.
British Ambassador PHILIP KERR, MARQUESS OF LOTHIAN, *Speech at Baltimore, December 11, 1940*

President Franklin D. Roosevelt's foreign policies—from the outbreak of World War II to the bombing of Pearl Harbor—were shaped largely by his response to the shattering events in Europe and Asia and to the swiftly changing world conditions. No set plan existed to deal with the crises beyond placing the United States on a limited national-emergency basis.

But in his actions, Roosevelt was guided by certain important convictions. Axis aggressions and Hitler's ambition to obtain mastery over the European continent represented to him clear and unmistakable threats to the security of the United States. "You must master at the outset a simple but unalterable fact in modern foreign relations between nations," he told the American people after France and England declared war on Germany. "When peace has been broken anywhere, the peace everywhere is in danger." He warned that the events abroad could not be ignored simply because they were taking place thousands of miles away. "This nation will remain a neutral nation," Roosevelt declared, "but I cannot ask that every American remain neutral in thought as well. Even a neutral has a right to take account of facts. Even a neutral cannot be asked to close his mind or his conscience."

The President's task was one of persuasion, but he counted on the course of events to do the education. Roosevelt continued to be cautious. He was acutely conscious of Woodrow Wilson's failures, and he realized that a full disclosure of America's world responsibilities—which might mean facing the unpleasant reality of engaging in a war with the Axis powers—would alarm the public and create tremendous Congressional opposition. The one thing that he did not want to do was to risk repudiation, a repudiation that would surely doom America's allies. While he favored all help possible to the democracies, therefore, he stressed that keeping the United States at peace was his main goal. But, he argued, noninvolvement could best be maintained by aiding the opponents of the aggressors "short of war."

Roosevelt's immediate target was to scrap the neutrality laws. He sought to do this first by obtaining a repeal of the arms-embargo provision. Two weeks after the declaration of war, Roosevelt called a special session of Congress. He asked for authority to permit the sale of arms to the Allies. The proposal quickly elicited a stormy and historic debate. Although the administration did not state that its purpose was to help Britain and France, its intention was clear. Isolationists declared that active support to any belligerent would make America a party to the conflict. It was precisely this contingency, they said, that the neutrality policy had tried to prevent. The security of Europe and of Asia, it was maintained, did not affect the security of the United States, no matter what the President said. Hitler was Britain's and France's worry, not America's. If they could not stop him, tragic though it might be, it was still not the concern of the United States; that bridge would be crossed when America came to it. Hitler, they were sure, was not interested in attacking the United States. America's first and foremost requirement, the isolationists asserted, must be the defense of the United States; and this defense rested solely on the security of the Western Hemisphere—not of Europe or Asia.

Public opinion, although confused, proved to be on Roosevelt's side. The debate led to a compromise. In November, 1939, the Fourth Neutrality Act was signed; arms, ammunition, and implements of war could now be purchased by all belligerents on a cash-and-carry basis. Since Britain and France controlled the Atlantic waters and were the only belligerents capable of buying and transporting American cargo, the Neutrality Act was, in effect, designed to benefit them. While Roosevelt won an important concession on the lifting of the arms embargo, the isolationists insisted on and obtained certain safeguards: loans to belligerent powers were prohibited, and the President was directed to mark out "combat zones" which American ships and American travelers were forbidden to enter.

Despite the limitations, the Fourth Neutrality Act was a significant victory for Roosevelt. In his plea to Congress, he had denounced the First Neutrality Act of 1935. "I regret that the Congress passed that Act," he said. "I regret equally that I signed that Act." The breach in the neutrality wall marked the beginning of a revolution in American foreign policy. It led ultimately to an abandonment of America's isolationism and an acceptance of the principles of collective security. In the process, Roosevelt's policies were in time to represent a fulfillment of Woodrow Wilson's ideals.

In 1939 and 1940, the American people were not yet ready to accept the implications of the change in neutrality policy. "You will send munitions without pay and you will send your boys back to the slaughter pens of Europe," warned Senator Borah. Antiwar sentiment remained strong. Roosevelt's role was to offer reassurance. A great radio performer, a first-rate showman at press conferences, and an eloquent orator, F.D.R. possessed an ingenious sense of timing. He was most adept at using the mass media of communication. By his folksy fireside chats, by his sharp and dramatic speeches, by his humorous jibes at the old-fashioned isolationists, but above all, by the feeling he imparted of being on top of the job, Roosevelt imparted a sense of confidence.

Quietly and secretly, while the country expressed its worry about the future and the President calmed its fears, he initiated a project which was to destroy America's continental insularity and climax the revolution in American foreign policy. Professor Albert Einstein at the Institute for Advanced Study in Princeton, had written the President a brief letter at the request of several scientists, including Niels Bohr, explaining the possibilities of developing a new bomb of unimaginable destructive power. At first, Roosevelt did not indicate very much interest. But in October, 1939, a colleague of Einstein came to Washington and discussed with the President the progress that had been made in the field of nuclear fission. He stressed the fact that Nazi Germany had made major progress in working on this new bomb. Roosevelt delayed no longer. During the next six months, plans were made for the future Manhattan Project. The gestation period began for the atom bomb.

Though President Roosevelt aimed at supporting the Allies to the limit of America's capacity, he did not tip his hand before the summer of 1940 and chose to deal with each situation as it arose. His caution stemmed from the healthy respect he had for isolationist sentiment and, more particularly, from the acute awareness that the powerful isolationist bloc in Congress could frustrate his policies.

During 1940, isolationist groups mobilized their forces to resist any further encroachments by the President on America's neutrality. Supporters were drawn from many segments of the population. They included sincere anti-interventionists, superpatriots, conservative rightists, German-Americans who did not wish to fight their brethren, and fascist and communist sympathizers. The major attack, however, came from the America First Committee, whose leading supporter was Robert E. Wood, chairman of the board of Sears, Roebuck and Company. Prominent figures joined the America First crusade, including the famous aviator Charles A. Lindbergh, railway magnate Robert Young, automobile king Henry Ford, Connecticut business executive Chester Bowles, labor leader William L. Hutchinson, and a number of writers and politicians. The America First Committee tried to divest itself completely of crackpot isolationists, Nazi Bundists, and communist organizations whose support of the aims of the committee was extremely embarrassing. But disassociation sometimes proved difficult, and the result led to a weakening of popular support. Principally backed by conservative businessmen and reactionary newspapers, the America First Committee obtained financial support from banking and industrial sources. While the impact of the committee's propaganda and influence was considerable, it was not as great as was generally believed. Most Americans wanted the United States to remain at home and stay clear of the war, but they were equally unwilling to accept the proposition that no aid of any kind should be given to the Allies.

Promoted by a famous editor, William Allen White of the Emporia *Gazette,* an important pressure group—the Committee to Defend America by Aiding the Allies—arose to counteract the America First propaganda. The White committee favored all material aid to the Allies short of war. However, early in 1941 a split occurred in the ranks of the membership when a faction advocated outright participation in the war. White resigned, and the committee became more outspoken in its interventionist views. The political battle lines between the isolationists and interventionists became more sharply drawn.

THE WAR IN EUROPE

From the fall of 1939 to the spring of 1940, the United States watched the war in Europe with anxiety. At the outset, the general expectation was that the pattern of conflict would be similar to that of World War I. It seemed almost as if the European powers were picking up where they had left off in 1918. It was thought that the German, British, and French forces would settle down to a protracted period of trench warfare. British and French strategy, in fact, had been based almost completely on maintaining a defensive position. Little attention had been given to the use of tanks and airplanes. Despite the fact that Hitler had tested *Blitzkrieg* tactics in the Spanish Civil War and used it in a devastating fashion in Poland, completing the annihilation of the country in six weeks, the British and French were not unduly alarmed. And, indeed, early German conduct seemed to warrant such confidence. In November, 1939, a lull—the so-called "phony" phase of the war—set in. Hitler had wanted to begin at once an attack on the Netherlands, Belgium, and France, but he was dissuaded from doing so by his generals, who urged that the offensive be delayed until the spring of the following year so that the German armies would not risk getting bogged down in a winter campaign. Hitler reluctantly agreed.

Meanwhile, in the early period after the outbreak of World War II, the United States concentrated its attention on the security of the Western Hemisphere. Military officials were convinced that if an attack against the United States were made, it would come from Central or South America. "We have set our mission as the defense, not of our territory alone, but cooperation in the defense of the Western Hemisphere," an American General Staff report stated. "This mission requires the provision of means with which we can deny the enemy bases from which he might launch military operations against us or any of the democratic nations of this hemisphere." It added that this policy was designed "to reduce to a minimum the likelihood of accepting war upon our territory."

America considered its immediate "danger zone" to be the Caribbean region and the Panama Canal. "Certainly for the safety of the approaches to the Canal," said Frank Knox, a wealthy newspaper publisher and Republican candidate for the vice-presidency in 1936—and soon to be Secretary of the Navy in F.D.R.'s wartime bipartisan cabinet—"we must make of the Caribbean an American lake. . . . One of our most obvious foreign policies should be the acquisition as soon as may be of every one of those West Indian islands." He suggested sounding out the British and French at once.

In October, 1939, the first meeting of the Foreign Ministers of the American Republics met in Panama, and the machinery for consultation established in the Lima Conference of 1938 was put into effect. An immediate result was the Panama Declaration, which created a "safety belt" around the Americas south of Canada, ranging from approximately three hundred to one thousand miles in width. Belligerents were warned to refrain from naval action within that area. Britain, France, and Germany promptly rejected the Panama Declaration. It was ignored completely; the belligerent powers continued to sink each other's ships within the proclaimed "safety belt."

The idea that the European war could be kept away from the Western

Hemisphere was wholly illusory. Germany's destructive submarine attacks on Allied shipping and the Allied announcement of a long-range blockade in retaliation quickly brought the conflict close to the shores of the Americas. These actions led to repeated violations of America's "neutral rights" in much the same manner as during World War I. The United States protested the restrictions on its shipping; it objected to the forcing of American ships into British control stations; and it complained of the practice of "visit and search." But these protests—largely made for the record—were not taken too seriously either by Britain or the United States.

Emphasis on hemisphere defense was not wasted, despite the flagrant disregard of the "safety belt." Before 1939, America's strategic policies had been largely passive. The actions of the belligerents contributed to the adoption of a more dynamic and positive course. The first "Rainbow Plan"—the Joint Army-Navy Plan I, approved by Roosevelt in October, 1939—recommended the "sending of U.S. task forces if needed to South America, and to the eastern Atlantic." More interesting was the fact that it also proposed eventually sending forces "to Africa or Europe in order to effect the decisive defeat of Germany or Italy or both."

After the Nazi war machine halted in November, Stalin decided to bolster his own defenses against Germany. Despite the Nazi-Soviet Non-aggression Pact, Stalin was concerned that Hitler might negotiate a peace with Britain and France and reverse his drive toward the East. He promptly occupied the Baltic states, and suddenly made demands on Finland for territory and for military and naval bases. Finland, however, resisted Russia's territorial claims. To the world's astonishment, she engaged in a war with the Soviet Union.

American sympathies immediately went out to the "brave Finns" who had dared oppose Communist aggression. Enthusiasm for Finnish relief was boundless. Congress promptly approved a $30 million loan, but to avoid involvement the money was limited to nonmilitary purposes. Under the circumstances, with guns and tanks needed, such a loan was of little help. In February, 1940, Stalin sent twenty-seven divisions into the country. They quickly crushed the three Finnish divisions which opposed them. The following month, Finland sued for peace; a treaty was signed in which she was forced to cede the entire Karelian Isthmus, together with islands in the Gulf of Finland. While Stalin did not destroy Finland's national independence, he obtained what he wanted: territorial cessions, naval and military bases, a right of transit across the country to Norway and to Sweden, and a demilitarization of the northern coast.

During several months, while American attention was riveted on the Soviet-Finnish War, Hitler was temporarily ignored. But the Fuehrer was not completely idle. Somewhat disturbed by the Soviet movement in the direction of Norway—both Norway and Denmark had been viewed as important bases for the German navy—Hitler undertook to prepare plans for Norway's invasion as early as January, 1941. Apprehensive about the possible loss of Norway, Britain decided to mine the Norwegian waters, even issuing orders for British troops to occupy the Norwegian ports if Germany interfered. The mining operation irked Hitler. In April, 1940, although his general staff opposed a campaign against Norway, Hitler took matters into his own hands. He directed that an offensive be launched at once. The invasion plans were carefully worked out, and with the help of a few traitors, led by the Norwegian Nazi Vidkun Quisling—whose name became synonymous with "traitor" —the campaign, timed to coincide with an invasion of Denmark, was brilliantly executed. Denmark was overrun within a few hours. British troops tried to resist the Nazis in Norway, but with Germany controlling the air and holding off the British navy, it was only six weeks before Norway was placed under German occupation. Germany's control over Norway gave her an important base from which she could undertake air and naval attacks against the British Isles.

The disastrous loss of Denmark and Norway led to a British political crisis. Prime Minister Neville Chamberlain resigned, and a coalition government was formed under the leadership of Winston Churchill. On May 10—the day Churchill assumed office—Hitler launched his invasion of Luxembourg, the Netherlands, and Belgium. (The Netherlands was to fall in four days, Belgium in two weeks.) On May 11, the German armies quickly swung into France; outwitting the French commanders, they swept around the much-vaunted Maginot Line and raced down the Somme Valley to the Channel. The French and British expeditionary armies which had been rushed into Flanders to support Belgian resistance now found themselves cut off from the main French forces and threatened with annihilation. Then ensued at Dunkirk the heroic evacuation, when the British assembled a vast fleet of vessels of every conceivable description and succeeded in saving some 300,000 French and British troops.

Early in June, the Nazi mechanized forces smashed toward Paris. Panic gripped France as highways became clogged with fleeing refugees. Loud Stuka dive bombers added to the hysteria. Paris was promptly declared an open city to save it from destruction. As the German armies advanced toward the capital, Mussolini declared war against France.

"The hand which held the dagger has struck it into the back of its neighbor," President Roosevelt declared. After the occupation of Paris, the French meekly surrendered. On June 22, Hitler, in a frenzy of ecstasy and joy, danced a jig as he witnessed the French sign the German-dictated armistice terms in the same railway coach and at the same spot where the Germans had been forced to accept Allied armistice conditions on November 11, 1918.

The fall of France was a staggering blow. Britain fearfully awaited an imminent German invasion, but Hitler delayed his assault on the British Isles until August. Meanwhile, the United States reappraised its defensive position. "No combination of dictator countries of Europe and Asia will stop the help we are giving to almost the last free people now fighting to hold them at bay," Roosevelt declared. "We have learned the lessons of recent years. We know now that if we seek to appease aggressors by withholding aid from those who stand in their way, we only hasten the day of their attack upon us."

Roosevelt asked Congress to increase America's armed forces and to step up production of war material. He made a dramatic plea for 50,000 military airplanes. *Life,* shocked by this request, printed 50,000 dots over several pages to try to convey some idea of what this huge number meant. But Congress, shaken by Hitler's triumphs, did not quibble about the defense appropriations. The largest peacetime military budget was passed; Congress authorized over $5 billion for national defense, and provision was made for future outlays for construction contracts which brought the total to nearly $18 billion. When it came to manpower, however, Congress hedged. Finally, in September, the first peacetime selective-service act was passed over the vigorous objections of the isolationists.

The fall of France induced two other unprecedented steps. At the second meeting of the Foreign Ministers of the American Republics, it was unanimously decided that territory of European powers in the Western Hemisphere which might fall into unfriendly hands should be taken over and administered jointly by the American republics, pending its final disposition. In coöperation with the Latin-American republics, America assumed responsibility for protective custody of the colonies of Holland and France in the West Indies. As a further measure in protecting the security of the Western Hemisphere, Roosevelt met with the Prime Minister of Canada in August, 1940, and arrangements were made to set up a Permanent Joint Board of Defense. Later, measures were taken to coördinate the production facilities of the two countries for their own defense and that of Britain.